THE MEANING OF THREE

UNDER

THE MASK

Sandy Sela-Smith
June 2012

BOOKS BY DR. SANDY SELA-SMITH

THE MEANING OF THREE: UNDER THE
MASK
A TRILOGY

THE MASK (2008)

BEHIND THE MASK (2009)

UNDER THE MASK (2011)

*

E PLURIBUS UNUM: OUT OF MANY...ONE
(2004)

WWW.INFINITECONNECTIONS.US

THE MEANING OF THREE

UNDER
THE MASK

DR. SANDY SELA-SMITH

authorHOUSE®

AuthorHouse™
1663 Liberty Drive
Bloomington, IN 47403
www.authorhouse.com
Phone: 1-800-839-8640

First published by AuthorHouse   05/17/2011

ISBN: 978-1-4567-5747-2 (sc)
ISBN: 978-1-4567-5748-9 (e)

Library of Congress Control Number: 2011905428

Printed in the United States of America

Any people depicted in stock imagery provided by Thinkstock are models,
and such images are being used for illustrative purposes only.
Certain stock imagery © Thinkstock.

This book is printed on acid-free paper.

Galaxy photo on the cover used by permission of ESA/Hubble
Cover copy-editing contribution by Michael Scialfo

To Rachael

10-1992 to 10-13-2010

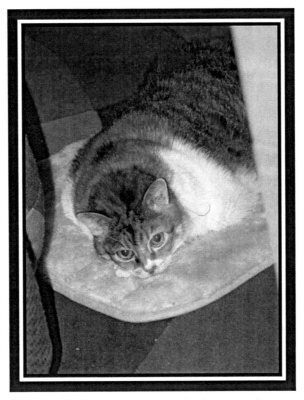

For teaching me more deeply how to love with
connection not attachment, to live without fear of being
alive, and to open to life by embracing death.

"You are it. The whole sense of these religions…is to evoke in the individual the experience of identity with the universal mystery, the mystery of being. You are it. Not the 'you,' however, that you cherish. Not the 'you' that you distinguish from the other."

Joseph Campbell

CONTENTS

ACKNOWLEDGMENTS

Saying thank you to the many people who have contributed to the creating of a book is a gesture that can hold great meaning. And, these special people listed here represent just the tip of the iceberg of all those who directly and indirectly made it possible for this trilogy to make its way to completion. While explicitly acknowledging those named, there is also an implicit recognition of all who supported these people, as well, making it possible for the ones named to support me, as they have done. Taken together, we all have created an intricately amazing web that, in the end, reaches out to everyone in the universe . . . including you, the one reading what is written here. So, in advance, I thank you, too, as I acknowledge:

All of those who were acknowledged in the first two books: My heart continues to appreciate who you are and all you did to make this trilogy a reality.

Bill: Thank you for offering me the gift of your insight into the deepest recesses of my unconsciousness, and your willingness to reflect back to me what you have seen, so that I might see, as well.

Clients: Over the years, I have been gifted with many amazing people who have invited me to walk with them, some for but one session and others for many sessions over the years. Each one came at exactly the right moment to weave with me what you and I were learning about what it is to be a unique spark of god in human form. Thank you for the privilege of being invited to join you on your journey.

Esther: You have been an integral part of my life and my writing from the beginning of this trilogy to the present. Without your tenacity in asking for what you want and truth telling about how you feel, I would not have met the tattooed lady whose predictive message opened the door to the meaning of three. And I would not have experienced for myself the value of truth telling in maintaining connection with those outside me, as well as with *Sandy God Essence,* a most significant contribution to *Under the Mask.* I am grateful to you for your part in this book and the two that came before.

Film Makers: The Cohen brothers, Cormac McCarthy, and Peter Roger: You all deserve special thanks for bringing to consciousness so many levels of what it is to be human by asking the deepest of questions that many of us would never consider asking without your contributions. Your profoundly deep films, *A Serious Man, The Road,* and *Oh My God,* became a significant part of the weaving of *Under the Mask.* Along with you amazing people are the writers, actors, and a plethora of others without whom films would never be made or offered to the public. All of you supported me in my efforts to bring a truth I have discovered in my journey to any who may be ready to go more deeply into their own selves to discover the meaning of three.

Jake: Even though our marriage did not work out, our lives together did work beautifully. I wish we could have learned the lessons and truths that grew out of our time together without so much pain, but despite our difficulties, I cannot imagine my life and my growth without your contribution. What we created, we did together, which on the deepest levels let us discover truths we could never have found without having experienced those things we lived through. Because my experience from aspects of our lives together were openly reflected in all three books of the trilogy, I want to express in this open setting my deepest apologies for all the pain and suffering I brought into your life, and I want to tell you I forgive you for pain and suffering you brought into mine. We drew each other into both of our lives to learn what we may not have learned in any other way. I now see we were living out patterns, repeating stories we lived over and over too many times, and we lived so many generational stories, as well. I am grateful that we won't have to repeat these stories with each other any more. I will always love you.

Jenny: My little 4-legged companion who has been with me through all the changes in my life for the past 13 years. You put up with being on the covers of the first two books, and didn't seem to mind that Rachael became the focus during this last in the trilogy. Thank you for reflecting back to me so many things I needed to learn about myself. My heart smiles that you have chosen to stay with me, still.

Longmont Astrologer: Thank you for coming into my life exactly when you did and telling me what I needed to hear in a way that impacted me exactly as it needed to happen . . . three times. You offered a gift of understanding that helped me see what I hadn't seen for decades.

Luke and Patty: I am and will be forever grateful for your open hearts and your willingness to offer the gift of the Inipi Sweat Lodge ceremony that was an integral part of my healing as expressed in the writing of *The Meaning of Three* trilogy. Your unconditional love and kindness, visible when you announced that I am a member of your Inipi family, touched me so deeply. From you, I have learned that it is safe to love and safe to be in a family setting where I am free to be myself . . . seen and known with all my wonders and all my flaws. I thank you for creating a place where so many other lovely people who have come to the lodge over the years are now my family, as well. As each of us asked for, or supported those who asked for healing, we all became infinitely connected with each other in our ongoing discovery that we are all aspects of the One, experiencing being a unique expression of *Universal God Essence* in human form. And of course, I thank all the angels, guides, spirits, totems, and departed loved ones who have entered the lodge to support us in our journey to experience the only thing that is really true, which is that even if it appears to be otherwise, unconditional love is the only thing that is real.

Michael Scialfo of Wolf Camera in Littleton, CO: Again I thank you for your spectacular skills in editing to make the front and back covers production-ready. You are so gifted in intricate shifting of visual energy to create that very valuable final touch.

Mother and Father: I came into this life to find a way to balance the light and the dark, to "dance with the devil" without being absorbed by it, to further my awareness of darkness while holding the light within me. As I look at your lives, my parents, I can see the struggles and the pain you endured, and I can now recognize that the life you offered me grew out of what you experienced in your lives. I also recognize that I could not have learned what I learned and may not have connected with *Sandy God Essence* for many more lifetimes without you. Writing this trilogy has allowed me to have compassion for you both and to be able to say that I truly forgive you, love you, and wish the best for you on your souls' journeys.

Oregon David: I remain forever grateful to you, my dear and beloved friend. You have been not only a significant part of all books in this trilogy, but you also have been an irreplaceable being of light in my life. Sharing our thoughts and our truths, which led to many discoveries reflected in not just *The Meaning of Three,* but in everything I have written since we met, also transformed my life and opened my heart. I will always be grateful that you answered Spirit's call to be my loving and trusted friend.

Saint Michael: I honor your steadfast dedication to the healing art that has been an integral part of your life for decades, and for being your authentic self while working with me. More than any other, you have been the one who has continued to give the single message to turn within, without which this trilogy would never have been written.

Shar: Your work that touched my life as the writing of *Behind the Mask* was coming to a close became an integral part of *Under the Mask*. I am grateful for your ability to be present and support my healing of so much that had been hidden deep within for far too long. I cannot imagine having completed the trilogy without all you contributed.

South American Shamans: Your work is so important in a world that has forgotten the spiritual understandings of our ancestors. One of the great lies I carried with me for lifetimes was that I did not belong. Without conscious knowledge of my intention to know that I do belong, you prepared a place for me and became a channel for *Universal God Essence* to speak to my heart, reminding me of the truth of my belonging. I humbly offer my gratitude to you and those you represent through all time, throughout human history.

Terry: Anyone who writes appreciates the value of a friend who knows how to be honest and reflect that honesty in critiquing, as well as in relationship. You have been such a person in my life, letting me experience what it is like to have family that speaks from truth. You loved Rachael when she was practicing the fine art of being unlovable and have the scars to prove it, and I will always hold that gift in my heart.

The Lone Ranger: Even though you are a fictional character, you represent all the roles and characters who keep hope alive in the children of the world until they are able to grow into the truth that the rescuing they seek is in themselves. I am grateful for the writers and actors, as well as all those who supported the role of *the masked man* allowing little Sandy to live beyond her childhood and into the woman I have become.

***

Another group of beings that deserve acknowledgment, are ones that have been in physical form in the past, but not now, and others who seem not to have been in human form, but none-the less have been irreplaceable in the awakening of not just me, but of many of my fellow travelers. These special beings deserve acknowledgment for all they have done to support me on my journey, and the journeys of all humanity, often without our knowledge or our appreciation. I know of a few who have impacted not just the writing of this trilogy, but my entire life, and among those are:

Carl Jung: You came into this world at a time when so few were able to understand the depth of your message about being human. Your work opened the hearts and minds of many who came after you to understand the great complexity of the human psyche and you were willing to challenge the accepted Cartesian world-view that ruled the Western interpretation of what is real for hundreds of years. By being willing to search deeply within yourself and offer your findings to those of us who followed after you, you allowed us to see what we would have been blind to before we read what you wrote. There is nothing in this trilogy that would have been possible without you and without the contributions of those who built upon your work. Thank you.

Great Grandmother Sarah: I acknowledge you for choosing to live into freedom to be yourself instead of living trapped in a life that was destroying you. Not only did you contribute to our family system the idea that it is possible to step out of a life that does not fit, but also, you contributed to my understanding of reality being far more than I thought it was by your mystical and magical participation in the synchronous events that became a beautiful part of *Under the Mask*. You, also, let me know there is something much bigger than my individual self that I can trust to lead me exactly where I need to go. If I drop into doubt, I can return to the three amazing ways your essence showed up in my life, exactly when I needed it.

Library Angels: Dr. Allan Combs recently introduced me to the name library angels, first mentioned by Arthur Koestler in his book, *Roots of Coincidence*. And now, I have a name for you special beings who've been visiting me for decades, delivering messages that led me to read exactly the right books needed to help me understand what was necessary for my next step in becoming conscious.

Synchronicity Angels: You are the special beings, sometimes seen, but mostly unseen, who communicate with the *Unique God Essences* in individuals to be sure we will be in the right place at the right time for those who are awakening or are ready to awaken from the collective dream. Your profound weaving has caused so many of us to release the belief that we are alone. Your presence offers reasoning minds the gift of recognizing cause and effect cannot explain so many of the mysterious, magical, mystical events that take place in our lives.

Part One

Before the Trip to The Northwest

Connecting to Courage
Speculations and Reflections
A Serious Man
The Road
Oh My God

Chapter One
CONNECTING TO COURAGE

We all possess courage; some choose to tap into it, while others withdraw, usually, out of fear of what accessing courage might require of them. Those who become afraid and withdraw, focus on what they fear instead of what they love, and in their search for safety and security, often sacrifice what they love. Turning away from courage disconnects us from the power that comes from being supported by love, and does not give us the security or safety we hoped would result from our sacrifice.

REMINISENCES OF THE MASKED MAN

Trumpets sounded the oh, so familiar *March of the Swiss Soldiers* from the finale of the *William Tell Overture*, as a masked man dressed in cowboy-white and riding a beautiful white horse raced along the trails, into the mountains, and onto the open plains of the untamed Western territory. The program began with an announcer speaking in that special way that sent chills of anticipation through the millions of attentive viewers, as the sounds of a charging horse and the exhilarating music blended with his intense and fast passed words, *"The Looooone Ranger…A fiery horse, with the sped of light, a cloud of dust, and a hearty Hi Ho Silllverrrrr."*

3

When I was a child of about ten, I lay on the floor in front of our brand new television set watching what I had only imagined before when the same music and words were broadcast over the radio. My heart beat in excitement as the masked man who came to enforce justice across the West carried with him the promise of rescuing people in distress, righting wrongs and, perhaps, on one of his many adventures, just maybe…saving me from the unspeakable wrongs of my childhood. But once again, after another half hour episode came to its end, the masked man rode off into the sunset, with another *"Hi Ho Silver, and away…"* leaving only a silver bullet as evidence that he had been there, and I continued to be left behind in my cold Alaskan house, waiting for him to come back someday to protect me as he did so many others.

As a little child, I had no idea who the masked man was, but I knew under his mask was compassion, kindness, justice, light, and…dare I say it…love, something I heard in his voice when he was on the radio, made visible in his eyes when I watched him on TV. And there was no doubt about his kindness revealed in the way he treated the women and children he came to rescue from some horrible injustice. As I reflect back on my life, I can now understand the importance of looking into eyes to see what was under the mask, as I continued my search to find someone who could save me.

When I was 16 going on 17, no longer watching the programs of my childhood, I looked into the eyes of a young man in my class, and saw the most beautiful light in him, illuminated more clearly by a ray of sun streaming through a window at the end of the hall. And not too many months after that experience, Jake stood on the porch of my parents house holding a gift of a powder blue electric blanket that he had purchased to keep me from getting sick as I did so often from the cold that permeated my house on so many levels. His most beautiful gift was wrapped in compassion, kindness, and love. I called him my knight in a tweed coat because on that very cold Christmas Eve night, he was wearing a long tweed coat that made him look more like a man than a boy. Five years later, I walked down the aisle to become the wife of the man my young-woman-self believed was her prince, her knight with whom she would live happily ever after …the man my child self believed was her long awaited Lone Ranger.

But the image of the knight and the Lone Ranger did not last too very long. If the truth be told, the images had begun to fade for both the 16-year-old, and the child long before I married Jake, but back then, it was my pattern to push away anything that did not match what I needed to believe was true…until there was just too much to push away.

When much more of what he had hidden behind his mask began to emerge and obscured the kindness, justice, light, and love that my teenage self first saw, she made herself forget what didn't match the image of her knight. But the time came when my child self realized Jake was not the Lone Ranger, and began to search other eyes to find the one who would rescue her, while my adult self kept trying as hard as she could to bring back the light that seemed to have gone missing in Jake's eyes. But, after 20 years of failure, my adult self finally let go of trying.

***

There are times when a single choice results in fairly unimportant changes in our lives, but other choices can lead to significant life-changes that we could never have imagined before we made the decisions. And there are other times when we consider making a choice that we know, without a doubt, that once we make it, our lives will never be the same. Though there were many of those small decisions in my life, there was one monumental choice that had been on my mind for a number of years that I knew would change my life forever. When it came down to actually making the choice, for a few profoundly painful minutes, I struggled.

September 25, 1986, late in the evening following my grandmother's funeral, I was driving north on Interstate-5 after leaving my mother's house to return home. My husband had not attended the memorial service honoring the life of a woman I had loved so very much, claiming that he couldn't get away from work, something I could not accept since he was the owner of our business. His most common response to most of my requests for support was, *"I can't get away, somebody's got to work*

5

around here," insinuating that anything I did that was not related to our business was unacceptable, including taking time out to go to a funeral. I felt deeply betrayed because he wouldn't reach out to me at I time I really needed him to be my knight, if not my Lone Ranger, and he could be neither. While I was driving and wiping away unwanted tears, the night seemed darker than usual, and there was too much traffic for that time of the evening. I believed the man who was supposed to be my partner had failed me so greatly, and this last neglectful act felt like the capstone of a whole series of his failures at being the husband I needed.

I knew I had a choice to make, and the moment I'd have to make it was quickly approaching. I could continue to drive the 17 miles north and take the 175th street exit that would take me to our house, or I could take the Interstate 90 exit that would take me East over Lake Washington and into Bellevue where another man, also named Jake, was having a birthday party. There was a profound war going on inside. The part of me, who had always followed the rules and always tried to do what was right, was committed to the northbound road, but another part of me, who had stopped trying to see his light under all of the painful patterns behind my husband's mask, was equally committed to taking the earlier exit and driving eastward.

As the lighted green freeway sign indicating the eastbound exit grew larger, I turned my head to the left to avoid looking in the direction of the sign, while that other part of me took hold of the steering wheel and turned the car onto I-90. The split second decision was called in favor of the one who wanted to end any more attempts to find the goodness in my husband and begin a new life. I drove to Bellevue, and after sitting in my car for some time in front of his house to see if I was really committed to the terrifying choice, I slowly walked to the front door and rang the doorbell. The other man, also named Jake, opened the door, and the surprise on his face turned into a joyful welcome. He opened to embrace me as I melted into the arms of a man whose eyes sparkled with love and light. Though this other man was not the person for whom my child-self had been searching—in time his own shadows from behind his mask emerged, as did mine—he was the catalyst for my literally making a decision between two roads, one that would return me to my husband and the life I had known for two decades, and the other that would take me away from my husband into another life that was totally unknown. Much of what I wrote in *The Mask* and some of what I wrote in *Behind the Mask* told the stories of what happened before that profoundly significant September night, as well as what followed that monumental decision to turn eastward.

Though I never married the second Jake who asked me to be his wife on Cannon Beach, Oregon while ocean waves crashed behind me against Haystack Rock, I did leave my husband and placed nearly all my attention on healing my internal wounding through psychological and body therapy. My total focus was to become free, not just from the outer chains, but from the inner chains, as well, that bound me and kept me from knowing my true self and prevented me from doing what I wanted to do with my life. Though I did drive back to my home later that night, I had set the energy in motion to eventually leave my husband to create a new life for myself, on my own. During the years of inner healing that followed, I began extensive travel that eventually took me all over the US and into other countries to study more ancient and spiritual healing practices, something I wouldn't have done had I continued the drive north on that September night.

***

Not long after I had begun psychotherapy, I received one of those messages from deep inside me by way of a dream that communicated to me I would be going to China. Three years and three months after the decision to go east on I-90, I was preparing to leave for what turned out to be nearly two years living in the East, in the middle of the Middle Kingdom, in Baoji City, Shaanxi Province, in the People's Republic of China. There, I taught English and studied Chinese Energy Healing from a circle of Qi Gong masters, and discovered a new life in a world so different from anything I had ever experienced before, which is a story for another time.

After returning to the US and relocating to Florida, I was drawn to study Alchemical Clinical Hypnotherapy in Naples, Florida and New Zealand, followed by a decision to enroll in Graduate School to get a

PhD in psychology. My practice grew substantially, but after 15 years of living in the Sunshine state, another message from the inside directed me to leave Florida…but I didn't get the rest of the directive telling me where I was supposed to go, other than seeing images that had told me I needed mountain energy. In late autumn of 2006, I discovered a carriage house in the foothills of the Rocky Mountains of Colorado, the Continental Divide. This was the backbone of America and I knew this place would help me reconnect with my backbone. But I didn't know why it needed to be exactly that place, not until the summer of 2007, when a Florida friend came for a visit.

***

July 23, 2007, nearly two decades after that momentous decision to turn east, I made what would've been called an insignificant decision, which changed my life in the most dramatic of ways. And now, I cannot imagine my life without having made it. I was on vacation with Esther, a dear friend of nearly 20 years who had come to visit me in my home away from home. For as long as she could remember, she had a fear of heights and asked if we could do two things on our travels around this beautiful state. She wanted to go up in a hot air balloon and wanted to take the Cog railway to the top of Pike's Peak, 14,115 feet above sea level. Standing on the cliff's edge at the very top of the mountain with an unobstructed 360-degree view of the smaller mountains and valleys below, Esther faced her fears there, while I understood how this peak was a marker for so many travelers who were headed westward a couple of hundred years before. And, soon after that peak experience, I came to see how the mountain was to become a personal marker, not just for Esther, but for me, as well, a marker of a very different kind.

After we descended Pike's Peak that rose above the picturesque mountain village of Manitou Springs, we wandered through the town and came across a storefront-sign, advertising for psychic readings. Esther wanted to go in for a reading, so I decided to join her without knowing that a momentous event was about to take place.

Near the end of the time I spent with her, the psychic asked me if I knew the meaning of three, a number she kept seeing, and after a few more comments, she gasped from one of those "ah-ha" moments and told me that I was going to write three books. When I heard her words, I knew what she said was true; the knowing came from that same place inside where I received very clear messages about what was going to happen or what I needed to do. While none of her other predictions came true, at least not as of this writing, the story of the *Tattooed Lady* and what she told me became the second chapter in *The Mask,* the first of the three books she predicted I'd write. Without any doubt, I knew these books would become important to my life, and I sensed they could be important in other people's lives, as well.

It didn't take long for me to discover that what I was writing, was really writing my life. It seemed as if each book had its own pulse, its own sense of time and was waiting for events to happen so I could take the roads those events created, which would then lead me to whatever it was the writing wanted me to discover. Events over a 16-month period—from the summer of 2007 to the fall of 2008—needed to unfold for the first book to be completed and published, and 12 months from November of 2008 to November of 2009, one year from beginning to end, for the second book to be completed. When I began thinking about the third, and last book, I assumed that *Under the Mask* would be finished within a year and before the end of 2010, but that was not to happen. Because the writing of this book was no different from the first two, I needed to wait for unknown experiences to take place before I could begin writing. For six long weeks, I didn't write anything, but simply lived a story; it took another 12 months from Christmas 2009 to Christmas 2010 to write about what unfolded in my life that grew out of those six weeks.

THE SIX WEEKS BETWEEN BOOK TWO AND THREE

In the fall of 2009, while *The Meaning of Three: Behind the Mask* was being readied for publication, I made arrangements to travel to the Northwest. I thought I might find inspiration and courage to begin writing this third and final book in the trilogy by making a couple of appointments with Michael, a gifted Rolpher and body therapist from Bellingham, Washington. He had worked with me nearly every week, for close to three years, from the beginning of 1987 to the end of 1989, supporting my journey in life when my mask was crumbling and what was behind my mask was pouring out. Following this intense time, I relocated to China for nearly two years, and then moved to Florida in late 1991 without having reconnected with this amazing healer until the mid 1990s.

A few days before Christmas of 1996, my father died, and I returned to the Northwest to be with my family. While I was there, Michael was willing to schedule two emergency sessions with me just a couple of days before Christmas, which allowed me to release some of the still-buried pain around decisions my father had made in his life that led to his inflicting insidious damage on me in my growing up years.

Over those earlier years, from 1987-89, I learned to trust Michael's healing abilities, as much as I'd learned to trust messages from within, which gave me direction as to what I needed to do, even if I had no idea why. And the message to schedule the appointments with Michael in '96 and then, again, 13 years later in the winter of 2009, were a part of that trust. So, I contacted Michael, and made plane reservations for a short trip to the Northwest for the second week in December. I couldn't have guessed what was to happen in the weeks between the completion of book two and the beginning of book three, and though I hoped the trip might stimulate my writing, I had no idea that everything around and within the trip itself would contain the foundation for what would be my life for the next year, and what was to be included in *Under the Mask*.

Three Storage Places

When Jake and I divorced in the fall of 1989, I sold most of my furniture, discarded or gave away many other possessions but stored the remainder of the items in two large walk-in crates Jake had built for that purpose. He offered a space for all the things I didn't want to sell or give away, and I left for China, where I lived for close to two years.

While on the flight from China back to the US in the fall of 1991, I felt as if the time I'd spent in the Far East had made me strong enough to be able to rebuild a healthy relationship with Jake should he want to try again. I had grown so much in the time I was away and thought I could create more effective patterns, but when Jake picked me up from the airport, I discovered he was just a few days away from getting remarried. I was in shock and didn't quite know how to react. So I responded as I'd done whenever something overwhelming happened in my life; I became calm and accepting of the situation and knew I'd have to go in a much different direction than originally planned.

Before the surprising information about Jake's remarriage, I intended to accept a position I was offered at a Junior College near Seattle and planned to look for a place to live somewhere between the Cascade Mountain Range to the east of Seattle and the Olympic Mountains on the peninsula to the west. With a new place to live, I could reclaim all I had placed in storage two years earlier to partially furnish a new home, and then I thought I'd work on rekindling a relationship with Jake. But instead, I added many items from my life in China to the crates that contained the remnants of my first 45 years of life. I let go of the idea of living in the Northwest, accepted a position in a college in the sunshine state, and began a new chapter of my life in Florida.

***

After the long drive from Seattle to Clearwater Florida, my plans included finding a home in the state on the opposite end of the US, after which I'd arrange to have the stored possessions sent to me. But in the 15 years I lived there, I never found the place where I wanted to put down roots and stay. Every year, when a new lease needed to be signed, I thought it would be the last before my departure. For a number of years, I went on a month-to-month contract because I thought the inner guidance to leave was imminent, so shipping things to a temporary home didn't seem practical. On-and-off, over those years, I thought of doing something about all the "stuff" stored in Seattle, but nothing ever came of it.

In the early summer of 2006, I received another one of those inner messages, this one telling me that the time had come for me to leave Florida. But I didn't know where I was to go. All I saw was an image of mountains, tall trees, rivers, and animals, but I didn't know which mountains or which state. When I left Florida near the end of August of '06 to take a trip without a known destination, I stored the vestiges of my life from the 15 years in the sunshine state in three large storage units and began a journey to a place I didn't know. After a long drive to Seattle, from one corner of the country to the other, then down the West Coast to Los Angeles, and finally part way across the country again to Colorado, I found the place in the mountains above Denver that I knew was the place I was supposed to be, at least temporarily. A half year after that decision to settle in for the winter, Esther came for a vacation and I finally understood why I needed the isolated place in the mountains surrounded by tall trees and wild animals, where I could open my window in the summer to hear the sound of a stream that flowed within a few feet of me and to see beautiful hummingbirds that learned to be safe enough to fly into my space hovering so very near me as I wrote the trilogy.

I thought it would be good to make decisions about all I had in storage in both Seattle and Clearwater, but the right time to deal with it all did not come. Over time, I pared down the three units in Florida to one unit, but every month when I paid the storage bill, I revisited the thoughts of letting go of what remained in both locations. After finding the writing place in Colorado I traveled back and forth between Colorado and Florida, but neither felt like my permanent home. I was sure another place was calling, but its voice was still too distant for me to hear. By late fall of 2009, I had possessions split among three storage places: Washington State, Florida, and Colorado. I'm sure there must be some important metaphoric *meaning of three* somewhere in all this, as well, though at the moment, I don't know what it is.

Jake's Request

With the economic downturn of 2009, Jake's business had fallen off, making it necessary for him to close down his warehouse, which meant he would no longer be able to maintain a space for all I had stored. He offered to ship everything, but that didn't make sense since I was living in two places. Florida was still the state of my legal residence, though it never felt like home to me, and Colorado felt only temporary. The Rocky Mountains contained what for me was the backbone energy of the US, and I felt my carriage house was the place to regain strength in my own backbone. I knew this is what was happening while writing this trilogy. But I wasn't sure if I would make the mountain state my permanent home, either. It was my writing space that provided the container for healing by way of what I wrote in the books, or perhaps more accurately, what the books wrote in me.

I told Jake I'd come as soon as possible to take care of everything, and then changed my travel plans for the sessions with Michael to include dealing with my belongings in Seattle; it felt good that I could finally solve the problem of what to do with all the stuff reflecting nearly a half-century of my life stored in those two gigantic walk-in crates.

I ended up changing the trip on both ends of my original plans. The first part of the trip would be dedicated to going through nearly 50 years of my life, sorting through and deciding what to keep and what to give or throw away. The second part of the trip was to experience sessions with Michael. And though I still didn't know the reason for making the appointments, I knew working with this special therapist would be important, and I had a sense that the work with him would also involve sorting through and releasing what might have remained inside me for that same amount of time. The third part of the trip was to visit a very dear friend, a man I have called Oregon David in the earlier books in the trilogy. I called him that because I have so many friends named David, and I thought it would be easier to differentiate which one I was talking about by attaching a location to the name. I really didn't have a purpose in mind for that visit other than to be with a dear friend I hadn't seen for far too long.

Three Films

The weekend before my trip to the Northwest, I did something I had never done in my entire life. For some inexplicable reason, I felt compelled to see three very unusual films, showing at different theaters in Denver, all in one day! The first film titled, *Oh My God,* was a documentary inquiring into the nature of God. The narrator, Peter Rodgers, traveled to 23 countries and spoke to many ordinary and some non-ordinary people from all walks of life, asking, *"What is God?"* There were many answers; some said there is no God, others' gave answers that seemed to be memorized from their particular religions' tenets, but three stood out for me, one of which was the most common response, *"God is Love,"* a comment that has a phenomenal depth of meaning when one opens to the idea of God in verb form or God as being, unrestricted by the limiting ideas of God as noun. A second intriguing answer was, *"God is the space between us"* and the third was that *God is us.*

The film director indicated that the purpose of his film was not to define God but to look for common threads among many people, perhaps leading the viewer to decide for him or herself how to answer that question. My answer was based on what I've experienced all my life, but never quite articulated so clearly for myself until I saw the film. The best descriptor for me is that *God is the ineffable experience of love that exists not just between us, but also in us…and is in the spaces between the spaces, which form the patterns that create the matter of all that is, as well. There is no place, no space, no energy, no matter, no existence, no experience anywhere in the Universe that is not an expression and reflection of God… and that this Godness is in all aspects of all that is, including us.*

As a result of the internal work I have done with myself over the past quarter century, as well as the work I have done with clients over the past two decades, I have come to an understanding that God is not some creature we can point to, a person, perhaps in robes, very ancient looking who rules the world with *his* iron hand from *his* throne in the far reaches of the universe or is a larger than life human being who rides in chariots across the sky waiting for the time he has chosen to destroy the world. I do not believe that God wishes us to suffer or is waiting to punish us for being who we were created to be. I do not believe that God is an object to study, but rather, is known through the *experience of love*, an idea honored in the mystical elements of most every religious and spiritual tradition. Love eternally exists, and whether or not individual consciousness has forgotten its connection to Love, God is still there.

I believe that God's essence exists in the flow of the universe, but is not the universe. Lao Tzu, the Chinese philosopher and author of *The Tao*, said, *"The Tao which can be expressed is not the unchanging Tao; the name which can be named is not the unchanging name."* God is experienced, not defined.

From the perspective I hold, each of us in the physical form is like a metaphoric cell in that universal body; each of us carries the essence of a unique expression of the essence of that which we call God. As each cell in our body is a unique expression of us that carries all of us; we contain and, also, are a part of the essence that is universal.

The thoughts that rose up in my mind as a result of watching *Oh My God* became a foundation as well as an unexpected capstone for the next two films.

***

The second movie I watched during that marathon day was *The Road*, a grimly dark story of a man and his young son as they trekked from some inland location in the US to find their way to the Atlantic Ocean. The boy's mother, the man's wife, instructed them to head for the ocean as her last directive before she walked into the dismal darkness of what seemed like a god-forsaken world, toward her apparent death. This destination she gave them held their only hope of refuge after a dreadful apocalyptic catastrophe devastated the world, which left everything in dusty grey; some places were much darker than others. Grey *was* the environment—ash covered ground, burnt lifeless trees, grey dusty sky with only a hint of light. Gray death had filled the hearts of the very few survivors, with the exception of the young boy, who had never seen anything but the lifeless world he inherited from those who were alive before the apocalypse, and the boy's father when he was protecting his son. Yet, the boy continually expressed a rainbow of love and light from his heart despite the obvious absence of love in the world around him. This film seemed to fit as a shadow side of the first as a depiction of life when connection to what I have come to call *God Essence* is forgotten. Without experiencing love that comes from connection to this essence, our lives crumble and our world falls into lifeless grey ruin, a metaphor for us individually, as well as collectively in our world today. This depiction of disconnection from essence created the link to the next film.

15

***

The third and last film in the trilogy of movies I saw before leaving for a three-part trip to the Northwest was *A Serious Man*. On one level, this film, set in the late 1960s, is the story of a Jewish man faced with his personal world falling apart around him. His life seemed to be a metaphor for all those who attempt to create order out of chaos by living according to the rules when rules are supposed to make sense of what does not make sense. Rules are supposed to make what does not fit to fit, or what is out of line, to line back up again, and they are supposed to make what is not supposed to be, to go away. Rules are supposed to make everything work right. In the story, this man who does what he is supposed to do, no matter what happens to him, loses everything, and from all appearances, he continues to believe in the rules, even as his world is crashing in on him and, perhaps, is coming to an end.

On another level, one might interpret this film as an inquiry into the meaninglessness of beliefs about what things are, how things should be, and what it is that we are to do to assure that everything will be as it supposed to be. I came away with my interpretation of the film's message: *Order cannot be created out of chaos by rules, and being serious about following the rules cannot create a good life. When we discover that the rules cannot save us, we have to decide what we will do.* I concluded that since disconnection from love is what creates chaos, re-connection with love is needed to release the limitations of rules and the destruction that can come from both the rules and the chaos.

On the long drive back to my mountain cabin, I reflected on the three films, and noticed how each one gained deeper meaning when seen as a part of the other two. I was surprised to see how each film reflected aspects of *The Meaning of Three*, something I had not known before I saw them. I saw the man who lived his life so seriously—trapped by the rules of his life, his religion, and his time—as being a film representing *The Mask* we put on expecting it to protect us from an unfriendly world, but in the end we can't cover what seethes deep inside us behind those masks. And, certainly, what we as a collective of human beings have spent millennia covering *Behind the Mask* was well depicted in *The Road*. The viewing audience does not know what caused the Earth to turn into a near lifeless planet where people have lost their humanity. They rob from each other and kill anyone who might compete for the right to cannibalize the survivors they capture. We are led to believe that those few left alive have a future of only more gray lifelessness that eventually will destroy all who remain ...unless love is found, again.

With the movies as a metaphor for our own lives, any of us, who have lived or are living the life of a serious man, know how empty a masked life—holding on to what is supposed to be—can feel. And, for any of us trapped in the darkness behind the mask, we know what it is to live in the grayest form of the hopelessness that can eat away at whatever life we possess.

The third film, which was the first one I saw on that marathon day, seemed to be an attempt to understand what is *Under the Mask*, which is connected to what we call God. The question, *"What is God?"* seems to redirect attention from focusing on hopelessness and helplessness found in the chaos we experience when we live from *The Mask* or the grey lifelessness that plagues us when we live from what is *Behind the Mask*, disconnected from essence. When we live from the essence that is *Under the Mask*, we experience love, connection, and creative synchronicity instead of fear, separation, and cataclysmic destruction.

I knew experiencing these three films in the same day had a meaning that was profound, though at the time I didn't know what it would come to mean in the weeks and months ahead. I, also, had a sense that deeper levels of meaning would unfold as book three began its task of writing itself in me.

Three Parts to the Northwest Trip
Part One-Storage in Seattle

In the early morning of Saturday, December 5th of 2009, 20 days before I began to write this chapter and just a few days after that marathon movie experience in Denver, I stood in front of two very large storage units. I couldn't help wondering if I'd planned enough time for sorting through a lifetime in the form of boxes filled with items that had occupied so many spaces and places in my earlier life. Because a fire had destroyed much of what I owned from the time I was born to the time I was a junior in college, there were only a few boxes from my earliest years. I found my baby book and my high school annuals that I decided to keep, but I had a different response when I looked into a powder blue jewelry box turned dusty gray from the smoke and time. The dusty box held mementoes from my early childhood including a pair of glasses I wore from the fourth through the seventh grades. The little brown colored frames still had the black electrician's tape wrapped around the nose bridge and the temple arms, both of which broke when I was playing baseball the summer between the fourth and fifth grade. We had no money to buy a new pair at the time, so I wore glasses that separated and fell apart every time the sun came out and melted the adhesive, leaving a sticky residue on my nose and the side of my face. There were a few things from my teen and young adult years, including the graduation mortarboard tassels from high school and college and a yellow and orange butterfly pin I received from a boy I worked with at the Seattle Center, the summer I was 18. He liked me, and Jake had been in one of his dark moods, treating me badly. I thought of ending our relationship that summer, but chose Jake over the boy I had worked with for three months; however, I kept the pin he gave me. It is still beautiful, after all the years.

I thought about keeping the taped up glasses, but when I was a child, I hated them, as well as the time in my life they represented. After three years of suffering with them, I refused to wear the brown-rimmed spectacles when I entered the eighth grade. Each day, I left for school wearing my glasses, and once away from home, I took them off and put them in my locker. In time, my eyes became adjusted to seeing without glasses, and I didn't have to wear any eye support until I was in graduate school in my 50s, when so much time in front of the computer and in books led to reading glasses. It was painless to throw the still-scorched and musty smelling box and its contents into the dumpster, except for the butterfly pin.

***

Silverware, cooking utensils, pots, pans, and dishes were more than objects, as each item still held the memories that were intricately entangled with events in my life. Many of the items were wedding gifts given when I believed Jake and I would be married for the rest of our lives. But there was not enough time to hold each piece to recall and release anything particular about the past these items might have represented.

There were some things that stirred up memories, such as the gold-rimmed, ivory Lennox dinnerware my mother-in-law picked out and placed on a list for a bride's registry at a number of local department stores. I didn't like the idea of a registry, and couldn't make myself comply with her wishes to sign up with various department stores selecting the things I wanted people to buy for me. I believed a gift should have meaning because the giver knows and loves the recipients; gifts from business associates and acquaintances of family members who gave out of social obligation felt too cold to me. Everyone I knew who received these kinds of gifts usually put them away in cupboards or in storage and seldom, if ever, used them. Those who had fine china usually put the pieces in a display cabinet to use only on special occasions; however, using the dinnerware for holidays made everyone uncomfortable at the thought of chipping or breaking one of the special and usually irreplaceable dishes, a worry that spoiled so many holidays for me.

Despite months of pressure from Jake, I am sure because of months of pressure from his mother, I didn't sign up for the department store bridal registry. But Jake's mother believed the registry was necessary; it was one of those rules that properly raised brides-to-be just had to do. And if she was going to maintain the approval of the serious women in her circle, I had to be on a registry. I imagine she must have had as much difficulty understanding my resistance as I had understanding her insistence. A couple of months before we were married, gifts began to arrive, which included many settings and specialized platters and bowls of that one pattern of Lennox, more than enough sets of matching silverware, and many silver serving pieces. We, also, received many color coordinated towels and sheets. I discovered my soon-to-be mother-in-law had registered for me. Part of me felt defeated by her actions, and another part of me was filled with joyful excitement in arranging all the beautiful gifts in the cupboards, in drawers, and on shelves of a brand new apartment that would soon be the beginning of a totally new life, unlike anything I had ever experienced before.

A year or so after we were married, when we moved from our second apartment to our first house, one of Jake's friends accidentally dropped a large box filled with the biggest, specialized Lennox pieces. He had been raised with all the rules regarding social expectations and knew how important china was to properly raised women; he was obviously distressed over the many broken pieces. I smiled and told him it was no big deal, although I was sure he did not believe me, but I was telling the truth. I felt more comfortable using everyday dishes so no one would have to feel upset should one be chipped or cracked, and I wouldn't have to feel any stress if something broke. When I found the boxes containing what was left of the Lennox, I placed them in the "give to Goodwill" pile...and it was still no big deal to let go of what was left.

What did cause feelings of sadness were the few remaining pieces of dark brown earthen dinnerware that I had begun collecting from the dollar store when I was in college and completed when Jake was in the military. I began to buy plates, bowls, and serving dishes as a way to give me hope that there would be a marriage in my future, especially when events happened that caused me to wonder if our relationship was over. And after we were married, when my young husband was in Vietnam, I bought additional pieces as a way to assure myself that he would be coming home.

***

Inside the second of the large crates, clothing had been piled up on the top of a huge number of boxes of books. The designer clothes I wore in the late 70s and 80s that went into storage in 1989 reflected the high style of my professional life. Ranging from size 6-10, a size range that would probably be called size 0 to 2 in the finer stores, today, these beautiful clothes belonged to bulimic Sandy, who later became anorexic Sandy. Classic in style, which made them almost timeless, they were still in immaculate condition, but I felt no need to hold onto them. Many large plastic bags were filled and placed in the Goodwill pile. Each piece carried the energetic DNA of happy times and sad times, of days I felt strong and days I felt weak.

One form fitting, grey suit held memories of the day I introduced the Governor of our state to a large audience, and another day Jake invited me to join him for lunch along with the woman with whom I was sure he was having an affair. After I became upset when I found out he had planned to go to lunch with her, supposedly a business meeting, he said he wanted to prove to me that there was nothing going on between them. Earlier, I had found a perfumed card she had sent to him inviting him out for drinks when I was on a business trip. Her first comment about me when Jake and I showed up for lunch was how lovely I looked, said in a way that felt condescending, as if she thought I would be ugly or dowdy. As we ate, I watched the subtle glances between them and felt the energy they could not hide. I had no doubt that my suspicions were correct. However, I pushed the suspicions aside and tried to live as if nothing were wrong. And then, I began to put on weight again. The slender Sandy who fit in that classically tailored grey suit grew much too big to wear it anymore. Sometime later, Jake acknowledged that he had an affair with that woman. For most of those 17 years, his girlfriend had expected him to leave me for her, but when he didn't, she increased pressure on him, and his negative behaviors toward me increased. Finally, when I filed for divorce, he seemed not to want the divorce anymore. However, by that time, I couldn't find the place inside that wanted to be married. When I was preparing to leave for China, I decided to save the clothing, thinking that perhaps, someday, I would be able to fit into them again.

The nearly two years I lived in China, which required riding a bicycle everywhere and eating a diet mostly of fruits and vegetables, resulted in significant weight loss and a restoration of my physical health. But I didn't reclaim those clothes when I returned. It was still too painful to wear clothing connected with a life I was still mourning. I thought I would come back for them later, but that didn't happen. I began to put on weight, as before, still trapped in the pattern that has captured so many people in our world today. I kept hoping I'd lose weight and would be able to wear the clothing worn by slender Sandy.

While filling the bags with clothing for Good Will, I realized that part of me wanted to keep a few of my favorite things for a future time when

I would finally be free of the patterns that created Fat Sandy and my body would be slender and healthy again. If I didn't give everything away, I could have a few beautiful, timeless pieces of clothing. But, it occurred to me that when I healed the Fat-Sandy-patterns that held me captive for too many years of my adult life, the *Transformed Sandy* ought not to have to wear hand-me-downs from the deeply tormented bulimic and anorexic Sandys of the past. Letting go of the grey suit and the rest of the clothing from the 70s and 80s was easier than I had thought it would be.

***

All my life, I had a strong identity with books. Despite the fact that my college texts were scorched and damaged from the house fire, I had kept them, and also kept the ones from the 12 years I taught at a Christian high school. I had stored boxes full of self-help and new age books that I read when my mask began to fall away and I needed something to hold me together. Years before, I had pulled out the most meaningful ones, brought to me by what a colleague, Dr. Allan Combs, called *Library Angels,* a name coined by Arthur Koestler in his book, *Roots of Coincidence.* He believes these special emissaries bring to us the books that contain ideas we need to know, ideas that were never taught to us during our more unconscious lives and, as a result, weren't a part of our conscious minds. When we are ready and finally do read them, the messages these books hold seem to ring so deeply true that we can't imagine not having known what was in them.

After I took the very few books I wanted, Jake helped me divide what remained into two piles, one to throw away and the other to sell to *Half-Price-Books.* I didn't need them to take up space in my external world because their messages had already become an intricate part of my internal world. It was not difficult to let these books go, either.

***

Music was a very important part of my life in my early years. The first piece of furniture Jake purchased for us right after we were married was a beautiful dark walnut stereo console, but I suspect he wanted it for its appearance rather than for the music it could produce. In the first years of our life together, when I returned home from teaching, I played my favorite classical recordings, something that made my heart feel full, but as soon as Jake came home, he told me to *"turn off that noise"* and in time, I stopped playing music. When I separated from Jake in 1987, I purchased a beautiful sound system to fill my new world with music, which had been nearly absent for most of my married life. But the intensity of therapy with Seattle David, and later with Steven, and body therapy with Michael in Bellingham was so very overwhelming that anything incoming from the outer world was too much for me to handle. I couldn't watch television or listen to the radio, and even playing music overloaded my internal system. For the nearly three years I was living on my own, all I could do was go to therapy sessions, though for a time, I was able to go to choir practice at the Unity Church, and sing on Sunday. I did sing with a quartet that, in time, became semi-professional. But, most of the time, I needed silence, darkness, and isolation, especially when I was in my apartment. However, in the two decades that passed since I made that purchase, technology advanced so profoundly that there was little value in saving a nearly unused stereo and speaker system. So it was not difficult to let that go, as well.

A couple of years before I left Jake, he took me to the Bellevue Street Fair, where a company that made and repaired stringed instruments demonstrated the hammered dulcimer. I was drawn to the beautiful sound and kept returning to listen to the players. Something in the sound made my whole body feel like dancing and singing despite the depression that lived in me nearly all the time back then. The next Christmas, Jake purchased a most beautiful dulcimer for me. A few weeks after I received the gift, I took a class to learn how to play my new instrument. When the teacher heard the sound of my dulcimer he exclaimed that he was its maker and considered it to be the very best one he had ever made. It had an ethereal sound like none other.

When I opened the jacket that protected my lovely dulcimer, I found that, in the years of storage, when the crates had been moved several times, somehow, the bridges for the strings had been broken. I pulled out a phonebook to see if the manufacturer was still in business. They were…and after looking at the instrument, the craftsman in charge of restoring instruments let me know he would be able to repair the damage, clean it, and install new bridges and strings. My heart was so happy…it was time to bring music back into my life, not time to let it go; I arranged to have my beautiful dulcimer repaired and shipped to me in Colorado.

***

In only a few hours, well-over 95% of what I had owned in my "previous life" had been either thrown away or placed in the give away pile. The only large piece that still needed some decision was the heirloom table that had been in my father's family going back at least to when my grandmother was a little child in the latter part of the 1800s. After my grandma died, grandpa came to live with my parents and gifted the old oak table to me, asking me to keep it in the family should I ever decide I didn't want it. With its extension leafs, it was bigger than most people's dining rooms, and I didn't know what to do with it. It had been dismantled and had not served anyone for a very long time. I decided to call my brother and ask if he would make arrangements to pick up the table, which he did. Like every material thing that exists, the table contains a history of both positive and negative experiences when family members sat around it and shared the best and worst energies for 150 years or more. I don't know if that heavy oak table will become firewood someday or will be refurbished and weave itself into some future generation's life.

The last of what I needed to go through were photographs and boxes of letters I had written and ones that had been written to me over the years. It looked as if it would take a very long time to go through them to decide what to keep or not keep. So I decided to put them aside, perhaps, to sort through when I returned to Colorado. Making that decision to not throw it all away, something I could have done but chose not to do, put me in touch with another time of throwing things out, when it felt like I didn't have that choice.

When we were in college, Jake and I went to separate universities for our first two years and we wrote letters to each other several times a week. When he was sent to Vietnam a year after we were married, we wrote to each other nearly every day. I had saved all those letters in two shoeboxes, and kept them on the upper shelf in my closet.

For some reason, a couple of years before we separated, Jake decided he wanted to do a major cleaning out of what he considered to be unnecessary junk we had collected over the years. After throwing out what he didn't want, he went into my closet and pointed to my boxes where I had stored his letters; he told me to take them down and put them in the bag to take to the dump. I explained that the boxes had my letters in them, and they were important to me, but he demanded I get rid of them. I couldn't understand why he insisted so adamantly that I trash something I highly valued, and those boxes took up such a little amount of space, but I was an obedient wife and did what he told me to do. With pain in my heart, I took the two shoeboxes from the shelf and placed them in the trash bag, which he put in the back of the truck. I didn't have a chance to look at any of them, but when the bag was dumped, one of the boxes fell open and I saw a number of photos from our young lives, including ones he had taken in Vietnam. While he was busy dumping other things, I salvaged a few photos before the rest were swept into the public dumpster. It was as if he wanted to erase all the loving things he had ever said to me in the past. Much later I found out that the on-and-off affair he had with the woman, the one who thought I looked lovely in my grey suit, had begun again and was likely the impetus behind his getting rid of all the evidence that reflected his past emotional attachment to me.

***

As the last of the items from the crates were divided between the give away and throw away piles, I put thousands of photos that went back into the lives of my parents and grandparents, the photo albums reflecting the 28 years Jake and I had known each other, letters I had received, and journals I had written into more sturdy boxes and planned to go through them later. As I worked my way through one of the boxes the night after letting go of so much, I found a photograph that touched a memory that will always be with me.

My grandfather had suffered a debilitating stroke when he was living with my parents in his last years. Near the end of his 92-year life, a distant family member had sent a box full of photographs to my grandfather. Grandpa sat in his wheelchair with his one good hand hovering over photographs, flipping through them, one after another.

He stopped for a breathless moment, pulled a photo of a woman to his chest, and he began to sob like a tiny child. In all the years I had known my grandpa, I had never heard him cry. He held the photo against his heart as if something so deep, so painful had exploded within him and only that picture, which brought him such pain, could also bring solace. I had no idea who the woman in the photo was, but it was very clear she was deeply important to him. The commotion brought my mother into the living room, and when she saw him, she snatched the photo from his hands and demanded that the box be closed up. I don't believe grandpa was allowed to look at the box or that photo ever again.

Later, I learned that the image he held against his heart was of his young mother, the girl who had been exchanged by her parents for a gambling debt when she was barely in her teens. Her father, my great-great grandfather, had lost a card game and he had no money to pay for the hand he had lost; he traded his young daughter for the debt. She was sold into white slavery, made socially acceptable by the family arranging for her to become the child-bride of a man likely close to three times her age. Her job was to keep the house and take care of her "husband's" needs. By the time she was 16, she had given birth to my grandfather, and by the time she was 23, she had birthed three other children; the youngest died shortly after its birth.

While her husband, who was really her slave owner, was away on a business trip, this young woman dressed her three children in their best clothes, pinned letters to their jackets, and took them to the station where she bought tickets for the train to take them to live with their aunt. My grandfather, the eldest of the three, fought back his little-boy tears because he knew his mother would no longer be in his life, and he would have to be the man of the family. She took a later train in the opposite direction and, in time, built a new life for herself. Her eldest son was still holding back the tears and the pain when his mother died some 50 years later, when he—grandfather to me and seven other children—refused to go into the hospital to visit his mother on her deathbed.

I was a little child of six at the time of my great grandmother Sarah's death, close to the same age my grandfather was when his mother put him on the train and escaped from her captive marriage, begun when she was a child of about 12. I sat with my grandfather in his old Nash car, while his brother, my great Uncle, walked across the busy street and into the hospital to bid farewell to their mother who was 93. The well-protected little boy inside the man didn't cry as my grandpa sat in silence until my great uncle returned a short while later. Thirty or more years after that incident, an old man, debilitated by two strokes, wheelchair bound, and unable to speak, held a picture of the woman he so dearly loved, a woman who had crushed his heart when he was so very young, and for the first time in over 80 years, the old man finally allowed himself to cry the anguished tears of his child-self. The photograph of my great grandmother belonged in the box of saved pictures that I packed tightly and mailed back to myself in Colorado.

The storage crates that had been filled with thousands of stories and memories were empty. Because of the speed at which I released items that represented 50 years of my life, I may never find an opportunity to remember and release anything more. But somehow, that felt okay. If anything really did need to be dealt with, I trusted that I would draw to me what I'd need to remember, allowing me to take care of whatever that might be.

There must have been something healing for Jake, too, in releasing so many pieces of a past we shared together. He showed kindness in his willingness to help me unpack, unload, and release some of the last of the material things that had been a part of our many years together. And we both had the opportunity to let it all go.

Three Parts to the Northwest Trip
Part Two-Saint Michael

Heading north on Interstate-5, driving from Seattle to Bellingham I became deeply relaxed, as the scenery of the beautiful Northwest seemed to fly past me. Along with the changing view from my window, came memories of many excursions Jake and I had taken during our married years. And I recalled memories of my own Shamanic training adventures in the back woods of Indian Territory not far off the freeway. In the three years between my separation and divorce, I participated in drumming and prayer circles, while learning about Native American healing practices. I, also, recalled the many times I drove that same freeway to see Michael, the wonderfully gifted body therapist who provided invaluable support to me while I was living through the most scattered and shattered time of my life. He became my source of grounding, as my mask and all the rest of me began falling away faster than I could pick up the pieces.

From 1986-88, I had worked with the psychotherapist I called Seattle David to find a way to save my broken marriage, and during that time in the spring of 87, I began having sessions with Michael who used a body therapy method called Rolfing. The foundation of this method is for the therapist to look for areas of alignment and misalignment as a way to become conscious of the various holding patterns caused by unresolved trauma. Even when a trauma event is very small, a holding pattern can be formed, resulting in restricted movement. This restriction in one part of the body causes the rest of the body to adjust to the unreleased pattern by counter-balancing with another restricting misalignment. After a lifetime of holding patterns, the body can become rigid and movement outside a narrow range of motions can become painful, if not impossible. The Rolfer puts gentle, thoughtful pressure on a point where the misalignment first began to organize to help it realign itself, which is then followed by releasing of the counter-balanced pattern. It is not unusual for whatever memories and emotions related to the trauma that caused formation of the pattern to come forward for release, as well. However, any change in alignment or any expression of the trauma is usually met with resistance because the pattern was created as a way to defend against whatever happened, and at times against recall of memories of the original trauma and the feelings and meanings that were attached.

Michael was exceedingly skilled at identifying the locked patterns my body held and knowing exactly what needed to be touched to trigger an avalanche of responses, which led to major releases. When the release took place, it was not uncommon for a flood of memories from my childhood to erupt. Not only was Michael a gifted body therapist, he was as good as any psychotherapist I have even worked with in being able to sit with what was coming up for me without getting overwhelmed by it or expressing a need to quiet it or stop it. He was able to hold the space for me to find my way to healing what had been buried for decades deep in my tissues.

Early in our work together, he found, I was unable to fully turn my head to the left. The muscles had developed a pattern of rigidity. He told me that he could force my head to turn to the left, and parts of me would be relieved to finally have that pattern broken, but other parts would never trust him again, because he had forced them to do what they were not prepared to do. Then he quietly asked if I would turn my head as far as I could to the left. After I turned, he gently asked, *"Can you ask the part of you holding your muscles tight so you can't turn any further, what she is afraid to see?"* My whole body began to tremble and tears streamed down my face. A little girl part of me had been holding my neck tight so she wouldn't have to see a terrible murder that was happening to her left. Because it is not uncommon for one muscle group to hold a number of memories of events from the past in deeper layers, later I found that my 4-year-old self had also buried the memory of the initial rape in the forest outside my family house in that same place. My child-self was sitting on the forest floor, making paths in the dirt when father approached her from the left. She looked over her shoulder to see who was coming and at first was so happy to see him, but then when she saw his expression, she went into fear, followed by terror when he shoved her to the ground and raped her. A child might reason that bad things won't happen if you don't turn your head.

For three years, Michael worked with hundreds of patterns that had subtly become locked in my body, holding it in rigid form. Over my life, I was able to override some of those patterns, and could force movement despite their presence, but not without putting terrible stress on tendons and joints. Had the patterns not been released, they may have developed into arthritic conditions that would have caused me to live my later years wheelchair-bound as my mother's mother had done or extremely weak and unable to walk as happened to my mother. Or,

I could have become hunched over with painful stiffness, as was the case for my great grandfather, grandfather, and father as well as many members of my extended family on my father's side. It is, also, possible that many other diseases could have arisen out of the restrictive patterns that threw my body out of alignment and limited the flow of blood, fluids, and movement within me.

Pushing against body patterns, as in *mind over matter,* can result in chronic inflammation that impacts the cardio vascular system, and can inflame tendons, joints, muscles, and tissues. Holding on to the protective pattern in the body while the mind is attempting to make the body move despite the pattern, creates an internal war. Because we have multiple layers and aspects of both mind and body, it is possible for many parts of self to be at war with many other parts of self as we attempt to live our lives. The result over time is a depleted immune system and vulnerability to illness, both physical and psychological.

Michael's gift extended past seeing body patterns; he was able to identify child parts that lived within the patterns and create an arena of safety for them. He had a profoundly gentle way of touching these most separated parts of myself, encouraging them to be seen and known until the time they were ready to discover their connection to my whole self, as one. I recorded many of those sessions in a book I had written in 1991 called, *Melting the Chains,* a book I had never published. When Seattle David left the state and I no longer had a psychotherapist, Michael became my bridge to the second therapist with whom I worked for over a year. Michael continued to work with me until 1989, when I began preparing to leave for China. He worked with me, again, in December of '96, a few days after my father died. I cannot imagine my healing process without having had Michael in my life.

***

Though 13 years had passed, almost to the day, he looked much the same, with only a little touch of gray in his hair and a balding spot in the back that I don't remember being there before. For a little over an hour, Michael worked with my body, and with his most perfect timing, he quietly suggested that parts of me might be remembering who he was;

with that comment, a tear spilled down my cheek. The tear was one of joy arising from parts that were touched for being remembered.

In those first three years of working with him, all parts of me came to know they were safe with the man who had known how to love and respect every one of them as he navigated the, often, turbulent oceans of inner energy systems that had been ripped apart from the many earthquakes, hurricanes, and tidal waves of my childhood. That first session seemed to be about reintroductions, and remembering how to allow the energies of another to work with my energies on the deepest levels to create connectivity within and peace in my heart.

It wasn't as if I hadn't been blessed with many gifted body therapists over the years, but there was something very special about Michael as the first person my body allowed to work with what it had hidden for so many years. There was a bond that ran deeply into all the levels and layers of my body consciousness.

Because this was a time of significant releasing, I thought working with Michael might bring up unaddressed issues resulting in painful but cathartic releases. However, like the first, the second session was incredibly gentle, with a sensation of quietly following the sensation of energy patterns as they accepted the invitation Michael offered to turn inward to reconnect with my center instead of being focused outward.

As a way to explain what Michael had done for me in that second session, imagine that there is a large family of a dozen or more people who have been under attack from some outside enemy for a long time. Each family member has spent the entire time of the siege at a window or door fully focused on the outer threat, fighting for his or her life against intruder after intruder. Even though the other family members are in the same house, each person is responding, not to each other but to the immediate threat just outside the window or door, remaining generally unaware of the condition of the house or what the others are facing.

Now imagine that after a while, the siege ends, but everyone remains focused on what might still be a potential threat outside, unaware of what is happening in other places in the room, or in the rest of the house. Then someone everyone trusts, calls in from the outside that the threat is over, and the call encourages each to turn away from the window or door, releasing the expectation that another invader could rise up and attack at any moment. Finally, each family member can shift attention to the others to see how they are doing after that long battle and to rejoice in the fact that they all survived. One-by-one, each embraces another, until the dozen or more separate people feel reconnected with the whole family again.

During that session, Michael became the voice from the outside. Even though the siege had been over for decades, there were parts, and even entire systems within me, that continued to hold an external focus and didn't notice other parts of me, at least not on a visceral level. Although I had experienced what is called *integration* from *Dissociative Identity Disorder* (DID) in June of 1994, a process that focuses on divisions of personality of the mind, psychological integration does not always include shattered feelings held in the body. The 2009 session with Michael focused on body feelings and sensations.

***

As a sidebar explanation of dissociation based on my experience of this disorder, I believe we are all dissociative. Everyone has the capacity to have multiple aspects, as Jung identified as archetypal patterns showing up in individuals as dominant and sub-personalities, and Freud, in a more limited fashion, identified as the Ego, the Id, and the Super Ego. When the child experiences a fairly consistent world, he or she learns how to respond to that external world by putting on a mask that meets with the approval of that world to which it can attach. In time that becomes the personality. However, when an infant experiences love and hate, acceptance and rejection, safety and lack of safety, and so many more opposing messages from parents or caregivers, the child has a difficult time with what research identifies as *attachment*. The child needs to learn how to respond to a volatile outer world based on an extremely inconsistent and ever-changing environment. The little one learns to organize multiple, complex behavior patterns based on inconsistent circumstances, responding to each circumstance in different, if not opposite ways. I believe that many of the personality disorders people experience later in life are directly related to problems around attachment early on in life. This ability to change patterns of interaction with parental figures who drastically change their responses to the child creates splitting in the little one. When there is confused attachment, coupled with extreme trauma between the ages of 4 and 7—the time personality is jelling—many personalities, or masks are formed instead of one mask.

After the mask-personality has been set in early childhood, most people retain that basic set of response patterns to the outer world, enough for researchers to have identified personality types. But for the child who first had to deal with extreme changes in the external environment and then was traumatized during that critical period of personality jelling, many personalities or masks had to be formed. Which mask would be donned would be based on external triggers, giving the impression that the person with what was called Multiple Personality Disorder (MPD), now Dissociative Identity Disorder (DID), had no core self. My experience with this disorder, in myself and in many clients, is that there is a core self that is like a conductor, unseen by the audience, who points his or her wand to a particular instrument in the orchestra to take the lead, switching and changing the lead based on the music that is being played.

The outside world sees the changing of the masks as evidence that the person is shattered into lots of parts (dissociated or multiple) without knowing there is a deep level, almost always unconscious orchestration going on, based on the pattern of having formed any number of personality patterns to deal with the outside world, instead of the more common single personality pattern, or, what I identify as the mask.

It is possible the reason the "cure" rate for persons with DID is much higher than most other personality disorders is because the core self is not so attached to any one mask, while persons with a single mask disorder may be much less willing to release attachment to the only mask they identify as who they are. My work has brought me to the conclusion that nearly all humans are wearing a mask, and because of this, we all need healing, requiring a release of attachment to the mask and an embrace of the god-essence within, which is the core or true self. Until we turn within to recognize who we truly are, we experience life dissociated from ourselves.

***

For days, weeks, and even months following the two sessions with Michael, I experienced an energy movement of turning inward, which I felt as an internal embracing among parts and systems that had been fully unaware they'd been living separately. Consciously and energetically turning within caused me to viscerally experience connective oneness to a depth I had not felt before. All the parts were turning deep within to notice and connect with my core being, what I have come to call my *Sandy God Essence*. It was powerful and continues to unfold, even now as I am writing this.

I have no idea if I will see Michael ever again, but I do know that he will always be with me. If hearts issued sainthood decrees, certainly, this amazing, gentle man would be called Saint Michael, named after Archangel Michael, whose names means, *one who stands up for children*, and without a doubt he did that for all the child parts of me for so many years of my life. As I left Bellingham in December of 2009, I knew those sessions with Michael that reminded me to turn inward were very important to whatever was happening in me and in my life.

Three Parts to the Northwest Trip
Part Three: Oregon David

The day following that last session with Michael, I was on the Amtrak Cascades train headed south to Portland, Oregon to visit with my dear friend, David, likely my most vocal cheer leader, who has always encouraged me to break free of any last constraints and melt any remaining chains that prevent the real me from living fully in my body and in the world. As much as I wanted that, too, there were parts of me that still resisted being set completely free. These parts reminded me of film images of concentration camp prisoners who seemed too afraid to leave the cells that held them captive for far too long, not sure they could trust the liberators who had come to rescue them from the terror they had lived with at the hands of their Nazi captors. Others may not have trusted themselves to know how to live in a world free from all they had suffered, a world that had changed so very much since they had been snatched away and imprisoned. They may have identified with the patterns that had kept them alive, and were afraid of create new patterns in a world they no longer knew. I wanted freedom and, yet, I feared it, too.

***

As a sidebar explanation to my use of the word, *I*: when a person says, *"I,"* there is often little understanding that *I* is really a collective word with many levels of meanings. In fact, there are many parts of any one of us that could claim being I at any particular time. It is possible for one I to want to reach out to another person with love while another I holds back and presents as a distant, reserved person. The part of self that most identifies with thinking can keep the feeling part of self in an inner prison, and one I can say I am not very emotional, while the feeling I might break out of prison and say something the other I would normally never say or do. A part that feels like the true I when it finally finds a way to speak might not be acknowledged or even know by the other I.

When something slips out, quite unexpectedly, the I attached to one way of being may say, *"I have no idea where that came from. You know that is not me."*

Some aspect of I can allow what I call God Essence to come out during important interactions that call for wisdom, and at other times another aspect of I will not allow the essence to come out in the world when coming out seems much too threatening to another part of I.

One of the masks that a person wears can become so powerful that the conscious mind believes it is the only "I" and attaches to that mask as the real "I-self," as in "I am the role I play, I am father, I am mother, I am professional, I am . . . and there can be multiple masks and multiple I-masks, with or without conscious awareness of the multiplicity. Certainly, we can have many I parts that exist behind our masks, completely unknown by the I attached to the mask, and when we stumble into one of those parts of us, saying or doing something foreign to other parts of us, we can be shocked that such a thing was in us.

The conscious "I" can have a difficult time dealing with the buried parts behind the mask that are usually unconscious to the conscious mind's I-self. We all have multiples of I-parts, but most of us don't let ourselves become too aware of the complexity within us. As a result, we believe that when we say "I", it means only one thing, and it very seldom does.

***

So, back to my story…I had left Bellingham and was headed to Portland via the train to spend a few days with David, the man I described in books one and two as being an athlete, a litigation psychologist, a shaman, and much more. He is a master of the inner workings of the mind and soul and has spent many years developing programs to support people to find inner healing. Among the many things being his friend has taught me is to honor my thinking and the discoveries I make when journeying into the deepest places within. He has been one of the main people in my life with whom I can share my ideas and listen to his. He has encouraged me to reclaim my physical health and strength, as well as to discover the joys of living.

David has known me in my periods of darkness and light, in my successes and failures, and through my ups and downs of weight and, in all of it, has remained a valued and true friend. He has encouraged me to discover my healthiest, happiest self. When he visited me in Colorado in August of '09, he went fishing, while I climbed around the rocks taking pictures of some of the most beautiful landscapes in the world. On one of the days, we drove to Boreas Pass and began a hike that was too much of a challenge for me, so he went on ahead, and when he returned, David challenged me to hike up the 14,000' mountain on the other side of the highway the following year. A part of me wanted to be able to lose weight and get myself in shape enough to make the climb with him in 2010, but another part did not believe I could do that.

I began a search for better fitting hiking boots, but new ones still left me with blisters and a heart that felt as if it would fall out of my chest. From early September to the end of November of '09, my focus was on the completion of book two that just never seemed to get finished while I resisted, struggled with, and then opened to the parts of me that needed my attention before the conclusion of *Behind the Mask* could occur. As a result, exercise, hiking, and releasing the excess pounds had been put on the back burner. Finally, the second book was completed in November of '09 and I was determined to begin the final book in the trilogy immediately afterward. By the time December arrived and my trip to the Northwest was at hand, I was not strong enough to venture out on any long hikes with my dear friend. Though I was not the heaviest I had ever been, I was still 100 pounds overweight and my muscles had not been properly toned.

A few days after I arrived in the City of Roses, which was ice-covered and frozen from a pre-Christmas storm, David suggested that we take a walk through the very hilly streets that surround his home in the foothills above Portland, it was quite clear that I was unable to keep up with him, and though I suggested that he walk ahead, as he did that previous summer, he slowed down so we could continue talking. We began a conversation that led to us talking about *"Fat Sandy."* He believed she had been given responsibilities far beyond her ability to master them, which wasn't very fair. Instead of just being in charge of what came into my body, she had been given charge of nearly every aspect of my life… everything was dependent on her to earn a living, to write, to keep me safe, and so much more, which made it impossible for her to focus on my body and the energy patterns that could create health. Instead, she bore the pressure that if she failed to do one thing right, everything would come tumbling down on her. As an example, she was given the job of assuring my safety, which to many little girl parts of me meant that I had to be fat so men would not find me attractive and hurt me, yet she was also in charge of getting me to lose weight so I would be healthy. She was in charge of maintaining invisibility, which is often the case for people who are fat, but also, she had been given the job of finding ways to make me known. It seemed as if most of the jobs she carried had built-in opposites, meaning that her life was overwhelmed with responsibilities that by their very nature would fail, whether or not she succeeded. If I exercised as David encouraged me to do, the pain connected to past experiences arose into my consciousness, revealing what other parts needed to cover over and insulate with fat. David told me that he finally understood how devastated Fat Sandy must have been when he suggested that she take on another responsibility of making sure that I walked or did some significant exercise for one-and-a-half hours every day.

When David asked what responsibilities *Slender Sandy* had, I was as surprised as he was when some part of myself answered, in disdain, *"Almost none!"* Many aspects that made up my I-self had declared Slender Sandy to be incompetent and perhaps even too dangerous to allow being in charge of anything in my life. Some parts of me still blamed her for having ruined my life by being attractive to those evil men when I was a child and blamed her for liking herself enough to become slender and then becoming disenchanted with Jake after I had lost weight that allowed me to fit into size six suits when I was an adult. They blamed Slender Sandy for ending my 23-year marriage and creating all the problems I experienced following my divorce. Because Slender Sandy still seemed to be a threat to many aspects of me, she was not given charge of anything. Later, I discovered that it was not Fat Sandy that made me fat; it was Slender Sandy that ate to stop the pain related to feeling judged by the rest of me for being slender. Fat Sandy had to live with the results.

The following days, I communicated with all the resistant parts and asked them to be open to David's challenge, and I exercised nearly two hours each day and felt very good. During those days in Oregon, David took me to a Christmas Concert in downtown Portland and asked me if I was still singing. I told him I had no music in my life, and hadn't since I had moved to the mountains. The intensity of the writing over the previous two years took full focus, and I had no time for anything else in my life but writing. He knew how important music had been to me in the past, and offered to pay half for an *I-pod* if I thought I would allow it to bring back music, something that had delighted my soul and opened me to wanting to be in my body and dance. It seemed to me that my writing self had been too afraid to let my singing and dancing self out for fear the writing would stop. And, there was also fear that if I reconnected with singing and dancing, I might just lose weight, which part of me wanted to do, but other parts were afraid of letting that happen.

The last morning of my visit, David and I took a long walk on the frigidly cold and icy road along the Skyline ridge overlooking the city of Portland, and we ended up at a cemetery. We decided to walk on the path within the cemetery because it seemed less dangerous than the street. At the time, I was simply enjoying the crisp air and the conversation, with my dear friend, while working very hard at maintaining my balance on the icy pathway. I had no way of knowing how significant that place was to be. And after the walk, David drove me to the Portland airport for my flight back to Denver.

Three Experiences Following the Trip to the Northwest
The First: Great Grandmother Sarah

Upon my return to my mountain retreat, I checked my email and found a message from a very distant cousin with whom I had been in only sporadic communication over the previous couple of years. My connection with him started when I had done an Internet search for Sarah, my grandfather's mother, while I was writing *The Mask* and found a man's name associated with her. I sent this person an email message and discovered he was my cousin, two or three times removed. Soon after my inquiry, I received information about past relatives, including the fact that depression and suicide had been a part of my family history, dating back long before Sarah's time. My understanding of family systems related to suicide is that the tendency towards these kinds of behaviors runs in families, so it was easy to see where such thoughts that entered my field now and then might have come from. It was helpful for me to know where I could direct my healing energies related to depression and suicidal thoughts to free myself of this family pattern, along with the many others that needed to be released.

I hadn't heard from this cousin for a year or so, and was surprised to have received his Christmas letter. In the holiday message, he stated that his searches of 2009 led to the discovery of family facts including the burial-place of my Great Grandmother Sarah in Portland, Oregon. When I typed in the name of the cemetery on a Google search, to my amazement, I found she was buried in a cemetery at 333 SW Skyline Boulevard, not so far away from where David and I had walked just that very morning.

As I thought about her, I reflected back to previous conversations with relatives when I was a child after my Great Grandmother had died. My relatives considered Sarah to be the black sheep of the family for what she had done to her husband, to my grandfather, my great uncle, and great aunt. The family believed she was a wicked woman for abandoning her children, despite the fact that she was a child, herself when she conceived them. When I first heard her story, I believed she was a woman of profound courage to have found a way to free herself from bondage despite the huge social constraints that would have preferred she remain captive. I couldn't see her as a wicked woman. Though her children experienced deeply felt, life-long pain as a result of her putting them on a train to live with relatives, likely, there would have been even deeper, unconscious damage to them if she had remained a captive slave in a loveless marriage that began when she was not even 13. No one seemed to notice what had happened to her as a child, when her father put her up as collateral in a card game and lost. I am amazed at the power of "social rules" that disregard the souls of those who are being so harshly judged because they dared challenge the rules.

By stepping out into the unknown, with what must have taken tremendous fortitude back in the 1800s, she provided an alternate answer to her family system's belief that there is no escape from life's cruel circumstances, except becoming lost in lifetime of depression or in committing suicide. Perhaps, it was her genetic contribution to me that encouraged me to challenge the social rules and not sign up for the bridal registry just before I got married when I was 21. And I suspect, it was Sarah that gave me the courage to leave what had become a painfully loveless marriage by the time I was in my mid 40s to create a new life for myself as Sarah had done in leaving her "husband" just 4 years short of a century before I left mine. Like Sarah, I chose to violate family and social rules that would have killed me, emotionally if not physically, if I had remained married and decided to create a life I could embrace, one that could embrace me, as well. I have come to believe that depression and suicide come from the belief that there is no way to change circumstances that seem intolerable. Sarah taught me that we have choice. We simply need to step into the courage to make the choice.

On that very significant trip back to the Northwest, while searching through the boxes of photographs, I had found that photo of Sarah, which was one of the very few things I decided to keep from all that I had stored in Seattle, and just a few days later, without knowing it, of all the places in this whole world, I was walking near her burial place. Then, when I returned to Colorado, I found out that though I had not been in her exact place, I had been so very close to her without knowing it, and my heart was even more deeply moved when I discovered that her resting place had an address of 333 SW Skyline. Since beginning this trilogy, the number 333 seems to have crossed my path so often. And, it was no surprise that in those few days, I had three connections with this powerful ancestor, by way of the photograph, the gravesite walk, and the email from my cousin.

Much later, I noticed more parallels in this whole experience. We had both made a decision to leave and step out into the unknown, despite how much our decision violated what was expected of us, and we both built new lives for ourselves. After leaving her husband, Sarah became a world traveler as a buyer for a huge Paris-based department store and later was a secretary for Cecil B. DeMille, one of the most famous filmmakers in history. I also became a world traveler after I left my marriage. When she died, I was a little girl, waiting with my grandpa just down the road from her, not unlike my being just down the road from her grave site on that icy Portland morning in December of 2009, well over 50 years after her passing. I felt that somehow, the two of us reached across time to experience a connection. I was not in exactly the same place or in the same time as she, at least based on our three-dimensional interpretation of reality, but when viewed from another perspective, we were not really so separate and not so very far apart.

Three Experiences Following the Trip to the Northwest
The Second: Christmas Eve Astrology Reading

In mid June, just about 6 months before the December '09 trip to the Northwest, I made an appointment for an astrology reading with a highly respected practitioner in a nearby city. I had come with a notepad and pen to write comments and discoveries, something that caused the astrologer to laugh and comment, *"How Libra of you!"* followed by her assurance that I wouldn't need to distract myself with taking notes. She explained that she would record our session and give me a CD at the end of our work together. It was my practice to bring a notepad to any encounter, not just as a way to write thoughts that struck me as significant, but, also to maintain full concentration and remain present. This was the first time anyone ever countered my practice by communicating a preference for me not to take notes. I put the pad and pen away, and we began the session. Despite the uncomfortable beginning, the session was extremely powerful. On a number of occasions, I was deeply moved by the experience, as if there were places inside me that were seen and understood for the first time in my life.

When the reading came to a close, the astrologer went over to her computer to burn a CD, so I could take it with me; however, the look on her face told me that something had gone very wrong with the recording. After her initial shock response that I felt vicariously in my body, she smiled and told me she was having trouble completing the task because this was a new system but assured me her son would make the copy and send it to me right away. Something in my gut told me that she was not telling the truth, and somehow, she had failed to record our session, but I didn't say anything.

After a couple of weeks, I called and left a message letting her know the CD had not arrived. I left another message, and when she did not return my calls, I sent her an e-mail message, but she didn't respond. Several weeks later, she finally returned my call without apology or explanation as to why it took so long to answer. Assuring me that she had sent the recording of our session quite some time before, she said she would make another copy, right then, and she put the phone down; however, in a just a moment, she got back on the phone and told me that her computer had somehow deleted our session. I sensed she was attempting to cover up her original mistake by, again, telling me something that was not true. She offered to give me another session to review the main points from the original reading and said she would get back to me to schedule a time, but she didn't call me back for another month. Finally, in mid August, she provided a much shorter make-up session by phone, and in a week, I received the replacement CD.

When the small package arrived, I felt disenchanted by the whole experience because I knew the second reading was not as complete or as spontaneous as the first. I kept seeing her expression at the end of that first session, and I felt she had not been truthful to me in all our interactions since. I didn't open the package for several months, until I felt one of those inner messages that came to me on Christmas Eve of 2009 directing me to open it and listen to the CD.

For several hours, I listened intently to the recording, stopping often and taking notes as I heard her comments and predictions for the third time. One thing she told me during that first reading really moved me to tears, something she repeated during the make-up session a couple of months later. It impacted me on the second hearing, but didn't register as deeply as it did the third time I heard it four months later on the Christmas Eve listening. She told me that I've struggled so hard to complete my life purpose, but what I needed to understand was **my purpose has already been completed...and I am the only one who hasn't gotten that I've finished with it**. It seemed as if I needed to hear this message three times for me to finally get it.

With nearly all my planets clustered together—3 in Virgo, 3 in Libra, and 2 in Scorpio—my chart reflected that I had come into this world with three major objectives. One had to do with being a healer whose focus was on purification, cleansing, and perfection. The second was I came to create balance in myself and balance between the world and me, and the third involved a fascination with the dark side. She commented that the first and third impulses might seem to be polar opposites—one of healing through purification coming from the light and the other, attraction to the dark side—but the balance and harmony coming from my Libra aspect provided a way for me to bring together my soul-level concerns that on the surface seemed opposite. All three of these intentions woven together led me to take on the deepest darkest possible wounds in my early years without closing my heart. She pointed out that in surviving my childhood and in fully embracing the healing process in my adult years, **I had accomplished the balance between the light and dark.** Though I might still have work to do with some of the energies I had to grapple with, I had completed the task of creating the balance and contributed this vibration to the world, already.

She told me that my chart reveals that I was built to play around in the dark, to try to understand it and uplift it. She said I have found peace with darkness; I have danced with the devil and then created a boundary with darkness, not allowing it to invade me. She told me that I've taken on the collective Karma with darkness, which was not personal. However, I believed because I experienced such depths of darkness, I needed to be punished, a belief that simply is not true. Instead, I needed to learn that, as a soul, I had offered to be of assistance in surrendering collective wounding related to darkness, something that would allow us all to embrace our spiritual essence. When she spoke those words, I knew that this is exactly what *Under the Mask* was to be about. Even though I had heard her say those things twice before, the first time in the actual reading that may or may not have been recorded but reported as being *lost* in the mail, and then in the second that was a shortened version on the phone, it was during the third listening on Christmas Eve I understood it.

When we began the first reading, the astrologer knew very little about me; she didn't know that I had written about the deep darkness of my childhood that ended with thanking my parents for living their parts in the drama of darkness so effectively that I was able to learn what I needed to learn. Yet, she said my chart revealed the depth of darkness that was my childhood, and that I had come through it all in victory. Without knowing me, she said my chart also revealed my drive to deal with the soul splitting events to bring balance into my heart, mind, soul, and life. And it revealed the drive I have felt for years to bring what I have learned to any who had ears to hear, or eyes to see.

Because I had responded to her with judgment instead of acceptance when I suspected she was not telling me the truth, it took three times for me to really hear what she had said…I guess I didn't have ears to hear or eyes to see the first two times. There was also something having to do with synchronicity in all this, as well, because I had to really get her message on Christmas Eve, as everything was coming together to begin writing *Under the Mask* not six months earlier when I was still finishing *Behind the Mask*. I was ready to finally get the messages on Christmas Eve of 2009 after all the other things had happened that needed to create exactly the right ingredients for what was to be included in *Under the Mask*.

Three Experiences Following the Trip to the Northwest
The Third: Calls from Three Davids

I spent Christmas Eve pondering the astrologer's words that had been given to me three times, and later on in the evening, I went for a walk in the Colorado snow surrounding my mountain retreat. When I returned, there were three messages, one after the other, from three of the Davids in my life, each calling to wish me a Merry Christmas. I turned to the dedication page in *The Mask*, written over two years before, in which I had expressed my great appreciation to the Davids who had provided me with so much caring support on my journey that began when I finally ended my marriage and committed to find my true self and discover what my soul wanted to do in this world. What I saw was how each represented courage in embracing the true self so important to me as I was preparing to begin the third book in the trilogy that is about the true self.

Oregon David, a long time friend, received the dedication in book one because he had accepted me for who I am with all my wonderful qualities and all my flaws, and he saw in me a strength I didn't know I had. In that dedication I wrote, *"There are only unspoken heart words that can convey the love that I feel for you in being my true friend, for your standing beside me and reflecting to me the strength that I possess, a strength that exists in all of us if we would but look within."* Receiving his message on Christmas Eve was a reminder that I am capable of facing whatever fears and overcoming any resistance I have had in writing *Under the Mask*. David had encouraged me from the beginning of our friendship to accept all aspects of me, as well…those parts who are comfortable with the light and those that still hide in the darkness, afraid to come out from inner prisons and reconnect with the world. In accepting myself, as Oregon David accepted me, I was learning to accept other people's complexity, as well. I understood the meaning of David's words that called me to be comfortable with both the light and darkness within me; for the first time in my life, I could do that because I had become consciously aware that I have a third aspect of my being that knows how to balance the light and the dark without the dark destroying me…and I had finally gotten it because only a few hours before, I had completed listening to that message for the third time… apparently the third time was, in fact, a charm.

I, also, received a message from Connecticut David, letting me know he was thinking about me. Hearing his voice reminded me of the courage he demonstrated in his life to be himself, willing to release the need to follow the rules society needed him to follow. In the dedication to him I wrote, *"There can be no greater gifts for any of us to give to each other than our vulnerability and our truth, for in the giving… we…can grow into our most authentic self."* This was exactly the message I needed to remember, as I was about to write what could not be written from any other place but from my authentic, vulnerable, and truthful self. Just as one cannot write about honesty from a place of dishonesty, or about courage from a place of fear, I could not write about what was *Under the Mask*, without coming from *Sandy God Essence,* my true and authentic self. And this message from David was letting me know that I would need to release my fear around what I believed people in my world required of me. Even though I am aware that I still have fear, I am confident that what this book is intending to write in me in the days, weeks, and months ahead will teach me to not be afraid of living and writing from this place of authenticity.

And finally, I received a message from China David, in Shanghai. In the dedication, I wrote, "*You taught me to believe in my own power to create what I believe. In living this truth, you showed me by what you have demonstrated in your living that we are all the powerful creators of our lives, as well.* David believed in his dream so much that he was willing to let go of what most people hold on to so tightly, and he dedicated every moment of his life to fulfilling his dream. Getting a message from him, right before I was to begin writing what I knew I needed to write, but at the same time resisted the very thing I wanted and needed to do, let me know I would learn to release the resistance and the completion of the trilogy was a dream that would be fulfilled.

All three of the Davids wished me a Merry Christmas and sent me their love. I went to bed that night, in the arms of *Sandy God Essence* who sent her thanks to all three of the *David God Essences* for preparing me to begin writing this first chapter of book three.

***

Though I knew I was going to write it, I realized that for a month and a half I had been hesitant to begin this first chapter. In reality, I had been afraid to write this third book from the time I first saw a glimpse of the trilogy in 2007. A part of me was afraid I would be rejected or perhaps more afraid I would be persecuted by those who hold a different image of who we are in our essence. I was afraid I would be lost and so very alone in this world, reliving the fears of my childhood…and part of my collective "I" had been unable to access the courage demonstrated in so many ways by all the Davids. After listening to these three angels in my life, I finally tapped into the courage that had been there all along; I released the fear and began this first chapter of book three on Christmas Day of 2009.

The Six Weeks

In retrospect, I can now see that I needed to have lived those six weeks to become ready to write. I needed to see the three films that were a reflection of the three books in this trilogy, and I needed to let go of so many artifacts that represented the first 50 years of my life, a metaphor for all that I held within myself, kept by the parts of me still attached to the past and living in inner dungeons and prisons deep behind my mask. I needed to experience the sessions with Michael, which became the reminder for all aspects of me to turn inward and reconnect with my authentic self who had been patiently waiting for my return. I needed to spend meaningful time with Oregon David and experience the synchronicities surrounding my Great Grandmother as a reminder of connection and interconnection of everything, unbounded by time and space, and I needed to hear, for the third time, the astrology reading that told me I had three powerful aspects to my chart that had already been completed. I needed to feel the support I have in this world, as shown in the calls from the three Davids, reminding me I can tap into my courage, I can embrace all of who I am, letting go of who I am not, and I can live from my authentic self. This amazingly significant sequence of events over six weeks was a reminder of the support I have, not only in this world, but also, beyond this three-dimensional reality for everything to have happened exactly as it did. And I wait with great anticipation to find out how all of this will unfold in the weeks and months ahead, as this third book, like the other two, writes itself into my life…and into yours, as you integrate in your own unique way, what you need from what is written, here.

Somehow, I know that the six weeks between book two and book three contain the whole story that will be told in this last book of the trilogy, even though, at the moment of this writing, I don't know how it is all going to unfold. Unlike the first two books that formed themselves as I wrote, with no sense of direction until they were completed, as soon as I finished the previous pages, I saw an outline of book three, and saw the headings of each of the chapters that were to follow, which involved the main events of those six weeks. But like the other two books, I am unable to see what this book plans to write in my life. I simply need to trust living into what is ahead.

We all possess courage; when we release fear, tap into that courage, and allow love to fuel our life's journey, we experience the bliss of living into our life's highest purpose.

Chapter Two
SPECULATIONS AND REFLECTIONS

From the present, we can imagine something of the future in the form of speculation; and though we lived through it, we can know something of the past, but not all of it, and even though we are in the present, we might not understand much of what we are experiencing, now. Sometimes it takes living into the future to understand a past we cannot fully grasp while we are living it.

SPECULATIONS ABOUT THIS THIRD BOOK

A month-and-a-half slipped by, between November 11, 2009 the sign off date for book two, *Behind the Mask,* and December 25, 2009, during which time I barely wrote anything, not even much in the way of emails to my dearest friends. And then, on Christmas Day of 2009, I began to write the third book in the trilogy, *The Meaning of Three.* As the words of the previous pages formed on the electronic pages of my computer, I was able to see that a number of things had to have taken place before I could write again. In some ways, I think I had resisted this third volume, even before I had begun to write the first book. I had to understand the resistance before I could release it and move forward.

As early as late summer of 2007 when the trilogy first entered into my conscious thoughts by way the *tattooed lady,* I had a feeling that *Under the Mask* would prove to be the most challenging of the three books to write, most likely, because I felt it might contain thoughts I had resisted acknowledging to myself, and I was sure those ideas would not only be challenging for me to write, but also, for some of you to read, as well.

Although I am just beginning to write this third volume, I intuitively know book three involves not just exposure of some of what remains behind my mask and, for that matter, the masks all of us wear, but I believe it will confront some of the most precious understandings we hold as individuals and families, as groups, cultures, and perhaps of the entire human species—understandings that have to do with who we have come to believe we are as opposed to who we truly are.

There have been times I have been afraid to acknowledge what I've learned from the path I've taken, and what I continue to learn, even now. Ever since I began this trilogy, the door to the inner spaces opened wider, giving me glimpses of the insights and understandings that exist deep within, and as a result, I have received fleeting awareness of what I believe the pages that are ahead will contain. Though I am in awe of the lessons, I am aware that a part of me has dreaded writing down what my journey has taught me for others to read, and I know there remains fear within me as I continue to struggle with what I've come to understand as true, at least what most of me has embraced as true at this time in my life.

Though I don't know the specifics of the path this book has planned for me—or for you, as well, as you participate in the journey through reading what is to come—I do know that, somehow, it will offer support for us all toward increasing out understanding, as well as our ability to experience more completely who each of us really is, not just as an idea or a thought, but viscerally in our bodies…and from that deeper experiential knowledge, allowing us to live in this world, no longer separated from our unique essence that has always been there under our masks, if we have the courage to open to it.

REFLECTIONS ON THE FIRST TWO BOOKS IN THE TRILOGY

In retrospect, though I know it was much more than this, now, I can see that book one, *The Mask*, was a personal story of mid-life crisis, something so many of us have experienced or will go through in our forties or fifties, and sometimes earlier, when we sense something needs to change, even if we don't know what it is. When we begin to feel there is something missing in our lives, perhaps feeling as if we have been masquerading as a real person, but not living from whatever is real inside us, we begin to question the answers we accepted when we were younger about how we ought to live our lives. Some of us go in search of new answers as we think about how we want to live, from this time of questioning, forward. *The Mask* disclosed a series of events, which caused the life I had been living to first crack and then crumble. It revealed what I went through to bring healing to the devastation that followed the cracking and crumbling, as well as deeper healing for what was buried from my past that created the formation of the mask and the false life I'd been living. It took experiencing the breaking up and falling away of the mask for me to find my true self I hadn't known since very early childhood.

The central story of the first book concerned my relationship with Jake, my high school sweetheart, who became my husband after we graduated from college. It revealed the life we shared, focusing on the painful patterns that grew out of a dysfunctional marriage and then moved beyond interactions we had in this life into past lifetimes. The story was about the mask I wore to protect me from knowing what was behind it, which was the darkness from both my childhood of this lifetime, as well as the dark side I believed I could not handle from many lifetimes in the past.

Even though *The Mask* told a story about me, on a deeper level, it was a story about all of us. Many who have read it reflected back to me that passages, and even whole chapters, seemed more about them and their life story than about me and mine. Some had to put the book down for a time to process what was coming up for them before they could finish reading it. I believe this kind of identification with another person's story can happen because *we are all living our own version of the same story*—one that holds a universal pattern. It begins with feeling connected, even if we have no conscious memory of that connection, but then, something happens that causes disconnection. The path many of us take to find ourselves, often called the hero's journey, begins with a struggle to restore connection in all the effective and ineffective ways we try. The most significant, yet least accomplished connection, is the one we long to have with our own authentic selves, our true essence. Finding this connection can be extremely difficult for us because most of us have pushed it far, far away, deep inside us, under our masks. For our own unique reasons, we become terrified to allow our true self to be seen or known, even by ourselves, and we come to believe we are the masks we wear, and then hold on to them with such tenacity.

This three-fold story-pattern of connection and separation, followed by a journey to find reconnection is replicated in fables, in our cultural and religious symbols and stories, in our birth process, in our personal life's journey from its beginning to ending, with a thousand, thousand stories in between, and on a far grander scale, any single story is reflected in the story of the birth and expansion of the universe, as it retells its own story in and through us. We are all living our versions of that universal story, although most of us don't know this is what we are doing. And, sometimes we can become stuck in one part of the story—repeating it over and over again—or we can repeat the whole pattern, each time hoping to finally get it right.

***

No matter what perspective ones holds to explain the origins of the universe as we know it, whether one believes in Genesis creation as presented in fundamental Judaism, Christianity, and Islam, or the explanations intrinsic to one of the many world religions or spiritual traditions, or has placed trust in the scientific explanation of the big bang that suggests all that exists exploded from one infinitesimally small particle into what is now the 3-dimensional universe, there seems to be a thread that flows through them all. The thread I see in each of the perspectives is that before its formation, what is now identified as the universe, contained nothing...*no-thing*. Though nothingness held all possibilities, much like a page that could have anything written on it, but is blank, the Universe had nothing written on it, and it didn't even have a page upon which something could be written. Science says something caused a massive explosion of a single something that was nothing, which eventually evolved into all that is. And Western religions—Judaism, Christianity, and Islam—say a word was spoken and a series of unfolding events over a week's time or, perhaps over timeless time, created our world, our universe. Both religious and scientific explanations attribute the explosive beginning to a word, a sound, or some kind of vibration, which caused something to be formed out of nothing. I've never seen these various perspectives as being so different from each other.

A blank page might contain anything. It can hold the possibility of becoming the first page of a book, the last page, or any page in between; it might hold writing, a map or a photographic image, or maybe a drawing that reflects the mind of the artist or the story of the universe reflected in a snapshot of a single life. There are infinite possibilities of what can be formed on or with a blank page. And the unformed universe, as well as the unformed you, before coming into being, held within itself infinite possibilities of what it could become.

More personally, before your father's sperm and mother's egg came together, the unformed-you contained all possibilities, like the empty page, or the unformed universe, but when the ineffable, vibrational spark that is you became one with the unifying sperm and egg, your infinite possibilities became limited by the genetic makeup of your parents and your soul's process of weaving together their DNA into your own unique expression.

During your gestation period, from zygote to infant ready for birth, the development process narrowed your possibilities. If your mother drank or took drugs, or if she was in a dysfunctional relationship that caused her stress, you were impacted both physically and mentally, an impact that would direct your development and your possibilities.

At the moment of your birth, the beliefs of your parents or parent figures—both conscious and unconscious—and those of your family system, community, social group, and the nation into which you were born narrowed more of your possibilities. The possibilities of how you could express your being were also limited by the moment in history that marked your coming into the world, and some would say by the placement of the stars, the sun, the moon, and planets in relationship to the place on the Earth where you took your first breath. Certainly, a girl baby born in America in 2000 compared to one born in 1800 would have a very different set of possibilities available to her at birth and beyond, into the unfolding of her life. And a baby boy born into slavery from a black slave woman and a white male plantation owner in 1830 in the US would have a very different set of possibilities when compared to a boy born in Hawaii in 1961 to a black Kenyan father and white mother from Kansas. Each individual story holds its own unique place in the world, and yet, *every story from the beginning of time to the present contains the same story*, each one coming from the perspective of its own unique sets of possibilities.

Book one, which told a part of my story, had been a challenge to write because I felt compelled to publicly declare who I am and what happened in my life, which caused me to confront the fear of being myself, as well as my fear of reopening the pain I still experienced regarding my childhood and my live with my former husband. *The Mask* included the details of a number of profoundly impacting events that happened in my childhood and the painful repercussions that followed, difficult to face because of what I believed it revealed about me, not just in this lifetime, but in past lives, as well, as stories from the distant past entwined with other stories from the more recent past in this life.

***

Book two delved more deeply into the dark side as represented by extremely difficult childhood events, the writing of which caused me to fear any who might judge me based on what I exposed about the underbelly of my early years, including what I called *the worst of the worst*. Book two was really the prequel to the first book, though I didn't know it when I began writing *Behind the Mask*. It probed much more deeply into my childhood and the extreme abuse that reopened soul level wounds. The wounding, itself, caused me to believe that I was, at the very core of me, too dark and too damaged to embrace goodness and too evil to ever be worthy of being loved, deserving of condemnation to an eternal dungeon or sacrificed to the will of others. And, it explained why I would have accepted the pain of my marriage and the mask I wore, which I'd written about in book one. It is important to mention that I was fully unaware of the wounds and the conclusions I made about the world and myself in my earlier years; I'd learned how to separated my conscious mind from knowing what happened in my past. Like an unnoticed backdrop in a photo that unconsciously impacts a viewer's impression of the subject being photographed, the wounding in my forgotten childhood influenced my impression of who I believed myself to be, an impression that lasted for decades, and from time to time, still can cause me to lose connection with my greater awareness of the truth of who I know I am.

Like *The Mask, Behind the Mask* was written in a way that included the stories of all of us, and what we all would rather hide than face. This book was my story told from the perspective of the possibilities into which I was born…and like all stories, mine, with its unique details, contain the same meta-story that we all live.

***

As I reflect on the content of first two books, without getting caught up in my own personal details, I can see my life—and for that matter, each of our lives—as a metaphor for the story of humankind, in which so many of us, if not all of us, came to believe in separation, something we keep playing out in our lives. Deep inside all of us, we carry the wounding of the painful belief in separation. Many of us believe we are ultimately alone whether or not we are consciously aware of it, feeling disconnected from what might have made us feel connected and whole. In our lives, we repeat the belief in separation by reliving it at our births and in myriad experiences through life, as well as when we near the time of our deaths. In the lives we live in-between birth and death, we often experience feeling disconnected from family, friends, parents, spouses or significant others, peers, children, and the world.

Even if we don't recognize we are doing it, most all of us spend a good part of our lives trying to separate from what we don't want or attempting to reconnect with whatever we feel separated, and yet, we create countless categories that separate us into we and they, categories that eventually leave us feeling isolated and alone. Too often, those we assign to *they* become enemies that must be defeated if we are to survive, or they are the ones upon whom we focus our attention and longings to try to find acceptance so we can feel all the good things we imagine about being connected. And even in our experience of being a part of what we identify as *we*, it is not uncommon for us to feel separated from them, as well, as we experience disconnection from our own families or groups.

For many, this belief in separation is connected to a belief in our unacceptability, or in some embedded flaw—our own or, perhaps, some horrible flaw in others—a belief that may well be completely unconscious. The nearly universal beliefs in separation between *me and you* or *we and they*, coupled with an often-masked belief in our personal unacceptability—of not being good enough, smart enough, pretty or handsome enough, rich enough, tough enough or any other self-judgments we might hold—can be projected out to become judgments of others, as well. The result of this belief creates a need to protect ourselves from outside threats, made dangerous because of *who we believe they are* or because of *what or who we believe ourselves to be*.

A universal solution to this fear of unacceptability, usually made long before we remember accepting it, was to put on protective masks to convince others, as well as ourselves, that we are whatever will make us feel acceptable and, therefore, safe. We might have decided that others, not ourselves, are the ones that are wicked or evil monsters who are out to destroy us or take from us whatever we believe we need to experience safety, security, and love. When we look at them, all we can see are the terrifying or radiantly beautiful masks we have projected on them. This mental process concretized our separation into camps of "*we and they*" and solidified our need to wear protective masks. As separation continues through life, even the "*we-group*" that was supposed to make us feel safe, secure, and loved, often fails to give us what we want and need, and in time it is *me against the world*.

A significant purpose behind the original masking of ourselves was to develop functional or, in far too many cases, dysfunctional personally traits that would lead toward feeling acceptable or simply safe. The personality, in actuality, is a constellation of protective patterns of behavior, some of which were formed to attract people to us, and others were formed to keep people away from us, whichever seemed more beneficial to our survival. Researchers and philosophers, who have studied the patterns of personality, have been able to categorize those patterns into personality types, which are far from unique and, most often, result in very predictable patterned responses to the world. The important piece of information, here, is that these patterned behavior responses are fear-based masks meant to keep people away or draw people to us—or both—and do not reflect who we truly are.

Once we donned our masks, we began seeing others with masks, as well. Some were hideous or frightening masks, which allowed us to separate from or attack the others because we believed we needed to protect ourselves from what we assumed they were, or we saw them with beautiful masks of perfection, as we longed for connection with them to help make us feel safe, secure, and loved.

Africans, who had been brought over to America as slaves in the early years of our history, were called so many inhumane names, allowing "slave-owners" to assign masks to the people who were given the names, both before and after slavery, as a way to justify treating fellow human beings with indignity and as less than human. And the same thing was done to Native Americans, when the masks projected onto them were of terrifying, godless savages. This allowed many European-Americans to feel justified in slaughtering them and taking their land. In Asian wars, beginning with US conflicts in the Philippines, circa 1920, and later in Korea and Vietnam, enemies from those countries were given the collective name *gooks*, which was a way to slur and depersonalize these people that American soldiers had been ordered to eliminate.

In all cases, the enemy could be seen as a *"they"* who were not really human, proved by what we believed we saw when we looked at the terrifying masks we projected upon them. It was not uncommon for those who were seen as wearing the masks from one group to also project masks on the other group, as well. What was little recognized by either side, however, is the mask we project on another is more about ourselves than the other. When I was little, my grandmother reminded me that whenever I pointed a finger at someone else, there were three fingers pointing back at me. It took my study of depth psychology and many years of inner work to really understand the complexity of the message my grandma, in all her wisdom, so simply stated.

In this whole masking process, it is also possible that we might have blocked ourselves from seeing what was behind the mask of another because we wanted to believe we could become attached to that other as a way to find safety, security, and love. It is not uncommon for abused children to block awareness of the cruelty of their abuser and see the one who caused such pain as wonderful, caring, nurturing, and kind. And certainly, when a person falls in love with another, so often what may not always be so well hidden behind the mask is blocked, and the one in love only sees what he or she wishes were the good qualities in the other, dismissing qualities, sometimes not too far from the surface, that might prove to be damaging later on in the relationship.

Based on many subtle and generally unconscious influences—cultural programming, social dictates, accepted theories or concepts, scientific world-views, metaphysical beliefs, family interpretations, religious doctrine, spiritual ideas, psychological perspectives and more—we look at ourselves and others, and we see what we expect, which gives us permission to act in whatever ways the masks would require, as if what we were told about ourselves and about others were true.

While some of us act as if we are superior or special because we are a part of what we've been told is a superior group, it is not uncommon to experience ourselves as inferior or unacceptable, and believe most everyone else in our group is better than we are, causing us to feel left out, and separated. And it is not uncommon for those who are told they are inferior to hate the label and, deep inside, believe they are superior to those who have judged them. But one of the offshoots of this kind of hatred, often, is the need to prove superiority, which is a category that demands separation from what is inferior. If we take on the beliefs of being superior, we can know there is a part of us behind our mask that feels inferior, and if we have taken on the stigma of being inferior, there is a place inside that feels superior, especially to all those who've dared to judge us. The creation of categories of opposites eventually leaves everyone experiencing the pain of being alone.

Many worldviews, including myriad religious perspectives, dealt with the dilemma of separation in human experience—from ourselves, from others, from our environment, and from God—by providing rules and giving direction that tells us what we need to do to counter the destruction that accompanies separation, especially if the separation is believed to be from God. We are taught that we can be saved from eventual demise if we follow the right rules, behave in designated ways, believe the right set of principles, accept a particular doctrine, or worship a particular god or *god-creature*, something I will talk more about later.

If we remain separated from ourselves, our disconnected lives will end in despair and disillusionment. If we remain separated from others, our personal lives will end in isolation and loneliness, and on the collective level if we remain separated, the world will be plagued with conflict and war, that might reflect what Seventeenth century philosopher, Thomas Hobbes, described as life in the state of nature, in which there would be *"war of all against all"* and life would be *"solitary, poor, nasty, brutish, and short."* When this belief is applied to 21st century technology, it is not a stretch to see this kind of belief in separation ending in great destruction or, possibly, the annihilation of our species. If we remain separated from our environment, the likelihood is that we will create a toxic world that will eventually kill us, or we will die in a world that can no longer sustain us. And if we remain separated from whatever we call our source, even if we see our ultimate source as ourselves, we may well experience life alone and as meaningless and empty, as those who adopted the nihilist philosophy suggested when they determined that life is without purpose and has no objective meaning or intrinsic value.

We might have embraced the idea that all is good, yet privately, suffer in what seems like experiences that are not good. We might have taken on the idea that there is only the One, and separation is an illusion, believing everything in the physical world is an illusion, while unconsciously experiencing being separate from aspects of ourselves such as our physicality or separate from our thoughts that might question the idea that all is illusion. While some of us may try to embrace the idea of connection, we might separate from those who believe in separation, including those questioning parts of us from which we have unconsciously separated, without noticing what we have done, despite our belief in connection.

I have come to believe that the human story, as reflected in any one particular story, such as the story of my life, contains the experience of disconnection from our spiritual essence, which is the *Spark of God* or *God Essence* in our core being, known only by ourselves or by others through experience. The aftereffects of our experience of separation from God Essence within have brought about the endless array of human stories, both personal and collective, filled with suffering, struggle, agony, pain, conflict, desperation, and more. My story—unique in its own way, yet, not so different from all the other human stories—contains the discovery of what I have come to know as who I truly am; although, I believe many people, as well as some parts of myself, remain unaware of what it means to experience the ultimate connection to the God Essence within, *Under the Mask*.

Knowing who you truly are takes courage because it requires that you not only allow who you thought you were to crumble and to fall away, which often feels like death, but also, it means all the structures and patterns you have depended upon to keep you safe, secure, and loved will fall away and die, as well. This can leave you feeling so very vulnerable, and unprotected, even when what you created didn't really give you what you hoped it would. But what releasing the mask opens to you is connection with that which truly provides safety, security, and love, rather than an imperfect replica that can never provide what is promised. Like a person holding on to a trapeze, who must release the grip on one bar, and for a time be suspended in air with nothing to hold onto until the release allows reconnection to that which will carry the person beyond where he or she was to a place on the other side, we each must decide if we will remain attached to the very restricted patterns that we have held on to for dear life for most of our lives, patterns that, in fact, prevent us from living the life we came to live.

Once we choose to let go of who we thought we were and what we believed we were supposed to do, we can finally open to the freedom of becoming who we came here to be.

Chapter Three
THE FIRST OF THREE FILMS
A SERIOUS MAN

We think we know who we are and what the world is, but for most of us, what we think, is not true. It can be terribly frightening to discover that the assumptions we've made about ourselves and the world, as well as the beliefs on which we have built our entire lives, are based on lies.

The three films that felt as if they had shouted out to me to see them before I left for the Northwest seemed to have totally different themes, separate stories, with little or nothing in common. One was set in the past, in the 1960s essentially about the life of one person, another was set sometime in a desolate future about a journey two people were taking after some apocalyptic event destroyed the world as we know it, and the third was a documentary about the present that featured many people answering a question about the meaning of God. I saw the films, one after the other on the same day. But not until I reflected on the meaning of the films, did I see they were significantly and intricately interconnected, not only to each other, but also, to the three books in this trilogy, as well as to what was happening in my life, and what needed to be included in this book.

THE FILM

Like most human life-stories, the film, *A Serious Man,* makes you wonder if you ought to be laughing or crying. This black comedy is set in a traditional, late 1960s suburb, somewhere near Minneapolis Minnesota, and tells the story of a professor whose life slowly begins to crumble when his wife informs him that she is planning on leaving him to marry one of his colleagues. As his longtime marriage is falling apart, the serious man has to put up with his selfish children and his seemingly useless brother who has moved in with the family, and inflicts his noxious behaviors on the family's life.

The lead character is an unassuming man, who apparently has been living an uneventful life until it begins to unravel. However, an astute moviegoer would be able to recognize that the cracks in the family-system had been there long before we dropped into his life via the big-screen.

Not only is the serious man struggling with his failed marriage, while putting up with the crazy-making demands of his children and their uncle, he has to deal with his son who is getting in trouble for breaking rules at school, stealing, smoking pot, and more, as well as his self-obsessed daughter who wants a nose job so badly she steals from her father to get it.

As his wife and his co-worker are making plans for her divorce and their upcoming marriage, the serious man's department chair lets him know he's been receiving a series of anonymous letters that have the potential to jeopardize the serious man's chance of becoming tenured at the university. On top of all these troubles, one of his students, who had failed a physics class, tries to bribe him into giving a passing grade, and at the same time threatens him with a lawsuit for taking the bribe that he didn't knowingly take, because everyone knows a man who follows the rules can't take bribes. Desperately trying to get his very disordered life back in order, the serious man becomes distracted by a beautiful neighbor who sunbathes in the nude in her yard, made visible when the serious man climbs up on his roof to adjust the antenna so his son can watch *F Troop*, a short-lived slap-stick comedy series from the late 1960s that mocks military order during a time when so many had turned to the military as the answer to world problems, and many others turned against the military.

Throughout the course of the film, the serious man seeks guidance from three trusted rabbis, one rabbi for each of the three sections of the film, but none is able to give him the help he needs. He tries to be serious, a goal that seems to be highly valued in his community and tries to live his life the right way doing the right things, but despite all his best efforts, everything is falling apart.

He wants to know the answer to significant questions regarding the meaning of life and how one is supposed to live. Should he trust that whatever happens is the will of God by taking both the good and the bad without question and simply maintain faith? Should he unwaveringly maintain his beliefs in right and wrong, and do only right, despite individual circumstances? Or, should he learn when to flow with the circumstances of life, letting go of absolute right and wrong, compromising in order to maintain some meager semblance of order in his very disordered life? These questions arise in the course of the film, but no answers are given.

One crazy thing after another invades his life turning everything into chaos as the serious man struggles to keep it all in order; his focus is always the need to do the right thing, to approach everyone with a controlled demeanor, and to never rock the boat, even when it seems like it ought to be rocked. With all of this insanity swirling around in his life, as the film is winding down a tornado looms over his town, quickly approaching his defenseless son and the boy's classmates, who have been sent outside to go into an underground shelter. They are all standing directly in its path, while an old rabbi unsuccessfully struggles to open the door to a shelter that could have saved all their lives had someone else less shaky been given the key to the shelter's door. But apparently, it is in proper order that the old man be in charge of the keys, and no one challenges the order of things, even when their lives are at stake. With this impending destruction approaching his son, the classmates, the school, and the synagogue, the serious man in another location, receives a call from his physician bearing tornadic-like news as the doctor strongly recommends that the serious man come in to discuss the findings from his x-rays … *immediately*! And we, the audience, are left with the impression that the serious man has a very serious illness.

In the end, we are given the words from the 1960s revolutionary philosophy, words that open the film, are repeated during the course of the story, and are offered to the serious man's son when he, not his father, is given an audience with the wise old—very, very old—rabbi. The holy man quotes from Jefferson Airplane with his own twist on the words, as he thoughtfully speaks to the boy and to us:

When the truth is found to be lies
And all the hope within you dies…
…Then what?

And, we are left to ponder our own answers.

THE PROBLEMS

The main character in this film could be considered the poster boy for the mask. He is facing problems that are universal; anyone seeing this film could identify with at least one, if not many, of the problems in the life of the serious man. We all have experienced periods of unraveling, or times we have feared such unraveling of our carefully laid plans even if they were not as all encompassing as in the serious man's life. It is easier to see the problematic patterns in the tragic, yet comedic undertones in a film set a half century ago, which permits us to distance ourselves enough to be less blinded by what we might not be able to see in a film set in our current time.

Those of us who were old enough to remember the late 60s can laugh at all the accouterments that made up that time in our lives, which, more than likely, we didn't notice when we were living in it all. And, those who were not alive back then can laugh at what looks like silly costumes, awful hair, and very bad design that made up the lives of over-the-top caricature representations of 1960s parents or grandparents. Whether or not we had direct experience with that time period, we all can find ourselves wincing or aching in sadness when we see the tragedy of being trapped in patterns that seem, unjust, unkind, unnecessary, and so insane, yet, impossible to escape for those caught in them. There can be little doubt that nearly all of us are unconsciously trapped by patterns no matter how much we may attempt to live consciously and free.

The serious man's answer to all that he faced was to respond to everything the way he was supposed to. So he hid what was authentic and escaped into the rules. He had become a pretend person. We have all tried to pretend something didn't hurt us, when it did, not unlike the serious man who felt pain when his wife announced she was planning on leaving him for one of his friends. Instead of expressing his hurt and anger, he tried to take it *like an adult*. He didn't reveal his hurt when his wife and her boyfriend suggested that he move into a motel, for appearances. And later, when he returned home, he didn't react when his son didn't welcome him home or acknowledge him in any loving way, but, instead, ordered his father to fix the TV antenna because the channel the son wanted to watch wasn't coming in. It was clear that the boy expected his dad to go up on the roof to fix the problem. His family treated him like he was a servant, deserving of no respect, and apparently he agreed with them because he let them treat him so badly. With a contrite spirit, he fulfilled the needs of everyone else without expressing his own needs or his suffering. He took the job of being a man very seriously. He was trying with everything he knew to become what was expected of the mask that he wore…instead of being himself.

At one time or another, most of us have done that, too. Instead of being real, we search for what is expected of us or what is normal, and we become that. The hurt we felt, but didn't acknowledge, might have come from seeing a childhood or a teenage heartthrob hold hands with someone else, or it might have happened when we discovered that someone we trusted betrayed us. We might have entered some sort of contest, and lost or worked very hard for something, but failed, and tried to pretend that it didn't matter, when whatever happened caused us to feel heartbroken. Like the serious man, we might have felt used and abused, but didn't let anyone know what was going on inside. Like him, we might have felt terrified about some threat in our lives or we may have felt ragingly angry at some injustice, but acted as if everything was okay, when it wasn't. We can play the role of one who is not hurt or not angry for so long that we lose the ability to know we are hurt or angry. And we can take on the mask for so long that we believe that is what we really are.

When we pretend that we don't feel what we are feeling, especially to ourselves, we are living a lie. But, far too often, we would rather live a lie than let others, or even ourselves, know how much their behaviors impact us. To admit that we can be made to feel weak, needy, sad, afraid, angry, confused, or lost would mean that we were not in control and, therefore, vulnerable. For many of us, to be vulnerable means we can be destroyed or we can destroy what we see as the cause of our being vulnerable, which in turn, creates a fear that compels us to maintain an image of one who is unshakable, unbreakable, and invulnerable. After a while, almost everything we live becomes a lie.

The serious man looked at the structures and rules to guide how he let himself think and feel, without considering what was happening inside him. He lived in his mask and everything he did was based on what his world expected of him, and what he had come to expect of himself. His hope and his expectation was if he followed the rules and lived within the structures that told him how to live, he would have a good life. But the world he built could not save him when what was happening in his life was too big for any rules to give him direction and too overwhelming for the structures to keep him safe. Fully focused on what his social order demanded of him to see as true, he had no guidance from within. He was left with the question posed by Jefferson Airplane through the very old Rabbi in the words. *"When the truth is found to be lies and all the hope within you dies...then what?"*

SYNCHRONOUS REACTIONS

I had just finished typing the previous paragraph when I had to stop what I was writing to drive through the snow and ice for a chiropractic appointment. On the way into the doctor's office, I slipped on a patch of ice covering a slight rise in the ramp and fell on my left knee and hand, scuffing both on the concrete and very slightly dislocating my hip. Two women came rushing toward me; one picked up my purse and asked if

I was okay, and the other helped me up. I assured them all was well and that it was a good thing I was going in to see the chiropractor.

Though I was wincing with pain and told both women it was really nothing, which it really wasn't in the big scheme of things, a little Sandy was very near tears, but I didn't want to acknowledge those feelings and laughed about the whole thing. I walked into the chiropractor's office and told him I'd need a bit more adjustment than originally planned. It didn't feel appropriate for people around me, who I didn't know, to see me cry when they wouldn't have known that my child self was even there or what was breaking her heart. And, except for the obvious, I didn't know, either.

So after the adjustment, I got back in my car and on the drive home, I told my child self that it was okay for her to cry; she did, and I felt better. The tears allowed her to feel comforted and in the comforting, she sent me a memory of a time I was playing baseball when I was about 9 years old. I was an outfielder going for a high ball when I slipped on a rise in the ground, a very similar feeling I had when I slipped on the ramp not long before. Without a glove, the ball made a direct hit on the top of my finger, knocking it out of joint, and then, the ball ricocheted into my face and my glasses, breaking them in two places. I let out a howl cry for the pain, and the neighbor kids booed me and called me a crybaby. I was so filled with shame that I never played baseball with the neighbor kids again.

The 9-year-old needed to feel loved and experience healing from that event, so I intervened into the memory and embraced the little girl. I kissed her finger and explained the salve I was applying on the dislocated joint and bruised muscles would help her heal quickly. And not until this writing did I realize that she had hurt her hip, as well. So I put the salve on her hip, which helped it to feel much better. I rocked her in my arms and in only a few moments, her finger and her hip were as good as new. I asked if she would like to have a baseball glove to play with other children who knew how to care for their teammates instead of boo them. She liked that and tried on a glove that was a perfect fit. We went to a baseball field in alternate reality where she was welcomed on a team that had been waiting for her.

As she was getting to know her new teammates, I asked the Sandy who had to wear the broken glasses, repaired with black electricians tape, if she'd come forward. She approached me with that kind of reluctant shyness, as if she both wanted to come but was afraid of being ridiculed. I asked her if she would like me to take her to a store to get a new pair of glasses. She was so overwhelmed that she began to cry. She cried until her tears turned to laughter and the two of us went into the store where there were hundreds of frames from which she could choose. She was amazed to see that there were nearly weightless glasses, and they could be made to fit her face perfectly. She picked out a gold-framed pair that had a lovely golden braid-like design on either side, which made her feel that wearing glasses didn't have to make her feel ugly. I let her know that there would be a time in the near future when she'd not need glasses anymore; she would just know when the time was right and could look forward to that experience, too.

She reconnected with baseball Sandy, and together, they were very good at focusing and catching fly balls. And I was surprised to see how well the little girl could hit when it was her time at bat. She really liked to play. After she had what seemed like a full afternoon of playtime, I talked to her about the children in the other game that made fun of her. I let her know the likelihood is when those children were hurt and cried sometime in their past, they were ridiculed as being crybabies, which hurt them so badly, they couldn't be around someone who was crying without feeling their own pain. In booing little Sandy and calling her a crybaby, the other children had become just like those who had previously ridiculed them. She was able to feel compassion for those who ridiculed baseball Sandy, and for the first time since I was 9, I was able to release not only the physical pain in my finger, but also, the emotional pain in my heart, and my little girl-self wanted to play.

I brought the two Sandys back to the ramp outside the chiropractor's office where they could see adult Sandy falling down and scuffing her hand and knee; they both went to her side and kissed the sore places, reassuring all the parts of Sandy that the fall was really not so big and the scratches would heal quickly because of the kisses. I felt myself smile. When I saw myself tell the two women who had, in fact, come to my rescue in that present-time fall that it was really nothing, I could see the truth, because I felt it. Without the pain and humiliation of the past, it *really* was no big deal.

Prior to doing this inner work, I wasn't ready to allow vulnerability. There were still too many tears I needed to heal to be vulnerable in the presence of strangers. I wasn't there, yet. It took connecting to Sandy who was hurt and shamed while playing baseball and Sandy who felt such shame for wearing the broken glasses to be able to release their tears before I could experience a fall that, on its own, would likely not have resulted in tears.

***

When I returned home from the chiropractor's office and sat down at my computer to continue chapter two, I couldn't believe where I had left off in my writing. The incident that happened on the ramp and later in my car needed to be included here. I know I have more to learn about being vulnerable without being codependentally needy, something I avoided like the plague. I believe that people learn to fake it with the stiff upper lip, or the tough-guy response, *"No big deal,"* because of fear that if the door to feelings were to open, all the hurt that was never expressed would come pouring out and, it would never stop. They fear becoming overwhelmed with pain like a helpless victim, or perhaps, they fear being caught up in victim energy and being sucked dry by an overprotective rescuer or attacked for expressing their feelings to a ridiculing persecutor. Others might use some present incident to allow unexpressed pain to pour out, perhaps hysterically seeking the attention they did not get when they were children. My life, that day, had reflected the very point I had been making in my writing just a short time before I had left to see the chiropractor.

A case might be made for the appropriateness of putting on a mask and hiding what we are feeling in certain social settings, especially when we sense that those around us would misuse our authentic feelings and vulnerabilities. This could happen if we have not learned how to fully possess our own power. But it is a shame when we find it necessary to wear a mask in front of our loved ones and close friends, and it is a tragedy when we have completely identified with our mask and lie to ourselves about what we feel or don't want to feel.

So many of us grow up believing that we have to take life so seriously by following the rules and living from social expectations of what it means to be an adult, rules that often include the suppression of feelings and following social order set down as necessary. We believe that if we can make ourselves be who we are supposed to be, that our lives will be smooth, and we will be happy. But far too often these rules of adulthood cause us to disconnect from our authentic self, and we feel as if something important is missing. We discover that life is not turning out like we thought it was supposed to, and we feel lost. Our life feels like a performance instead of something experienced authentically, and everything we thought was true, we discover was a lie.

If we are to reconnect with authentic living, we need to let go of the rules we thought would help us to love and be loved. We need to let go of all the structures we built to guarantee our happiness because the rules we follow and the structures we built cannot provide us with authentically felt love and happiness.

Once we let go of living our lives by the rules fulfilling what others expect of us, hoping they will make us safe and secure, we can open to experiencing love, the only thing capable of creating authentic safety and security.

Chapter Four
THE SECOND OF THREE FILMS
THE ROAD...THEN WHAT

When we look out at the world or into our lives, we are seeing the stories that reflect back to us what we believe is true. Until we know what we believe, we cannot know whether or not our beliefs are true. And when we release the lies, we can transform our lives into something more worthy of who we really are.

In the previous chapter, before I took the verbal detour about pretending to not have been hurt by the fall outside my doctor's office, I was sharing thoughts about how we often try to live properly by following expectations and rules of conduct, directives from the outside telling us how to live our lives, as depicted in the film, *A Serious Man.* These directives try, but far too often fail to prevent the crumbling of a life such as the one that came to a tornadic conclusion at the end of that first film. The second film, *The Road,* presents what happens when all the directives that didn't work to keep civilization together result in the world falling apart with nothing left but terrifying and desperate clawing for survival; of course, what happens to civilizations also can happen in the lives of individuals. Both films ask the question, *"Then what?"* In *The Serious Man,* a tornado and a doomsday illness foreshadow destruction for one man who doesn't know what to do next, while in *The Road,* destruction has already taken place, as a man and a boy seek to answer the same question by taking a journey to the ocean only to ask the question again, once they arrive at their destination.

Everyone who holds on to a particular three-dimensional world as their source of safety, security, connection, purpose, and meaning has experienced or will experience the ending of that world as it once was for the simple reason that everything in life changes. Whether the change happens gently or catastrophically, nothing stays the same. Over time, most people grow from being children into young adults, through their middle years, and into old age. People we know move away or die; single people become couples and coupling shifts or ends. People have children and become parents; jobs are lost or we get new jobs, and we come into more money or lose what we had. Illnesses invade our bodies, and some of us find healing while others do not. And, we can feel betrayed by someone we believed would never betray us, or we, ourselves, might have betrayed someone who trusted us.

Natural disasters like hurricanes, earthquakes, tidal waves, and floods take away what we once had; community development changes what used to be into something new, and acts of human violence let us know that everything has changed. Fires destroy and nature rebuilds. Bad things, as well as good things happen to what we call good people and bad people, alike. The shifts in circumstances, whether gigantic or small or whether we believe they are for good or bad, change our worlds. Those changes can expand into transformations or they can bring personal or collective annihilation, especially if we try to hold on to what was when it no longer exists. Our authentic self and the life that emerges from this self exists *in* us; our safety, security, love, and significance come from our connection to the authenticity within us not in systems or things we hope will bring us safety, security, love, and significance. Eventually, everything in our lives that too often we depend upon for what we need in our lives will crumble. Often, it takes losing the false source we learned to cling to, for us to find the authentic source within us.

Sometimes we try to hold together what is crumbling in our lives or recreate what slipped away from us as a way to avoid facing the crumbling, and other times we try to embrace something new, but very similar to what used to be, as a way to replace what crumbled. Despite our desperate attempts to breathe life back into what has died, we cannot; the attempt at re-creation is not grounded in the energy of the present world because the world has shifted and what was in the former world has shifted, as well. The Beatles, Elvis, or John Denver impersonators are not the originals; the originals were a part of the energy field of their time, and while some people or things can span many decades, impersonations or recreations do not hold the vibration of the original. We cannot hold onto what was, no matter how much we want it or how hard we might try. I suspect this is why so many remarriages after divorces, fail again. Those who try to go back into the old relationship or into the old world without both making major changes and then creating something new, almost always experience failure.

When the past crumbles or fades away, you can spend your energies trying to recreate what is gone, or you can take the road that leads from the old world to a new one. If you have not, yet, experienced such a journey, there is a high likelihood that someday you will take your version of *The Road,* simply because life is about changes. You can walk your road looking back, longing for what is gone, resisting releasing the old, as the light goes out of your eyes and the spark out of your soul, a choice that leads to depression in a world that turns gray, and eventually, dies. If you choose to walk your version of the road with anger, violence, and aggression—you against others, and others against you—you will have created the world Hobbes described, that I mentioned earlier, one composed of *"war of all against all"* causing life to be experienced as *"solitary, poor, nasty, brutish, and short."* Resistance to embracing the new can also become a seedbed for anxiety about what the road and the new world will contain. Disconnected from your ability to create something beautiful, you can become absorbed in fear, a feeling that can eat at you until it consumes you. Or, you can decide to walk your path with acceptance of the learning from the past, with openness to learning from the present as it is, clearly responding to what your path holds, and with anticipation of what possibilities you can create in the world that is ahead for you.

THE FILM

The Road, begins with a dismal scene of a dusty grey world, as a man on a journey with his young son are living in the reality of an almost completely dead world; they are pushing a grocery cart carrying their meager belongings, like the proverbial bag-lady turned bag man and boy, wrapped in layers of tattered clothing and walking in shoes barely covering their feet. But then, in the middle of the desolation, the scene shifts as the man remembers the world that used to be. We enter a tranquil scene, drenched in the beauty of lush springtime flowers that sway in gentle breezes, as lilting melodies of songbirds hint of life in paradise just outside a lovely country home someplace in rural America. A young and very pregnant woman lives with her husband in this idyllic setting. But, as day shifts to night, the peace is interrupted by flashes of light coming from outside looking very much like explosions of fire that are the only indication that a major, frightening event has taken place.

And again we return to some future present day after several years pass between the flashback of abundant beauty and the future man and boy on a desolate road. The viewer can deduct that 6 or 7 years have passed from the time of the fireball explosions, since the child seems to have grown to about that age.

By way of a few more flashbacks, as seen through the eyes of the man, the viewer learns that some horrible event occurred to tear apart the tranquil life of the couple, and shortly thereafter, their child is born into a dying world. More flashbacks along the road let us know that the couple's life was filled with love, with beauty, and music, but all that ends with what seems like the dreaded apocalypse.

After years of struggle to survive in their home, the wife and mother can no longer continue living in constant fear that something even more terrifying than the apocalypse would come at any moment. She makes a decision to surrender to her death by walking out into the darkness without any protection, apparently to accept whatever evil is out there, and face the death she has been expecting for several years. Her only power left appears to be to choose when she will die instead of waiting for the unthinkable to choose death for her.

We can deduce that the family has protected itself with a gun from whatever horror exists outside the walls of their home, but only two bullets remain. She laments that she did not use the bullets when there were three left, and tells her husband that if it comes down to it, to use one bullet for their son and the other for him. And, as she departs, she gives her husband a last suggestion that he and the child head for the Atlantic Ocean, a place the woman believes life may still reside. She disappears into the darkness of the night, surrendering to her fate. She may be sacrificing her life as a way to save her husband from having to use the remaining bullets on her and their child, thus leaving him to suffer the unthinkable death that would await him.

In the film, it is the woman who surrenders in the face of doom. She is unable to counter an angry, aggressive, and dying world, an act that seems to be symbolic of the loss of the feminine, both in the film and in our world. When feminine energy is experiencing its power, the world experiences love, nurturing, and abundance of life, as was present in that first flashback scene of the beautiful country home and the pregnant woman. But when feminine energy is gone, a rainbow of colors turns to grey, abundance becomes scarcity, love turns to fear, nurturing vanishes and is replaced by aggression, and impending death eats away at what little life remains.

The disempowered feminine in any of us, whether man or woman, does the opposite of what an empowered feminine would do. She withdraws her ability to connect with others and may sacrifice herself to the needs of others in fear or hopelessness instead of surrendering and remaining open to receive others from a place of love. No longer capable of embracing all that is, she is unable to transform what comes to her, and what comes to her consumes her.

Reluctantly accepting his wife's decision to end her struggle by giving herself over to those who kill and eat anyone they find left alive, the man takes the boy and leaves what was their former safe home to go out into the dark and dismal world to face all manner of evil in their trek to the Ocean. What a metaphor this is for all of us who separate from the feminine—the part of us that rules the inner world, sees the infinite connections of everything in the universe, and nurtures those around her with affection, compassion, and understanding. The healthy feminine knows the outer world is safe because it is ruled by the healthy masculine, which is powerful and protective and is also independent, confident, and assertive. Because the masculine and feminine energies are interdependent, when one is damaged, so too, is the other.

Whether in a man or a woman, a damaged masculine energy is unable to protect the feminine within, and without that protection, the feminine energy is unable to surrender into being fully nurturing. A lack of nurturing creates abandonment, which further damages the masculine principle, and turns his protective energy into the dark side, becoming aggressive instead of assertive, separate instead of unique, isolated instead of independent, violent instead of confident, and forceful instead of empowered. With the breakdown of the masculine, the feminine withdraws nurturing and consumes or is consumed by others in her world. Embracing becomes withdrawal or smothering, nurturing becomes abandoning or self-sacrificing, and life giving becomes destructive consuming.

The feminine, damaged by the apocalypse, can no longer embrace the masculine that has also been damaged. The outer world, without the feminine, has been overcome with a life and death struggle in which winning requires others to loose in the most heinous ways.

***

If we pick up the newspaper, or watch any nightly news program, we can easily see, as metaphorically depicted in *The Road,* that the feminine energy is gravely ill or in some cases entirely missing in our world, and may also be missing in our own lives. Because of my personal apocalyptic childhood, I was unable to be the trusting, nurturing, all embracing person who could connect with my world and the people in it, including my husband, as I recorded in books one and two. I suspect my husband's inner feminine was damaged as well, leaving him to do what men often do without connection to their feminine aspects. He became an isolated loner, a man who spent much of his life working to make his way through the world to prove his worth based on his ability to survive and conquer what seemed to be a nearly unsurvivable and unconquerable world, just as the man traveling with his son on the road had to do. And…I not only expressed myself as the wounded feminine, I, also, had a damaged masculine that was not capable of protecting me from aggressions by other damaged people, as a healthy masculine energy would have done.

Each of us, man and woman alike, have experienced our own stories related to the absence of the feminine and damage to the masculine. Certainly, this is a story that has been played out many times in our history, not just personally, but culturally, as well. Since the world adopted the perspective of women being inferior and dangerous to the advancement of mankind, likely from the time religions blamed woman for the downfall of man, it turned against the idea of connection to the Earth and adopted a attitude of man's domination of the earth; our world, and especially the Western Culture, rejected emotion and compassion as inferior human characteristics compared to unemotional reason, observation, and judgment. It also adopted a masculine perspective that includes independence, mind over matter, and a focus on learning by disconnecting and separating instead of by experiencing the whole and seeing connections between and among all things. All of this has resulted in much of humankind experiencing life devoid of the feminine impulse, both collectively and individually experiencing the self abandoned and alone, having to fend for itself to find safety in what is believed to be an unsafe universe with the goal of survival as the final purpose.

The Road is a harrowing story of the dying of our planet, a metaphoric nightmare that tells the hidden story in all of us from the time we first believed we were alone in a loveless and god-forsaken world, whether it was just a fleeting thought or a life-long belief that stole decades of our lives. From work I did nearly 2-decades ago, I traced my own inner belief in painful abandonment to original creation. This experience, I believe is genetically in the DNA of all of us, carried as a story of aloneness. We all repeated the story when we went through the birth process as we literally separated from mother, and for far too many of us, did not find new connection with our biological mothers, with the feminine energies in our fathers, or in ourselves and in other humans in our lives.

The feminine energy unites and opens to the experience of Oneness with all, a feeling that allows us to know that we are never lost and alone. It is able to open and unite because it can trust the protective energy of the masculine. The masculine energy, which focuses on being unique in its creation of individuality, knows it is safe to be free and independent within the connective energy of the feminine. Masculine and feminine energies are opposite, and yet both are necessary for our inner spirit to experience unique lives within the support of connection, without feeling isolated and abandoned. If we have not reconnected with the loving, nurturing, oneness of the feminine balanced with uniqueness of the masculine within ourselves, we cannot connect with the spirit within us that expresses itself in the perfect, flowing balance of masculine and feminine energies. When our experience causes us to feel like we are separated from our feminine or disconnected from our masculine, not only are we out of balance, but we know something is missing; we feel as if there is an empty place deep inside us. We repeat the experience of separation and disconnection in our stories again and again, throughout our lives, resulting in the experience of a void within that seems never to be filled. And our lives so often are spent trying every possible means to fill the emptiness with something that seldom works for very long.

We remain in the story of separation that feels true until it brings us to the threshold of the void within. It is then that we finally realize we have a choice. We can take the leap into the void and bring healing to the experience of separation, or turn away and find something else to distract us from a journey that can feel as if it would be too devastating. The leap into the void of an unfathomable pit of darkness that contains all we have hidden behind our masks seems to be lying in wait to destroy us. But when we confront what is in the darkness, bringing healing love to it, and move through to the other side of the darkness we enter the place where our God Essence resides. If we choose the inner journey, though it can be harrowing, at times, we can finally reconnect with our true selves. However, if we attempt to get to the light within without taking the journey through the darkness, what is in the dark will continue to push its way into our lives, creating more crumbling and destruction, despite the best wishes of the light.

***

Have you ever reflected on your life story? Have you abandoned yourself like the mother in the film by giving up on the masculine energy in your world to protect you by walking out into a world that you believe will destroy you, feeling defeated even before you begin? Have you been living without the ability to embrace, with deep nurturing love, all those in your life, or have you separated people into *we-and-they* groups? Have you experienced the world from a place of being alone and forsaken, abandoned by what you thought would support you? Have you taken on the goal of conquering your world as your proof of your safety and your worth? These are all evidence of a life separated from the feminine and dependent on the broken, disconnected masculine.

Have you tried to live as if there was nothing to fear, when inside, you are terrified, finding that you just can't live like this anymore? Have you become one who believes that the only way you can survive is to eat up the competition in a world where there are only enemies and very few if any friends, though you pretend others are your friends? These, too, are products of a world disconnected from the feminine and attached to the wounded masculine.

***

In the film *The Road*, the boy, born after the apocalyptic event, contains both healthy masculine and healthy feminine energies in their child-like forms. Dependent on his father, the boy trusts the masculine energy of his father to protect him, which calls out the healthy masculine in his father to fully focus on the child's survival. Father tells son that he carries the fire, the light of life in the nearly dead world, and reminds the boy that he is one of the good guys. While the father often acts aggressively from the energy of the wounded masculine, separated from his feminine energy, the child is able to reach out to other people and can see their goodness. From his inner feminine energy, the boy offers

81

help when he has help to give and embraces the good when it comes his way. He sees colors and life in a gray and dead world and keeps hope alive in the eyes of ones he meets along the road.

In one poignant scene, the boy sees a rainbow in a waterfall, even though there are no rays of sunlight to create the crystalline patterns; the viewer can speculate that the light that creates the array of colors comes from the heart of the child. And in another scene, the boy is the one who finds a beetle, still alive, that flies off into the world when the boy connects with it. When father and son come across a nearly blind old man, it is the boy who pleads with his father to allow the old man to eat with them. The old man calls the boy an angel, and the father responds by saying his son is god.

In the end, the boy loses both his mother and father, and if we are to find healing, we, too, will be given the opportunity to release the wounding of our feminine and masculine aspects and embrace the potential for a future connected through the balance of the healed masculine and feminine to the God Essence that resides in each of us.

***

Other groups of people in the film were composed of those who were overtaken by fear and became predators or cannibals. They saw everyone else as enemy or as food for their survival. Their fear drove them to total disconnection from their humanity. Ruled by wicked aggression that had no foresight at all; they lost any connection with reason or compassion and became like threatened animals that gain advantage by appearing to be more powerful and threatening than their prey. When we look at upsurges in the numbers of people doing horrible things to others such as international terrorism, Ponzi schemes, corruption in nearly every human institution, senseless violence and murder of innocent people, as well as increase in the use of distractions such as drugs, disconnected sex, and alcohol that often connect to violence, we can see the damage of such predatory behaviors that have the potential to bring down, not just the Western world, but all humanity.

Looking closer, it is easy for us to see the marauding terrorists from the film as metaphors for those who would manipulate, not just strangers, but also, family and friends for their own benefit without any concern for the aftereffects of their actions on others, perhaps negatively impacting their victims for generations to come. But we can also see some of this behavior in less extreme manipulations of others when we maneuver to get what we want without noticing or caring about its impact on anyone but ourselves.

DIFFICULTIES IN FACING WHAT IS ON THE ROAD

The second in this trilogy of films, *The Road,* was difficult for many to watch, perhaps because it tore off the cultural *Mask* with which we have identified for generations and represents a journey *Behind the Mask,* which has been avoided by most of us for our entire lives, if not for many generations and lifetimes. But until we face what we have avoided for far too long, the human race may become stuck in its own version of *The Road,* and will not find our way to the end of the journey for a very long time, with the end of the journey, in reality, being the beginning of a brand new life in which our humanness is intricately connected with what is *Under the Mask.*

***

In the Eastern tradition, the Ocean represents spirituality, the place of Oneness and wholeness, and it refers to the unconscious or that which is hidden deep within. At the beginning of the film, before the woman abandons herself to the dangerous darkness, she tells the man to take the boy to the ocean, perhaps as a message to the adult and child masculine in us all to find out what lies beneath. The father dies beside the ocean from an illness he has had throughout the film, without discovering the deepest meaning of the ocean. However, after his father's death, the boy finds another family of both mother and father and a boy and girl. They reach out and offer him inclusion and their love, a sign that the healthy feminine still is alive. They, also, offer the child their protection, a sign that the protective, assertive masculine is still alive, as well.

Though we don't know the final outcome, we are left with a choice about the journey on our own road. We can choose to refuse to take the journey and die in our fear, depression, and anger, or take the journey that causes us to face the deepest darkest pain within us. We might choose to die before we find full healing, perhaps saving that experience for a future lifetime, or we might choose to move on until we have the chance to discover what the ocean holds for us deep within where the holiest of the holy lives, *Under the Mask*.

Some will walk a longer road in the gray desolation than others, or will experience an "eat or be eaten" world filled with violence for lifetimes, while others will walk on the road a very short time. The length of the road may depend on how long a person clings to the world that was or resists the one that is ahead, or how long one is willing to continue to look into the darkness of what is behind the mask to bring in light, love, and healing. No matter the length of the journey or how many segments it contains that can take you from the old to the new, it provides amazing opportunities for you to discover who you really are and what the purpose and meaning of your life is. Some may choose to go only so far in their journey this lifetime. Others may choose to keep going until all the segments are completed and the new world is formed. I sense that more people in the current world-climate are choosing to go far on their unique roads to experience the transformation and create their new world.

***

Though, at times, walking my road has been a very difficult journey, I do not regret that I chose to walk it because it has given and continues to give me the opportunity to discover truths for myself that are making transformations in me, truths that I now can share with those who are ready to experience their roads, their truths, and their transformations.

The lives we experience, both individually and collectively offer a gift that often does not feel like a gift, which is insight into what we have created based on beliefs about ourselves and about our world. When we allow ourselves to really see what is in us and in front of us, we can become conscious of what we believe. Only then can we decide if this is what we want to experience.

Chapter Five
THE THIRD OF THREE FILMS
OH MY GOD

Throughout human history, the idea of God has created cruel separations and long-held hatreds among peoples of the world, as well as wars that have been horrifically devastating to human life and to consciousness. However, the experience of God creates everlasting connection, love, and peace.

Oh My God, the third film I saw on that marathon day before leaving for the three-part trip to the Northwest, was not a story like the other two films. More of a documentary, the film presented a scattering of beliefs held by people from around the world about the identity of God. While reflecting on what I'd seen in the film, I wondered if the answers would have been different if the filmmaker had asked the interviewees what had been their *experience* of God rather than asking for a definition, which was more about the idea of God. And I began to think about my own experience of God.

LIBERTY QUARTERS AND GOD

If someone had asked me a question about my experience of God, my answer may have surprised the one asking. I would have said that my experience of God is in the feeling that fills me when I receive a Liberty Quarter. The backstory to the meaning of this coin, and the feelings related to it, some might interpret as sacrilegious, if not crazy.

But for me, when this particular coin comes to me what I feel is one of the most genuine experiences I have of *Universal God Essence*.

The story began back in the late 80s in a Laundromat. I had left my husband and moved into an apartment with no washer and dryer hook up, so I used the laundry provided by the apartment complex. On one unimportant day, I loaded the washers and then took out a roll of quarters to put the required number of coins in the slot. As I held the unopened roll in my hand, the fleeting image of a Liberty Quarter came into my mind. A short time before, I had gotten change after a purchase of some long forgotten item, and in the coins, I received a shiny new 1976 Liberty Quarter from a limited minting in '76 commemorating the 200th anniversary of the founding of the United States. It was so very beautiful and looked as if it had not been in circulation, though somehow had made it into a cash register and then into my hand. I put the coin in my pocket, intending to save it, but accidentally spent it in some unthinking moment when I needed change. I thought about the lovely coin with appreciation for all it represented, as I broke the roll open to feed the washing machine.

In the microsecond when I remembered the spent coin—not with any negative or sad thoughts and not with any wish for a replacement, but simply a thought of the beautiful quarter that made me smile—I took a coin from the roll and began to insert it into the slot, when to my amazement, I saw it was a bright and shiny Liberty Quarter. I began to laugh at the coincidence, and then another thought came to me that having received the coin was not just a coincidence, and a bigger smile came into my heart, a smile that filled my whole body with a kind of glow, as if my feeling-self knew something my thinking-self didn't know.

I had been learning about co-creation and manifestation in my church, and there seemed to be a message in the experience. I had no idea how important that message was to become, as it seemed to be communicating to me that something as insignificant as a quarter was to hold great significance in the years ahead. At the time, all that seemed to matter was that I thought of a Liberty Quarter and one came into my hand a microsecond later. I felt giddy with the warmth and the glow.

That feeling held the same kind of glow I still experience when I remember my sweet dog Sara, who will always be my puppy, running with her tiny Lhasa ears flapping in the breeze or her busy little teeth chewing up some toy making it squeak with each bite. I feel that same way when I close my eyes and remember the sound of my lovely, feisty cat Rachael purring from inside a large paper bag I had next to my computer. Her happiness was so powerful that her purring made the sides of the bag vibrate; it filled the room, and most importantly, it filled my heart with sweet loving tenderness and joy. She was totally content in her paper cave, and I can't help but feel every vibration of joy in my own body nearly a decade later when I recall the sound that was so much bigger than the paper bag. I feel that same glow when I think of so many moments I've shared with Oregon David, someone with whom I have allowed myself to love and trust more than any other person in my life. And, I've felt that delightful rush of warmth every time I have ever gotten a Liberty Quarter.

Not long after my laundry experience, I went to a workshop held in the mountains in Western Washington. The speaker, Alan Cohen, author of *The Dragon doesn't Live here Anymore,* had been presenting a long weekend training called *Dare to be Yourself,* and at the end of the time together, he asked participants who felt so inclined to come to the front and dare to claim a dream. I went forward to tell everyone that I claimed my dream to go to China to fulfill an actual dream I had a couple of years earlier in which I saw myself living in that magnificent Middle Kingdom. After the dream I'd received another Liberty Quarter and I knew I would go, though I had no idea how. A little over three years later, I was in China, where I lived for nearly two years.

***

Seventeen years after that first experience with Alan Cohen, and after collecting many Liberty Quarters at significant times, I heard that Alan was going to be a guest speaker at a The Center for Conscious Living, near my apartment in Largo Florida. I went to the service and when he announced that he was doing a weeklong workshop on Maui, I knew

I needed to go. The weeklong Hawaii Mastery Training was called *Oxygen*, named this because its purpose was to encourage people to take care of themselves first, like the airlines suggest we do when we are on planes and the oxygen masks fall down. Only after we put the oxygen mask on ourselves, do we take care of others. Self-care was seen as something good. I knew I needed to go to that workshop despite the fact that I had very limited income and was still making up financially from the 7-years in graduate school. Following the service, I went to the front, placed a deposit for $1000 in Alan's hand and told him I was following the path I had begun so many years before when I declared my intention to go to China while attending his *Dare to be Yourself* workshop, an experience that changed my life.

A few months later, I was in Maui participating in a soul altering experience, which included releasing energies around the dead zones that continued to occupy places in my body—energies that prevented me from being myself in the world. Despite the added expense, I chose to give myself a suite by myself. The bedroom had a tall cathedral ceiling and a large sliding glass door providing a view of the cascading forest that carpeted the mountains down to the Pacific Ocean. The bathroom was filled with tropical plants that surrounded and hung over a sunken tub, from which one could see the forest and ocean, as well. And, besides the gift of this private room, I decided to have daily bodywork sessions to compliment the work the group was doing with Alan.

The time there was transformative on so many levels, but as the week was coming to a close, I became concerned about how to handle my financial life after I returned to Florida. I had to smile from the center of my heart when I went into the laundry room to wash a few of my clothes and cracked open a role of quarters for the washing machine, but the roll exploded and the quarters fell to the floor, scattering everywhere. There, right in front of my feet was a Liberty Quarter and all of the oppressive thoughts melted away.

In between 1986 and 2003 when I had those two interactions with Alan Cohen, there were many other incidents when Liberty Quarters entered my life. Some came as a gentle touch to lift me out of a depression; other's came when memories from my childhood rushed forward, devastating me and causing me to believe I was totally alone in this world. The Liberty Quarter let me know that I was not alone. Other times, they came after I had significant dreams or visions, and I wondered if what I had experienced was connected to truth. One had to do with a vision I had of the original soul-splitting experience of humankind, another had to do with my decision to go to a Stanislav Groff *Breathwork* workshop where I saw in a dream what was to happen before I went, and the third had to do with a trip to Brazil for an International Conference on Shamanism, where I saw myself there in a vision before I went. Each time, right after I had finally made the decision to accept what I sensed was the right choice, Liberty Quarters came to me, as if reassuring me that I had made the right decision.

The first of these three liberty-quarter experiences happened after the night I woke from a dream that helped me to understand original creation. The dream was so vivid. I saw a form that appeared to be a man as he first became aware of separateness and went into shock. I watched the shock waves roll through him and then I found myself within the body, experiencing the pulse of the shock as it created cell level awareness of the primal explosion and scattering of matter. In that dream experience I was simultaneously inside and outside the form and knew it was fear that interpreted creation as meaning separation and eternal disconnection rather than uniqueness and eternal connection. As the dream continued, I saw myself teaching huge numbers of people in great arenas how to experience uniqueness and release the fear of separation and how to experience connection and release the experience of disconnection, which seems to have been encoded in our DNA from that beginning shock. I supported people in becoming aware that disconnection was an illusion, and then led people in a meditative visualization that let them experience connection to Oneness without losing uniqueness. It was a most profound dream. When I was inside the original body watching the expansion of the explosion, experiencing it on both cellular and universal levels, I knew I was watching original creation. Within the message of the dream was my teaching the ability to hold at once, both division and connection, both unity and uniqueness, truths that are in our DNA, as well.

As a human is being formed in its mother's uterus, a single cell divides and becomes two, and four, and eight, until the divisions become trillions of cells; yet, these divided cells create the unity of one body. Connected unity, together with unique differentiation, is necessary in the oneness of our bodies as human beings, a truth that is replicated in everything in nature, in which nothing is separate, although there are trillions upon trillions of unique existences within each person and unfathomable numbers within the universe, as a whole.

It was almost embarrassing to acknowledge to myself, much more to anyone who reads what I have written here, that I dreamed I'd be speaking on such a grand scale and wondered how I could let myself imagine such a future. The dream seemed too grandiose, but also, it seemed so real! I was thinking of the meaning of the dream when I went into the laundry room, very aware of my lowly status, a divorced woman, in therapy to heal a badly shattered life with no known path to becoming a community speaker much less a world speaker. I pulled out my half-roll of quarters—the other half had been used on the last laundry day—and tore at the plastic wrap, which unexpectedly exploded in my hand and quarters flew all over the washer and the floor. Like what would happen in Hawaii sometime later, the coin nearest me was a Liberty Quarter, liberty side up. The rest were ordinary quarters. I laughed so hard . . . Not only did I get a Liberty Quarter but it came to me in a scattering, so very similar to the dream from within the human where I experienced the scattering of original creation, and as if for emphasis, it was going to be replicated in my experience in Hawaii, also in the laundry room, and it was in a laundry room like the first time I began to notice Liberty Quarters.

Not long after that, dreaming vision, I met Sela, an experience I wrote about in more detail in *The Mask*. At first I thought Sela was an angel outside of me and then I discovered she was the part of me that exists on all planes, not limited to the three-dimensional level we often call reality. Sela introduced me to my light family, who are beings that live on multiples of planes including this plane, but their consciousness is from a much higher dimension. Their vibrational level is higher and I cannot see them with ordinary seeing, but they are around me all the time. I was really pleased to meet them, though it seemed I have always known them. In time, I came to understand everyone has his or her counterparts in other dimensions and on other planes, as well. These higher vibrational beings are able to flow towards us in this world as well as connect us to *Universal God Essence*, from which all of us emanate. I visualize this as the light of the universe, spanning out in streams of light like rays from the sun, and each of us is one of those rays of light; some aspects of those rays are very close to the sun and others much farther away, but none-the-less connected in the same ray of light. Within each of us is the ray of light, the spark of God, in its unique ray-of-light form . . . creating the *Unique God Essence* in us. At the same time, I thought I was losing my mind to believe in the existence of rays of light or light beings, especially when I began feeling a heart-connection with these beings that felt like my family and found it easier and easier to communicate with them. It wasn't something I could check out with a whole lot of others; actually, I wasn't sure I could ask anyone without significantly jeopardizing my intellectual and professional credibility.

While having a meal in a restaurant, I was thinking about all I'd been learning from my dreams and shamanic journeys to visit my light family in another dimension. The waitress took my payment while I was internally struggling with my thoughts. Wanting to believe in these internal experiences and chastising myself at the same time for even considering such incredulous ideas as being real, I asked Sela to help me know if what I was seeing and hearing was true, and just as I made that request, the waitress handed me my change, which, of course, included a Liberty Quarter. That rich delight returned just like before, as if my plea for clarity around accepting what had been given to me had been heard and answered.

About a year later I went to a psychic who told me lots of things that made me wonder whether or not I should dare trust what he said about my purpose for being in the world at this time. While doing laundry, I was mulling over the session and while the thoughts were still in my mind, the very next coin I began to put in the machine was a Liberty Quarter. I had two more $10 rolls so I broke them open and searched all the coins for another Liberty Quarter; there were no more. For weeks I searched every roll, and purposely gave cashiers payments that would give me two or three quarters as change, but none came. It seemed Liberty Quarters came to me only at very significant moments, not when I went in search of them or tried to control situations to make them come to me.

While I was still in Florida, I had experienced a very low income for a number of months and felt concerned if this were to become a trend. I had calculated what I needed to live on and things looked bleak. I wondered if I should leave Florida . . . for where, I didn't know. My light family assured me that I would be okay. They told me I needed to learn to trust they were looking out for me.

I noticed that when I was going through particularly tough periods that required focused internal work, my client load would diminish and when the concern was resolved, my schedule filled up, again. One morning, I had been communicating with my light family about my financial concerns on this plane while taking my dog Sara for her walk. My light mother explained to me that all I had to do was to be open to listen to truth and they would be able to support me far better. It was then that I got a distinct message to turn down a street I seldom took when I walked Sara, and certainly was not the one I planned on taking that morning. But hearing the message, I turned. Perhaps two hundred feet or so after the turn, I saw something shinny on the pavement. I walked up to it, picked it up, turned it over and saw it was a Liberty Quarter. I felt a joyful giggling well up from the inside, which exploded out into the world, sounding like something that would come from a two-year-old child's delight. The feeling stayed with me all the way back home and into the rest of my day. What seemed so important about this was I had heard a message, responded to it and a Liberty Quarter verified to me that the message was clearly about the concrete, three-dimensional world, not just coincidences in laundries or in change at restaurants.

Years before there were Liberty Quarters in my thoughts, I had seen the film, *The Miracle Worker*, the story of Helen Keller who was deaf and blind from the time she was 19 months old. She had grown up unable to speak when her family hired Anne Sullivan to teach the wild-child to be civil. The child actress, Patty Duke, played Helen. There was a magical scene when Anne had become impatient, if not exasperated with the rebellious, impossible child and dragged her to the water-pump to feel the splashing water on her hands as Anne kept signing the word water in in the child's hand, and forced the girl to feel the movement of her lips when she said water. In a profound moment little Helen finally connected the finger movements with the vibration in Anne's voice and the water splashing on her hands. Helen began to speak for the first time, allowing the first syllable to come out of her mouth. An explosion of awareness filled the child as she ran around touching everything she could find to learn what they were in sign language and voice vibration, and in one poignant moment, she touched Anne, to find out her name, and resistance turned to love.

Helen had discovered how to communicate with a world she had been separated from since she was so little. Helen's life was transformed; she went on to get a Bachelor of Arts degree, became a lecturer, as well as an author and political activist fighting for women's rights, and much more. For me, Liberty Quarters were like the water flowing from the water-pump. It was what my spiritual teachers from the light used to teach me that a simple thing like that coin could open my inner pathways to hear what my *Unique God Essence* eternally connected to and flowing in *Universal God Essence* had been trying to communicate to me, but I was blind and deaf to the higher vibration . . . until I finally got it.

In time, I didn't need the Liberty Quarters to verify the vibrations that were communicating direction and guidance. But every now-and-then, I would need a reminder that I was not alone and I could listen more carefully to that inner guidance of *Sandy God Essence*.

***

Sometime later, I had become aware that Stanislav Grof would be very important to my journey though I didn't know how for sure. I first learned of his work through my friend, Bill from Atlanta, while we were at a bookstore. Bill showed me Stan's book, *The Holotrophic Mind* and told me about some of the thoughts presented by this amazing man; I bought and read his book with an open heart. Everything in it felt so true. When I found out that Grof gave workshops, I decided to find one I could attend, but when I discovered the cost of attendance, I set the idea aside for a while.

As my 50th birthday was approaching, I was feeling sad I couldn't be with the people I loved who were so scattered around the world, so I sent out 50 invitations to a birthday party in alternate reality. I knew in my heart that there was a place in the universe for such an unusual party that was more a celebration of life than my particular birthday, though it was that, too. In the letter, I welcomed all the ones who received an invitation to invite anyone else they wanted to invite, and the only directions I gave were for attendees to close their eyes and wait to see a rainbow . . . and then they were to follow the rainbow to the party in an alternate reality.

When I arrived at the designated place, happy people had already arrived and were meeting others they had always wanted to meet and finding old friends that they hadn't seen for years or even for lifetimes. It was an amazing experience. Many who attended did so without their Earth-conscious counterparts knowing, but some entered the experience lucidly. Stan Grof came. I didn't know how he knew about the celebration, but I knew he was there. Sometime later I found that one of my friends in Florida had become close to Grof years before and had given him the invitation to this party held in a location in the collective unconscious, though I suspect neither of them were consciously aware of the invitation.

A number of months later, I learned of a Grof workshop from a dear friend who was thinking of attending a seminar in Kansas City where Stan would be speaking. I wanted to go so badly, partly because I wanted to meet Grof in physical reality and maybe discover how he would be supporting me in my journey, and partly because it would have been wonderful to participate in a spiritual conference with my friend I hadn't seen for a long time. I noticed that Grof would only be there for a couple of hours doing a talk and somehow that didn't feel right. But because my friend was going, I thought the experience would still seem worthwhile.

The week I needed to make my decision about going to Kansas City to qualify for the lower fee, I was asked to speak at the Unitarian Universalist Church in Clearwater, Florida, after which I was invited to participate in their metaphysical gathering. The discussion of the group was the work of Dr. Stanislov Grof. One of the participants had a magazine that listed Grof's upcoming conferences. When I looked at the publication, I found out that Grof was giving a breath workshop the same week of the Kansas City program in Washington D.C. Later that afternoon, I was standing at the checkout counter in a grocery store, and decided that it was the breath work I really needed and finally made the decision to register for the far more expensive breath workshop. While feeling a bit disappointed that I wouldn't see my friend, yet knowing the breath work was going to be important, I received change from my bill, and there in my hand among other coins, was a Liberty Quarter. The universe was validating my decision to attend the full workshop rather than the 2-hour talk.

Prior to the Grof workshop, but after I had made the decision to go, I stumbled upon a belief I held that suggested I was not meant to be in a love relationship in this lifetime. I discovered that belief as a result of doing inner work that took me into three lives in which I was executed for being in love. Those lifetimes taught me to believe my responsibility was to stay focused on my spiritual obligations and not allow myself to be distracted by love. The belief gave a directive that I must love others but was not allowed to experience someone loving me in return. In one of those lives, I was a young woman being initiated into a religious order and was being pledged to a priest. During the ceremony, I turned my attention to the right for the briefest of moments to catch a last glimpse of the man with whom I had fallen in love before my betrothal to the priest. I had to release the man because the priest had chosen me to be bonded to him. Before I had time to turn my attention back to the ceremony, my head was cut off with a saber, wielded by the priest, himself. A part of me remained stuck in the shock for many lifetimes.

A few days before the Breathwork weekend, I experienced a vision of myself looking directly into a man's eyes. I seemed to be in a reclined position and the man was to my right. It felt like he was very close, yet slightly above me. Somehow I knew it was Grof though I had never met him. I was about to experience one of those profound synchronous events that have come my way on so many occasions in my life.

Breathwork sessions begin with very loud and pulsing primal music that draws the participant into a deep trance state, and coupled with very deep breathing, consciousness shifts into inner arenas seldom accessed in any other state. If there are unresolved issues, it is not uncommon for the participant to be back in the experience as if it were happening all over again, but in the re-experiencing, there is support to move through whatever trapped a part of the self in the past. For me, five excruciatingly painful hours of inner work pulled me through some of the darkest experiences of this life, as well as through matching experiences from past lives. After the first hour, I believed I was finished with my work, but Stan stopped by to check on me, as well as those who were supporting my processing. He suggested there was more for me to do . . . and he was correct. I was not finished; the break was just a rest point. Two more times I thought I could do no more work, but Stan encouraged me to continue. The last time, I reentered the experience, and dropped into a very dark place. Grof remained, providing the support to move me through what felt like death was ready to snatch me out of this present, 3-dimensional world. In total exhaustion from the work, I lay on the mat face down, Stan was near, partially laying on the floor with his upper body a couple of feet above me. I turned over and looked into his eyes and in that moment, I realized it was Grof I had seen exactly like this in the dream just days before the workshop; however, the man I dreamed had a beard and Grof did not, but I recognized the light of his soul that shown in his eyes

I studied Grof's eyes and saw in them the gentle man from so many lifetimes ago, when I turned for the briefest of moments to look in his eyes as the sword held by a power-hungry priest severed my head. Something profound happened inside me. That shocking death thousands of years ago had held a part of me trapped in the trauma. The ability to love a person of my choice who loved me in return had been stolen in that distant past. In the powerful Breathwork session, I reclaimed what that priest had stolen so long before when I accepted the belief that without total submission to a religious leader, I would be given death. I brought back into myself, my power to choose to love. This wasn't about the man in that distant past life, nor about Grof and who he is in this life; it was about my perception of love, life, and death. That was why I needed to go to the Breathwork conference instead of the Kansas City lecture with my friend. I needed to reclaim the part of me that had been trapped in that experience of long ago, feeling separated from me and from truth that it was okay to experience being loved.

***

Not long after that powerfully significant Breathwork experience with Stan Grof, I learned about a conference that was being offered in Manaus, Brazil. I was in graduate school and had very limited funds, but something inside me told me that I needed to go. After struggling with whether or not I should attend the international shamanic conference, I finally decided that I would trust the inner message. The moment I made that decision, I was paying for lunch and, as before, in the change, I received a Liberty Quarter. Taking so many days off without income and spending so much, without knowing the purpose in going seemed crazy, especially at a time when my practice was low and I didn't have assurance of enough money to live on when I returned. Despite my fears, I made a reservation. Receiving another Liberty Quarter at the moment I decided to go meant that I could trust my decision. I understood that the universe was aware of my financial situation and would supply what I needed.

I made the conference, hotel, and plane reservations, but only days before I was to leave for Brazil, I had a heart attack, something I wrote about in *The Mask*. Despite the setback, I went to Brazil anyway. While at the conference, I received a most powerful healing from a Peruvian Shaman who had been invited to bless the gathering of 800 or so people. After the opening ceremonies of the conference, the Shaman left the stage to return to where he had been seated, and almost immediately, a throng of people engulfed him to receive his special blessings. So many people were pressing their way forward, but I didn't feel good about forcing my way through the crowd to get to him. After a few moments, the Shaman made his way through the crowd and came toward me; he spoke words in his language that only my heart knew. I kneeled down in front of him, partly because he was quite short, and partially out of respect for his position. He spoke to me as if I understood, and then place his hands over my heart. With his powerful touch, I felt a surge of energy flow into my heart and heal it; I learned to trust so much more deeply the messages I received about following the directions my heart hears in the vibration coming from *Sandy God Essence.*

There weren't a whole lot of people I could tell this Liberty Quarter story to back then. My felt sense was that they would have thought I had gone over the edge. I've learned that Liberty Quarters arrive when they are supposed to for me, *only when they are supposed to,* and I can't make them come, even if I desperately believe I need them. I can't tell you the numbers of rolls of quarters I bought over the years from stores or banks so I could find one. And in all those times, I never did find a Liberty Quarter. They aren't there until I need them, exactly in the moment that I need them, which is not the same as when I think I want one. Receiving these coins has been one of the ways those who love and support me from other dimensions have been able to communicate with me, sort of like someone dropping breadcrumbs to let you know you are on the right track.

Liberty Quarters may mean nothing to anyone else in the universe, and others might get these coins all the time, without any meaning attached. However, I get them only when something needs to be communicated to me. They are my sign to let me know that what I am experiencing is real. They are my assurance in a world that too often has offered me little assurance of the validity of what I have come to know . . . to believe . . . to feel . . . and they let me know I have made the most beneficial choice. They tell me that I am free . . . all I need to do is recognize that I am free and then allow myself to live as a free woman. They remind me that the universe supports my ability to be who I truly am. So, to me, the feeling that I experience in receiving a Liberty Quarter is so much like seeing my dog run with delight, or still, even after she is gone, being able to hear my cat purr with deep contentment, because these experiences open my heart and align all my Chakras with heart energy. The Liberty Quarter experience is like being in the loving presence of a dear friend or in awe of a radiant sunset, and in the center of all these amazingly ecstatic moments is my experience of God. Receiving one these coins is like getting a card from someone I deeply care for that says, *"I love you."* And, my heart responds with a joyful and silent, *"I love you, too."*

IMAGES OF GOD THROUGH THE AGES

Though I did when I was a child and during the time I was a young woman, I no longer adhere to a list of rules to regulate my life to gain the approval of others or of their perceptions of God; instead I am aware of what allows me to feel love, inner harmony and peace or what takes away those feelings, and that becomes my guide. The experience of God as love is far more beautiful, pleasurable, and authentic than the idea of God, which seems to produce the opposite effect, replete with rules and judgment. However, people throughout the ages have not recognized God as experience, but more often as an aggrandized image of themselves, much bigger, stronger, and more powerful than they are. And, that image is projected onto this imagined being they believe will intervene in human affairs, supporting those who are faithful and destroying those who are hated.

Those who have studied the history of religion have found that the evolution of cultural images of God can be directly traced to the social, economic, and political conditions of the times in which the images were formed. Earliest records indicate, when people were closely connected to the earth in hunting and gathering for their sustenance, the gods they worshiped were related to nature. The rituals they practiced had to do with rain and sun, hunting and gathering and later with the harvest, and especially with abundance and fertility. The majority of the earliest gods were female, likely, because the major concerns of the tribes involved fertility of the land, the animals, and the woman.

While some gods were believed to be sensitive to the needs of the tribe, others seemed to be concerned about the wellbeing of the individual who acknowledged that particular god. If a person had a request, he or she would give something to his or her special god in exchange for the fulfillment of the request. In many ways, gods seemed to be up close and personal, and looked very human or were a cross between animal and human.

These early religions were polytheistic, or what the Western religious perspective identifies as Pagan, in that there were different gods for different needs, and each held influence over particular domains. Rituals were developed to communicate with the various gods. Animal sacrifice had to do with slaughtering and cooking the flesh of the best of the herd, and offering it to the god they wanted to please, so in turn, the god would give them what they wanted. Gatherers and, later, farmers offered the best of the harvest to share a meal with the god they wanted to please for the same purposes as those who practiced animal sacrifice. In some religions, the sacrifice was neither animal nor plants, but was human, as in the sacrifice of infants, children, women, or warriors for the sake of the tribe. Some even considered it an honor to be sacrificed because the belief was that those who were offered in the ritual would immediately be transported to the presence of God, where they would be forever honored.

***

A number of years ago, while on an excursion into the Yucatan Peninsula, I entered an area where there were impressive pyramids, on top of which human sacrifice was performed hundreds of years ago. Hearts were cut out of living beings and the still beating heart was sacrificed to win the favor of the gods. I walked beside images of heads carved into stone blocks. Having their heads cut off as a part of the victory celebration immortalized the winners of sporting events, and their likeness was carved into squared stones for all generations to see and honor. This seemed to be their version of assuring eternal life.

Later, during that Yucatan adventure, I followed a path beyond the pyramids and game fields to the place where women and children were cast over a cliff into a deep, dark lake below as a ritual to promise abundance. When I stood on the ledge overlooking the dark green water, I felt my body begin to seize. I felt as if I were transported back in time as images from a past life flashed into my thoughts. When I was a small child in that life, the tribal priest had selected me to be sacrificed for the fertility festival. My mother was so proud that among all the young girls, I was chosen. She carefully braided my hair with white flowers and dressed me in a beautiful white robe. When it was time, people of the tribe came for me, and I was led to the rock from which I would be dropped into the sacrificial lake. I was given something to drink, which caused my body to feel heavy and my legs were unable to support me, and then I was ceremoniously thrown from the rock into the depths below.

As I stood on that same spot so many lifetimes later, I realized the belief held by many of the souls who died in a similar fashion was when they entered the water in the sacrifice, they would be lifted up to be united with god. Little girls and women believed they would be the bride of god. I had a very strong sense that many souls remained in the depths of the dark water still waiting, while their bodies decomposed and became a part of the tropical forest that surrounded the dark lake. I sensed that an aspect of my soul from that lifetime was among those waiting, so I leaned over and told the child that it was time for her to let go, and release her body from that lifetime. I invited her to come out of the water and return to the light where she could be reconnected with my full soul and return to me. I watched her rise up in a beam of light and in what seemed like a microsecond, I felt her energy enter my body and experienced a great expansion in my being. I then spoke to the souls of any who remained at the bottom of the lake and let them know that they could release the beliefs, the body and the lake from that lifetime, return to the light and rejoin the rest of their soul, wherever it may be in the universe. While in this deep state, I saw hundreds of people, mostly children, rise up out of the dark waters below and flow into rivers of light that took them to wherever it was each needed to go.

Later on during that trip, as I leaned against the railing on the ocean liner, I sent a message into the Caribbean Sea asking the water to carry a message throughout the entire world. The message was an invitation to any and all aspects of my soul that may have been trapped in some past lifetime and was ready to come back home, to release that past life and the body to which a part of me may have remained attached in that life, and to follow the light back to me. I gave permission for the bodies to release their energy into the Earth to complete the cycle. As I stood there, looking into the rolling ocean waves, I sensed the return of many missing parts of me; and was aware that some parts might require additional work to allow them to trust the message. I speculate that many people are living with aspects of themselves, separated and still attached to past life experiences, some of which may still be attached to religious rituals made powerful by the beliefs held by their families and cultures at the time. The kinds of horrific human sacrifice I learned about while in the Yucatan continued to be public practice for centuries until cultures changed their stance on such things. However new, more hidden forms emerged, many of which are still practiced today, despite the resistance of our culture to acknowledge that such things are still happening.

***

When societies grew larger and began to war against each other for control of a region, the god images that took center stage were those strongly connected to war, which for the most part, became reflected in the shift in gender from female to male gods. Even the early worship of one major god per tribe or nation did not negate the belief that there were other gods in charge of other concerns and gods that supported other groups of people. The allegiance to one's god didn't mean a rejection of the existence of others' gods. Each tribe hoped theirs was stronger than the other ones and would support them in winning the wars they conducted. The idea of there being only one God, not just above all other gods, but the only god that exists, came much later in the development of human religion. And of course, each religion claimed their god as the One God, worthy of dying for . . . and killing for.

Perhaps 3500-4000 years ago, during the time of Abraham, the one man who was accepted as the father of Judaism, Christianity, and Islam, there was recognition that each of the tribes and nations had their own gods. The god of Abraham, *Yahweh*, was one among many. And when the Ten Commandments were written and delivered to the people by Moses about 500 years later, one of the requirements was that these people have, *"no other gods before me"* a comment that indicates a belief in the existence of other gods that needed to be kept in their proper place by those who worshiped the God of Abraham.

Along with the evolution of the idea of a god who supported his people when they warred, came an understanding that god was more distant, someone who could not be known by mortal man and was out there in the universe rather than intricately involved in everyday life events of planting, harvesting, and hunting. These more mundane concerns were left in the hands of those designated as holy men, priests, or representatives of god on Earth, and for the most part, these were also men.

In the West, as societies grew from villages to states and into nations, national religions acted as a uniting force. When the connectedness of a group of people based on family and tribes no longer was sufficient to hold people together and leadership needed another way to create a sense of bonding for people who may have had little else in common beside their religion, the political leaders sought support from religious leaders to create unity. Because priests were seen as the representatives of god on Earth, it was almost a natural progression that they became entangled with political leaders offering ascendance to thrones by divine right for the leader who would then recognize a national religion. In some instances, the head of the religion was also the head of the nation.

From these roots, many came to believe God is an entity, entirely separate from us humans, most often seen as male, in charge of everything, and powerful enough to destroy all who do not worship him, either by his divine intervention or by using the hands and weapons of his followers, or in the judgment of natural disasters. More recently, because of the entanglements and apparent misuses of the word, *god*, to identify this unknown, unseen, ineffable source of being, many people have chosen to use other words to define the indefinable such as Spirit, Great Spirit, Universe, the Force, the Creator, the I Am, Christ Consciousness, The One, Oneness, and more.

When we look over the course of human history, it is clear that the needs of humans caused them to believe in gods who would fulfill those needs.

The modern world has not become exempt from the practice of forming images of god by looking into mirrors and determining the attributes of the being they call god by what they see reflected back in those mirrors. And, certainly, the needs of humans over the past 500 years have shifted from those of the previous 3000 or more years, causing the image of the god they see to change.

The last half of the second millennium in Western history, from the early 1500s to the present, has been a time of significant expansion and accompanying struggle at a far grander scale than the centuries prior to the discovery of the round world. The Western world saw major changes from living in the protection of medieval manors where people clustered around the powerful lords for defense against marauding plunderers. And, in exchange for protection, they sold their souls, their daughters, and their lives to the lord. The many manors grew into small kingdoms that warred against each other for increased power and wealth, into states ruled by leaders such as despots and kings, and then nations ruled by even more powerful leaders. Empires grew up, first as political entities that used invasion and war to conquer lands beyond their national boarders, and eventually they grew into economic entities that dominated markets through the whole world. In the latter half of the 20th century, the powerful, expanding entities took on the form of multi-national economic empires, spanning the globe, undefined by limitations of national boarders.

The last 100 year period, the bloodiest century in human history, was challenging for so many who lived and died during that time. There were two world wars fought only 20 years apart and horrible acts of genocide committed across the globe in the name of religion, and in between the world wars, the Great Depression destroyed more than the economic lives of multi-millions of people throughout the world.

While all of this was going on in the world, there was a major change in the American landscape that shifted the US and many other countries, as well, from being nations of little towns to ones of major cities and from family owned farms to corporate industrialized farms. In the US, local businesses grew into national corporations, which evolved into multi-national entities. And large extended families that lived and worked close together on farms turned into the nuclear family of parents and children, who no longer lived close to other family members, but lived in scattered suburbs. And in the present time, more and more families are composed of one parent and a child or two, while many people do not belong to families at all, living independently and in isolation. All of this has impacted the psyche of the culture, as well as the hearts and minds of individuals. These shifts have also changed the images many people hold of themselves, of religion, and of God, while others continue to hold images that belonged to generations of long ago, and for that matter, images from thousands of years ago.

THE GOD OF OUR FATHERS AND AMERICAN NATIONALISM

Without knowing where our beliefs about the world and ourselves come from, as well as our beliefs about religion and God, most of us simply adopt, with little or no questioning, the accepted world-view of our families, our cultures, our rulers, and ultimately, our species. The core of our collective beliefs grew out of the drive for survival. Some of them were based on the need to achieve superiority—as in the need to be able to say, *"My genetic makeup is superior to others, so I must fight to make sure who I am survives. If my genetics maintain superiority, I am more safe in an unsafe world."* For my genes to survive, I protect my children—in some cases my sons first, then daughters—and then I watch out for sibling's children, then my extended family. In time I attach this need to protect those around me to my race, my social or cultural group, my nationality, and if my consciousness has expanded far enough, I protect humanity and eventually all sentient beings, the land, the water, the Earth, and the sky. The need to protect self and others and the beliefs attached to them are passed down from generation to generation to guarantee safety. And, if they involve protecting me and mine against you and yours, they are fear-based, requiring actions inconsistent with believing in interconnection of all things.

As we collected into groups that evolved into extended families, tribes, states, and nations, we accepted the social constructs of those groups. In the Western world, the right of kings to collect taxes, maintain castles, and build armies allowed the peasants protection from invasion. Few questioned the right of kings to be kings, especially when the church acknowledged that God's will provided the divine right of being a king to the one that was on the throne.

Kings evolved into rulers, emperors, and in some cases, into prime ministers, and presidents, and the selection of the head of state shifted from appointment by God, to assumption by military power, and in some nations to the will of the people through election. The collective consensus within a country seldom questions the right of officials to take charge of a whole nation, even when the leader was Germany's Adolf Hitler, or Iran's Mahmoud Ahmadinejad, and even if the election was called democratic, but was fraudulently won. Whatever religion is the one accepted by the powerful, often became the religion of the masses.

It is easier for one group to see the inhumanity of other groups, without acknowledging it in one's own group, something true in the US, as well. While we have been critical of genocide in other nations, we seldom look at what happened in our process of nation building. The American dream included a concept of what historians called *Manifest Destiny*, a belief that it was the divine right—a right established by God—of the new Americans to claim the land between the Atlantic and Pacific Oceans, despite the fact that other people lived there long before, and we downplay the fact that millions of people died in order for European-American genes to prevail. If another nation in today's world did what European-Americans did 250 years ago lasting into the early 1900s, we would likely have a far different response to this kind of nation-building than we have to our own history.

Another belief deeply embedded in American culture is what came to be called *The White Man's burden*, which was a belief that white people needed to share with the Native Americans, the enslaved and then emancipated African-Americans, and in time, all those in the rest of the world, the religion and culture of the white man to *lift these others up from degradation to salvation*, though some groups still doubt that others outside their privileged group of white, Anglo-Saxon Christians can be saved. Many Americans took on the mantle of this burden by introducing those they considered to be the less fortunate of the world to the beliefs and benefits of Western culture. What is interesting is that it was not just the white, Anglo-Saxon Americans that came to believe in the destiny and the burden, but many of the minorities and people from other countries believed it, as well, especially when America seemed to be so blessed by the *God of our Fathers* the God the majority of Americans believed was the only true god.

A NATION UNITED AND THEN DIVIDED . . .
AND THE CRUMBLING OF THE IMAGE OF GOD

The US became more interconnected and unified in the 1950s by the highway system, which was begun by Eisenhower, and later by the development air travel, and the introduction of television, communication, and technology, and of course, the Internet, which connected the US with the rest of the world, as it had never been before. But, not only did this create a more united country and culture, it also produced the opposite effect. By introducing people to understandings, concepts, and beliefs of others, long held ideas and beliefs related to superiority of Western culture and religion no longer seemed infallible, especially in the presence of viewpoints of others that were in opposition to those held by the majority of Americans. Understandably, the recognition of the differences became most clear to young people who were growing up in this expanded and interconnected world.

It is common for any new *up and coming* younger generation to challenge some of the accepted beliefs and behaviors of the older generations. This allows new perspectives to change more rigid social systems based on new information and new circumstances without blowing up or disassembling the systems that came before or without rejecting the age-old principles, many of them related to religious beliefs, which act as the glue that holds the whole system together and protects the genetics of those committed to the system. For anything to maintain vitality, whether it is a human body or a human culture, it needs to have both structure and flexibility. The past patterns provide the structure and the present perspective provides the flexibility. Either component held onto too tightly can cause the system to become brittle or crumble or so flexible that there is nothing that holds it together.

Perhaps, because of the dramatic shift in the population as the *baby boom generation* came of age, youth's challenge to the old social order in the 60s had greater impact than previous generations when only a small percentage of the population challenged the system. The baby boomers—very large in number and interconnected by way of highways, air travel, expanded telecommunication, and advances in science and technology—were confronted with beliefs and systems very different from the social order solidified by the success of what historians have called *The Greatest Generation*, that came of age during World War II. It was this older generation that sang songs like *"Praise the Lord, and Pass the Ammunition"* that made patriotism equal to the American religion. Baby Boomer's parents were the people who pulled together more powerfully than any generation in the past to guarantee the survival of the nation, the beliefs, the way of life, to protect the genes of those who made up America. So when their children came of age in far more massive numbers than previous generations, the push was for more powerful flexibility that challenged the patterns of the past more than previous generations. The dramatic conflict between the solidified and stalwart system of the past and the overwhelming questioning of assumptions of the new generation acted as two tectonic plates under the Earth's crust, one careening into the other, instead of the simpler challenges of previous generations' youth.

Everything we thought or believed in as a culture was subject to re-evaluation, including nationalism, discrimination based on beliefs of superiority and inferiority regarding race, nationality, and gender, and beliefs about sex and sexuality, religion, human rights, social class, education, the military, war, peace, the environment, and so much more. The profound questioning brought forward by the young people of the 60s and unprecedented social upheaval was later accompanied by a backlash to the upheaval. This, in turn, caused other groups to attach to one side or the other; some who were closely connected to the American religion defended the old system even more strongly than generations in the past, while others wanted major revolution. The nation, if not the world, had become split between two oppositional camps that believed a healthy future was dependent on which of the two systems would prevail.

A problem can arise in any system when there are two nearly equally held, but opposite viewpoints about what is needed for survival. Instead of creating a sense of safety for its members to hold, the system might be interpreted as life threatening to one group, and it can feel like it is not capable of protecting the other group because there is such strong opposition to those ideas for which the system used to stand.

An entire population can feel as if its world is crumbling because of the other half of the people. This split can cause such significant disruption that the system cannot fulfill the expectation that it will protect those within it, and eventually, the system may collapse under the pressure of the split. The value of such core level disturbance in a disorder of this magnitude is that some people may begin to search for truths beyond those held by the system or by those who challenge the system. When outside structures no longer work, some might begin an inner journey to find deeper truths about the world, about safety, and about themselves than those they inherited. The words so aptly spoken by the old Rabbi, in *A Serious Man* can fit here: *"When the truth is found to be lies and all the hope within you dies . . . then what?"*

The Middle Eastern nations in the second decade of the 21st century are currently experiencing their own version of the baby boomer generation's 1960s revolution in America. Demanding an end to the old alignments that have disenfranchised so many, the youth that makes up over half the population in many of these nations are rising up to demand human rights. They have their own version of tectonic plates crashing against each other. The Phoenix that rises from the ashes of the collision between what was held to be true and the challenges that call those truths, lies, may well be found in the discovery of far greater truth in both the Middle East and in the West . . . or not. Time will tell.

***

Based on recent statistics, a majority of people in the US, claim to be Christians, and many of those believe that there is only one true God.

Many of these people believe that humans are by our very nature at least sinful, if not evil, and that if we live good lives or profess certain beliefs, we will be saved, where saved means that when we die we will leave this place that is not our true home and go to heaven to live forever with God. And many continue to believe America is the nation most blessed by God, something that makes Americans special, chosen, and superior to others, not because this is true but because that is what they were taught to believe. After all, so goes the reasoning: If God had not seen Americans as special, he would not have allowed us to expand across this land and would not have supported us to become the number one nation in the world. The justification for seeing Americans as the apple in God's eye is that America came into being to guarantee religious freedom, and the founders were God-fearing Christians who acknowledged God's exalted place in the Declaration of Independence, and on our currency. Of course, what has been called the *Greatest Generation* reiterated the honoring of God when they placed *One Nation Under God* in the Pledge of Allegiance following World War II.

This has the feel of a modern twist to the ancient belief that if we give the god of our tribe something we've decided he wants, like our best grains, our best animal, our virgin daughters, or our devotion, god will give us what we want, like victory in war, abundance in our crops or fertility among our women, and the current exchange is, if we declare our nation to have only the true God and follow his rules, this God will bring us back to being #1, in the world, something we lost when the godless revolutionaries of the 1960s, nearly destroyed us. What is too often not noticed is that the pre-1960s ideal America that was "lost" in the revolution and the volatile years that followed, was ideal for white American males . . . but even that assumption can be challenged in light of the millions of "serious" men of that time, who in their "winning" the prize of the good life for following all the rules, in fact lost themselves.

THE EVOLUTION OF MY EXPERIENCE OF GOD

Like many Americans, I was born into a family, a community, a culture that believed God favored America, and basically, all we did as a nation was good. I was taught to accept the many mixed messages in Christianity, including the "fact" that I was a sinner; evil was in my very nature, and, I deserved to be condemned to hell because of my sinfulness yet, God loved me, still. However, if I didn't take certain actions and profess certain beliefs, I would go to hell. Being good required me to not break the commandments, which, among other requirements, directed me to love God above anyone and everything else, to not lie, steal, or kill, to honor my parents, to remain chaste until I was married, and to be obedient and faithful to my husband until death parted us.

But when I began to see that my parents were living dishonorable lives, and when I didn't feel loved by my husband who was having a long term affair, I could not find a way to integrate what I believed and what I experienced. My answer was to push away what I saw and felt, and I began to live as if what was true was not true and what was not true was true. As I had written in the first two books of this trilogy, and in *E Pluribus Unum: Out of Many . . . One,* for me to be able to hold the picture that I needed to believe was real, I needed to dissociate those parts of me that experienced events that didn't match the picture. Splitting off what I didn't want to know and hiding it deep within me until I no longer consciously knew what I knew, allowed me to go on pretending until I could pretend no longer. Like the society around me, the *"I,"* who I believed I was, began to crumble from the inside out. I suspect that there are many who recognize this pattern inside them, as well.

But whatever people do to try to live with what does not make sense, eventually, leads to the collision of two worlds—the one we try to preserve as real, and the one that we try to push away as not real—not unlike the metaphor I used about the US in the 1960s and the Middle East currently of one tectonic plate colliding into the space of another plate. When the two finally hit, metaphoric earthquakes, hurricanes, tidal waves, and floods follow, shattering and scattering everything in the world we tried to hold on to as real.

As I wrote in *The Mask*, my underground plate shifted when an event caused my two worlds to crash into each other and tear everything apart in my life. I had been married for nearly 20 years, living as if all was well and I was happy. But deep inside my unconscious mind, and hidden in the recesses of my heart, I was disconnected and deeply sad. One day, sometime in the early 80s, my then husband became upset with me for something, although I have no recollection of what it was. He must have had his own inner plate shift and the collision of the worlds inside him sent him into a rage.

While I was taking a shower, unaware of his anger, he reached into the shower, turned off the water and then stepped in and pulled me out, dripping wet. He lifted me over his head and carried me through our bedroom. As he approached the stairs to the main floor, I began to cry, begging him to not carry me down the stairs. I was afraid that I might fall as I did another time when he was just playing around. But he continued to carry me down to the main floor and into our kitchen, where he performed a wrestling move called the helicopter. He held me up in the air and twirled me around despite my pleading cries for him to stop, and when he was finished, he dropped me to the floor. With a look in his eyes that seemed demonic, he told me, *"Now you will know who is boss."* The shock was so great that it literally caused my outer world to split apart and my inner world to shatter. The man who had held the *"divine right"* position of husband in my life . . . the one to whom *the God of our Fathers* directed me to be subservient and obedient, to love, to honor, and to remain with until I died, was someone I no longer recognized.

What I didn't know at the time was that my husband's treatment of me paralleled an event in my childhood that I had shoved down, and buried deep inside the darkest place behind my mask. Before an excruciatingly painful rape, my father twirled me around on a merry-go-round in the school playground that felt exactly the same as when Jake did the helicopter twirl 30 years later. The result of these two events crashing into one another was like a gigantic earthquake that cracked me apart. Aftershocks and tsunami force waves devastated my life and my world, and though I tried to live as if the old world were still there, I could no longer find the love I had once felt and tried to believe in for so many years.

Terrified to leave, I remained in the marriage looking for any way to repair the cracks and rifts. But it was not only my relationship with my husband that had been cracked apart; my relationship with my family, especially my parents split open as more of the horrific abuses of my childhood became conscious, and my understanding of and relationship with the *God of our Fathers* had also been deeply shaken. Of course, my understanding of the world and my place in it drastically shifted, as well. My post-shower behaviors were unrecognizable compared to the pre-shower behaviors. I was no longer the obedient, subservient wife who lived to support her husband; that woman died on the kitchen floor.

The more I tried to hold on to the world that, in reality, was gone, the less I was able to feel any form of comfort. I began to see a therapist in a desperate attempt to glue back the pieces, but the truth was, the shattering had been too extensive. Still hoping to find a way to make the old world work, I separated from my husband, but moved into an apartment less than a mile away from him.

***

Part of the shaking up of my world brought forward questions that I had hidden away for decades, which were only indirectly related to my marriage. Some of those questions were about God. If God was unchanging, how could there be a difference between the God of the Old Testament and the New. How could God have condoned the stoning of children for disobedience and then invite children to come to him because these are who will be in heaven. How could God order the execution of a child to prove the father's faith without considering what trauma the child must have endured when he was tied up, placed on the sacrificial fire and approached with a knife? How could God love all of us equally but decide that women had to be obedient to men and had to cover themselves in church, without speaking. And how could he demand that a woman be obedient to her husband, surrender to him, and love him when she is treated in the Holy Book like she has no value?

I didn't know how I could both love God and fear him at the same time. I didn't know how a God who loved me could condemn me to hell if I did something wrong, and apparently my inability to love my husband and remain in a marriage of religious obligation was something wrong. In an attempt to rebuild a real relationship with God instead of holding on to the old relationship that didn't make sense any more, I began to attend a Unity church that provided a much different picture of God, as well as a different picture of me. None of the images I had been taught to see since I was a small child seemed to reflect what was forming in my new world any more. I needed to find if perhaps there might be a new image that felt more real. While struggling with the destruction of just about everything in my life, I had one of those dreams that was profoundly transforming.

GODS IN THE MIRRORS

The dream that transformed my life seemed to have been going on for some time. In the dream, I am walking very slowly toward an open door at the end of a hall. It is necessary for my arms to be stretched out on either side of me so I can feel my way by touching the walls as I move forward. I take each step cautiously, carefully testing the floor in front of me before I put my foot down to take the next step. I am not watching myself as in most of my dreams, but I am the dreamer walking toward what seems to be a large room, perhaps an old attic-like room that is not well lighted, but somewhat lighter than the fully dark hall.

As I enter the attic room, I become aware of what seems to be a freestanding, full-length mirror that is a few feet in front of me, and in the mirror, I see the image of God. He is enormously tall, and is wearing ivory colored robes. He is carrying an ancient looking leather-bound book, holding it against his right side with his right arm. The book looks very heavy. Though I try, I cannot see God's face. I feel like a lost child who has been wandering the streets for as long as I can remember in search of something familiar and finally I recognize that I am home. I am filled with all the emotions of being lost and then being found inter-woven in the same microsecond. I tell the God in the mirror that I have felt so painfully disconnected from him all of my life, although I have believed in him as long as I can remember. I tell him that I have loved him since I was a small child and I want more than anything to dedicate my life to him.

In agony, I bow my head and tell God in the mirror that I have been so lonely for his love. It feels as if a lifetime of longing is pouring from my heart. I am speaking with deep emotion, but become aware that nothing seems to be coming from him. I am not feeling any love or empathy. He seems detached and unconcerned about what I am expressing.

I lift my head and notice that a second mirror has appeared to the left of the first one with the image of another God in it that looks exactly like the God in the first mirror. The two are mirror images of each other, but I know the two are not the same God. As much as I try, I cannot see this God's face either. A sense of horror fills me that I cannot recognize which God is real and which is false. I call to both of them, telling them that I want to follow the one true God. Franticly, I look back and forth between the two images searching for some sign that will tell me which of the two Gods is real.

Somehow I know that I must make a decision as to which one I will worship and which one I will reject. I beg the real God to come out of the mirror so I can know he is the one that is real. I wait, terrified and in silence, for one to come toward me, but neither moves. I know that if I select the wrong God, I will be condemned to eternal separation from God, which is death, forever burning in a lake of fire. I fall to my knees. I can feel mournful sobs filling my entire body as I plead for help. I cannot understand how God could put me in such an untenable position of having to make a life-threatening choice without being given enough information to choose. I awaken in terror.

After looking a little deeper into the meanings of the dream, I could see how the struggle I was experiencing in my marriage that was in the process of ending led to confusion of deeper feelings about the God I thought I knew from the time I was a very small child. The dream helped me discover that I didn't really know who God was. Much later I was to learn how the god of my childhood was a god that professed love, but was a god of rules and punishments. All the inconsistencies I had known about the god of my childhood were buried in some inner dungeon, and I didn't dare ask about them . . . until I had this dream.

RELIGIOUS BACKGROUND

I grew up in a small Alaskan fishing town nestled between the foot of majestic Mount Marathon and the shores of the beautiful Resurrection Bay. I was raised to believe in Jesus and his love, and to fear God, who somehow seemed different from Jesus. One of the songs from my childhood Sunday school experience had a melodic chorus that went some-thing like this: *One, two, three, four, five, six, seven. All the children go to heaven. When the master rings the bell, all the bad ones go to hell.* Another song I learned had these words: *If you don't go to Sunday school, you'll grow up to be bad. If you don't go to Sunday school, you'll someday wish you had. If you want the Lord to be proud of you, you'd better start today, cause the ones who miss the Sunday school, are on the downward way.* And still another song warned us, *"Oh be careful little hands what you do . . . oh be careful little hands what you do, for the great God above is looking down with love, so be careful little hands what you do."* Each verse reminded us to be careful of something, be careful little feet where you go . . . little mouth what you say . . . with a subtle threat that if I was not careful the great God would rain fire down on me and send me to hell for not being careful.

I spent my childhood years afraid that somehow my little hands were not careful enough for what they had done, and my little feet were not careful enough for where they had gone. And deep inside, I knew my feet were forced to go to some pretty horrible places, and my hands were forced to do some pretty horrible things. But they were my hands and feet, so it seemed that it was my fault for what they had done.

The religion of my childhood was one in which God seemed to have a split personality. My understanding was that the loving part of him is expressed in the person of Jesus Christ, God the Son, who came to give me an abundant life, who wanted little children to come to him and who loved all the children, *"Red or yellow, black or white, all are precious in his sight; Jesus loves the little children of the world."* The other split part of God was the one that ruled creation with cold judgment from a distance. He was the God above and looked down upon us, who had set the date when he would destroy the wickedness of the world, which meant eternal hell fire for most of us and I believed, I was one of those included in the punishment that would last forever. He was God the father who had already decided when he would come to judge the living and the dead. On that day, he would spew out of his mouth those who were lukewarm and slay those who were sinners. He would destroy the Earth and create something new for those who were obedient. So many comparisons were made between God, the Father, and our biological fathers, and if my father in heaven was anything like my earthly father, neither heaven nor earth sounded any better than hell. And yet, I was supposed to want to go to heaven.

If I believed in Jesus, loved him, and obeyed him, then the loving son would stand before me on judgment day, protecting me from the anger and wrath of his father. There was a subtle suggestion that the validity of my belief in Jesus would be established by my sinless actions for I was to *go and sin no more.* I was to *be holy even as Christ Jesus was holy.* But my child-self's heart knew I sinned, and I knew I was not holy. I struggled with the dilemma that if my actions were sinless, I would not need anyone to stand in front to protect me from God the father. I would need Jesus to stand in front of me if I had been sinful but my sinful actions would be proof that I did not believe, love, or obey adequately enough to deserve the son to protect me from the father. My bad actions would be proof I was not one of the chosen. And the fact that bad things happened to me was proof that God had already judged me. As much as I wanted to believe in the God of love, I was terrified of God the father. I was terrified of the moment after he counted to seven when the bell would ring out and I would be sent to hell.

After attending vacation Bible school at a local church when I was still in primary school, I began a practice that lasted for many years. Each night before going to sleep, I carefully placed my shoes in exactly the right position to be able to jump into them in a single movement in case the end of the world would come in the middle of the night. I knew that the end would come when I least expected it *like a thief in the night* based on the lesson I had learned in Bible school. I had images of Resurrection Bay, just a few blocks from our house, churning with boiling steam exploding off its surface and huge burning rocks falling from a blood-red sky and boulders tumbling from Mount Marathon, the mountain whose base came down to the very edge of our small town. My only safety would be to run to the mountains and call out to the *God of our Fathers* to save me from destruction, but even that would not work. I had gone on hikes part way up the mountain and knew that there was a whole section that was made of loose, sharp shale. Running up the mountain would cut bare feet, so the shoe placement became the solution to bring some relief to a child frightened to the core about the coming of God, the judgment, and the condemnation. It probably didn't help that God's coming like a thief in the night felt too similar to my father stealing into my room at night to take me away to the places where my hands and feet couldn't be careful for what they had to do or where they had to go.

I knew I was supposed to love the God whose deeds were told in another church song, a God who *so loved the world he gave his only son to die on Calvary, from sin to set me free*, and I knew that my heart did love God. However, I was terrified of the God who would not only send his only son to die, but could also tell his faithful servant, Abraham, to tie up his little boy, Isaac, butcher him with a knife, and burn him at the stake like a sacrificial animal. He had to do this in order to prove his faithfulness. I was deeply fearful of a God who killed Job's wife, all their children, and his livestock just to prove to the devil that Job was faithful. The Bible said that Job was rewarded with a new wife and children, but I wondered about the old ones. What made them so expendable, so replaceable? The woman and children must not have mattered at all to God the father if he could kill them for no reason other than to win an argument with the devil. It made no sense to my child-self that God—as powerful as the *God of our Fathers* was supposed to be—would have to prove anything to anybody, least of all the devil.

I knew I was supposed to love God with all my heart, my soul, and my mind, but I didn't know how to love someone for whom I felt such fear. If he could so easily send his son to his death, and order the death of

Abraham's son, and kill all the children of Job, then I figured I didn't have a chance.

In spite of my fears, for many years, I was God's faithful servant. I attended church and became an active member of the church youth group. I taught children in Sunday school and sang in the church choir. But when I was a young adult, I made a promise to God and later broke it. I remembered the warning from the Old Testament that we needed to be wary of making promises to God; breaking them would mean condemnation, and to me, condemnation meant hell. For a dozen years following my graduation from college, I taught in a Christian high school, teaching religious history, leading devotions, and at times giving Chapel presentations, all exhorting students to seek after the *God of our Fathers*, all the while believing that I, myself, was already condemned to hell.

In the mid 1980s my life and my marriage began to fall apart and the distant unloving God of my childhood seemed even more distant and unloving. The therapist I was working with at the time, knew how much my heart longed for spiritual connection with the creator of the universe and suggested that I might find a new age church to be a place to heal my heart and find God. In this setting, I heard about the God of love that more closely matched my sense of the God I sought from childhood. I began to attend regularly and felt as if I had finally found a church that felt like home. I took classes, sang in the choir, and occasionally led congregational singing for the thousands who attended the church.

From the perspective of this new church, there is only God and only good. Everything else is an illusion. When someone lives outside awareness of love, what is created is the experience of hell that is not real. Other teachings suggest that our thoughts create our reality, so if we are experiencing difficulties, it is our lack of faith in love and our belief in difficulties that cause these things to happen.

As I became more involved in church, it seemed that the judgment I found in my childhood religion was present in this new church, as well, and I found that people were as frightened and condemning in the new church as in the church of my childhood. Some of the people in the church of my childhood where involved in deeply dark activities that I shared with readers in *E Pluribus Unum: Out of Many . . . One* and more so in the second book in the trilogy, *Behind the Mask*. Much later, I discovered that people in leadership positions in the new church were cheating on their spouses, and the church was suffering from inner conflict and power struggles. I was as sad in the new church as I had been in the old one and my heart was still longing for connection with God. I was also terrified my very questioning of my fundamentalist upbringing was proof I had left the *God of our Fathers*, which was all the evidence necessary to condemn me to an eternity in the lake of fire. Though I thought I had found the God I had been seeking, I was to discover that this religion did not possess the God of my search, either. It was sometime in 1988, in the middle of this sadness and fear that I dreamed the dream of the Gods in the Mirrors.

The dream of the two gods in the mirrors continued to haunt me. The more I searched, the more disconnected I felt from God, and yet, the more I felt a deep calling to find the God who created the universe and who loved me. My heart believed in a God of love, but I feared I was chasing after false gods becoming just another fallen soul paving the way for the Anti-Christ to wreak destruction on the Earth and I'd be sent to hell.

The more I asked questions of myself and deeply investigated my inner world, the more I reconnected with what I knew as a child that had to do with my psychic abilities, my healing energy, my ability to experience shamanic journeying, and to dream multi-leveled dreams that often were prophetic in nature. I saw visions of futures, many of which came true, and dreamed a new path for my life that I began to take, but not without trepidation. These were things I wrote about in book one of this trilogy, *The Mask*.

In time, I re-entered the dream and returned to the room with the two mirrors and the images of the two Gods. Because I had come to understand that everyone depicted in our dreams are parts of ourselves,

I stood in front of the first image, the one to my right, and asked the part of me that carried the heavy book if she would be willing to put the book down and come out of the mirror. At first she seemed indignant and even hostile. A child's voice coming out of the God in the right-hand mirror began to condemn me, pouring out quotations of wrath from scripture verses I had memorized in my childhood. The book was filled with laws and rules that she believed would help her find God. She refused to put the book down as she continued to chastise me. After listening to her for a little while, I asked her if in all the years she had been carrying the book, following the rules, judging others and me, as well as herself for breaking the rules, had she found her connection to God. She began to sob. Her tears answered my question. I asked her if she would be willing to set the book down now and come to me.

She stepped out of the mirror and collapsed into my arms. I felt such a deep love for this little child part of me who had been so afraid of breaking the rules that she became the very God she feared. She was the holder of the bell, doing all she could to make it not ring to save me from sure death, yet knowing that it was her job to ring it, and to send me—along with her—to hell.

I turned to the image of the God in the second mirror and asked her if she was happy. She smiled and assured me that she was very happy. She told me that she loved me; she always had. She told me that she loved my father and she understood his agony that led him to do what he had done that had been so painfully damaging to me. She was the personification of innocence and saw the world filled with love.

After careful consideration of her words, I told her that something seemed missing in her belief that there is nothing but good. I asked her what attachment she had to that belief. There was a very long pause. She leaned toward me and almost whispered that to see it any other way was to see a universe with darkness spinning out of control. If there was both good and bad, and if the God in the other mirror was not the true God with all the rules and the answers, the judgment day, and the bell to ring, then it was possible for the bad to win, and all would be destroyed. But the condemning God had already condemned her, so she had to remain with her beliefs about love.

She told me that believing only in love felt so much safer. I stood in silence in front of the mirror on the left. This little child had spoken what I had felt for so long but had never had the courage to voice. I had known that to see darkness in the world would mean that there was darkness in me, and the most frightening thought that ever was in my mind was that there might be darkness in God, which was a thought that had been too devastating to consider. I broke the silence with a simple question. I asked her if it *felt* true that there was no darkness, no badness, and no evil in the world.

This child part of me began to sob as deeply as the first had done. She had experienced evil inflicted upon her in the darkness of other people's fear that had devastated so much of her childhood, and she spent a lifetime blocking awareness of what had happened. The more she understood of everything in our lives being reflections of parts of ourselves, the more she had been able to see her own darkness. She saw her own actions of goodness could come from a camouflaged need to control her world and her practice of self-sacrifice was subtle manipulation to hide her fear, her anger, and her pain. She had wanted so much to believe in her goodness that she could not allow herself to look at the darkness inside. I held out my arms to this part of me reflected in the second mirror. She looked into my eyes for what seemed a very long time and then she stepped out of the mirror and fell into my arms.

I held this frightened little girl part of myself close to my heart and told her that every one of us carries both good and evil, light and dark, from which we can choose, but the more we deny what is in us and in others, the more we become un-conscious of what we are choosing and doing, and much of those unconscious behaviors generate from the dark. As I rocked her in my arms, I explained to her that though I had an experience seeing where fear first originated eons ago, I don't understand where evil originated, but that I know it exists in the physical world. I told her I thought that maybe it grew out of fear related to the belief in separation, which must have led to seeing others as enemy, followed by a need to become defensive, and some forms of that defense evolved into evil. Since all of us are a part of creation, and all of us contain good and evil, it seemed to make sense that whoever or whatever created us must contain both, as well. I told her that I don't know how to explain God being everything and yet God not containing both light and dark, and explained to her that perhaps when we get to the other side of this life-experience, we will better understand. At that moment, that was all I could offer her.

The parts of me that were reflected as the two gods in the mirrors in my dream had appeared to be so powerful, so demanding, and so sure. The two stood in such opposition that no matter which I chose, I believed I would surely die. The blackness behind the mirrors that allow reflection, like my own shadow, had reflected back to me my projected split images of God. The first mirror reflected the traditional masculine image of God, who judged me and condemned me to death if I did not follow his way. That mirror on my right, I can see now, as the shadow masculine part of me that had adopted the god of my fathers. The mirror that appeared on my left was the feminine aspect of God, that wanted to include me, but did not know how to embrace all of me, including my shadow. The two parts of me, disconnected from each other, could only reflect separation that was both figuratively and literally tearing me apart.

With the embrace of love, the child parts from the mirrors flowed into my heart. As I walked closer to the mirrors, the two mirrors became one, and instead of two gods, as I'd seen before, I saw myself reflected back to me. I looked deeply into my own eyes and saw love and fear, sadness and joy, strength and weakness and the most beautiful light in the heart of my heart, a light that filled me with love so over-whelming that a powerful joyful sound rushed like a geyser from my chest into my throat. It filled my entire body and exploded into the room. I finally was able to see the dwelling place of God, creator of the universe. I knew that the heart of my heart was my eternal connecting place. And more deeply than ever before, I felt God in me. The connection I sought from the time I was a small child, finally happened, not from some being, some *god creature* out there who created me with both light and dark and then would cut off my head or send me to hell for having darkness in me; but I experienced something that I knew was true . . . *God Essence* was within me.

And, then, I watched as the blackness that created the mirror and the reflection began to melt in the light that flowed from the heart of my heart. I watched the image of myself fade away as the blackness behind the mirror melted, leaving a clear window that became a magnificent opening to the universe. It felt as if the weight I'd carried for thousands of years lifted off of me. My heart felt so full. Light and love seemed to fill the entire room and flow through the ever-expanding window into the outer-world. I felt love for my years of struggle, for my parents and grandparents, and all those who had formed religions to find God and all those who rebelled against religions, only to create new images, new god creatures, and new gods. My heart finally knew, not just in my head, but also in the experience of my body that God does not live in religion; *God Essence* that fills the universe, also, lives within me, and that is who I am.

I now understand that God is not split between an Angry God and a Sacrificed God and does not have a checklist like Santa Claus to see if I am good or bad, naughty or nice. Some great and powerful God did not kill sons, order the death of other people's sons, or kill wives and children on a whim. These stories of god were projections based on the storyteller's self-image, and therefore, became the gods they depicted. The images that had been in the mirrors in my dream were two sides of my own beliefs, one inherited from the religion of my forefathers, and the other from a religion formed in reaction to the one I had inherited. I realized that religions and followers of religions have bowed to gods that were images of themselves in their own mirrors, made visible by the darkness behind the glass, a reflection of the darkness within those peering into the mirror. For the first time, I felt safe, and my child-self realized that she no longer had to carefully place her shoes alongside the bed because she no longer believed that God would come like a thief in the night and condemn her to hell.

CONCLUDING THOUGHTS ABOUT THE THREE FILMS

Without knowing why I needed to do so, I watched these three films, *The Serious Man, The Road,* and *Oh My God,* prior to taking what was to become a profoundly significant trip back to the Northwest. Afterward, I was amazed at how these three movies were linked together. On some level, they all were a reflection of my own life. For much of my life, like the serious man, I lived by the rules as closely as I could until an internal explosion devastated my world, and I began to take a journey from what had crumbled to whatever was ahead of me. Like the two travelers—the man and his son in *The Road,* —I was terrified by everything in the world that was left after my personal apocalypse, afraid to move forward, but more afraid to stay where I was, and despite my fear, I moved forward.

And like the people from those 23 countries, from the time of my personal explosion, I reflected on my beliefs about God, which eventually transformed my understanding of God, of the universe, and my sense of myself, which I now see as being without separation from God Essence that exists within me, within all others, and in the whole Universe, a metaphor for you, me, and us . . . three in one, . . . and one in three. The three films allowed me to articulate the transformation in a way I had never been able to do before.

On reflection of all that I wrote in this chapter, when we examine history, it is easy to understand how gods who existed in the minds of humans evolved, but even when we know about these images, they tell us little about the origins and meaning of the world or of ourselves except for the myths that were spoken as stories and passed down for generations before they were written. Neither from science nor religion can we know the mechanics of whatever it was that brought into existence something out of nothing, whether it was the vibration originating in *Universal God Essence* that began the process of creation, or some yet unknown interactive principle, some vibration or sound, that caused an explosion, as proposed as the big bang, which eventually evolved into the universe and all that is in it. Even the big bang theory does not tell us what caused the bang and religion does not tell us of the origins of the God that is said to have uttered the words, "Let there be light." And as much as the most brilliant minds through all time have sought an originating "theory of everything," nothing has proven itself to supply the answer, though many have tried. But there remains something in the human spirit that continues to seek answers and continues to long for connection with something beyond our limitations . . . something related to the universe . . . what I have called *Universal God Essence,* and others have called the *Great Mystery* or whatever is their name for the originator of all that is. I believe the knowledge we are seeking about purpose and meaning, which many have hoped we would find by discovering our origins of the universe, is available to us from knowledge of another sort. This knowledge is discovered through accessing the unique essence we carry deep within our being, *Under the Mask*, available to us through experience.

POSTSCRIPT

In March of 2010, while working with later chapters in this book, I saw a news article about a man and his grandson. John Mayasich was on the 1960 US Olympic hockey team when they unexpectedly won the Gold against the favored Soviet Union team. Fifty years later, the old man had planned to be with the new generation of players at the Vancouver Olympics, but instead of being at the medal ceremony in case the US beat Canada, grandpa Mayasich was in a hospital room sitting with his grandson, who had been hit by a car during a 200-mile relay race across a portion of Arizona. The boy, Robby Mayasich, was a dearly loved lacrosse player for Brophy, his Parochial high school, and when his dedication to the game finally led to a place on the team, he chose the number 8 for his jersey, the same number worn by his famous grandfather a half century before. And the boy, for whatever reason, played with a pink lacrosse stick.

A group of boys were participating in the relay race where those who were not running were riding ahead in a van to meet the runner at a designated point ahead. At the change point, the runner would climb back in the van while a refreshed relay runner would begin his portion of the race. Though it was not his turn to run, Robby got out of the van carrying a bottle of water to meet the incoming runner, but in the dark of night, when he crossed the road to give water to his teammate, Robby was hit by a car.

John Walters wrote about what followed when Robby's father Dan Mayasich spoke at a candle light prayer vigil for his son shortly after the accident. Dan said, *"What we're experiencing is without a doubt every parent's nightmare. But this is every parent's dream. How odd, and yet how beautiful is it to have those two very different forces at play simultaneously."* The father was referring to the fact that in the middle of his pain for the life-threatening accident his son had experienced, he was feeling joy from being in the presence of hundreds of people who truly loved his son.

Walters reported, that two days following the father's message to those who gathered to pray for his son, Robby Mayasich died. He was only 18 years old. The following week, the Brophy lacrosse team played a game against Chandler High School and won. Each Brophy player wore a gray undershirt with the words "WE ARE ONE" printed on them, and all of them had the number 8, on their shirts. The teammates took turns playing with Robby's pink stick. One week later, Dan Mayasich talked about the gift he had received earlier when he spoke at the chapel before his son passed away. He said, *"I wanted them to know what an amazing and actually 'joyful' thing it was for us to be experiencing; how unusual or odd it could possibly be . . . but ultimately how lovely . . . to be using the word 'joy' in the face of such tragedy, horror, sadness. I then had them consider that this thing they're all seeing, this magic they're all feeling in the chapel, it's actually there in all of their kids, all of the time. They just don't realize it. It's like this invisible thing that shows itself only when it's called upon, but it's always there for everyone, not just our son. Perhaps THAT is God?"* This realization is not so different from the father's comment to the old man in the film, *The Road*, who saw the love emanating from the boy and called him an angel, but the father said of his son, *"He is God."*

The life-shattering discovery that what we thought was true about who god is and who we have believed ourselves to be is not true, may not feel like a gift, but nonetheless, it is. When we are willing to receive this gift, for the first time, we can discover who we truly are and know our place in the universe, as we experience God Essence within us. Although knowing the truth can set us free, accepting what is true can be terrifying, when it means letting go of what we held onto for so long. And letting go can transform our lives beyond our possible dreams.

Part Two

The Trip to The Northwest

Storage Crates
Michael's Message
Synchronicities

Chapter Six
STORAGE CRATES
A LESSON IN LETTING GO

When we are truly connected with another, there is no need to hold on. The attempt to hold on, something that we really cannot do anyway, is evidence that we have already lost our experience of connection with the person we thought we couldn't let go of or live without; we simply have not, yet, acknowledged or grieved the loss. The same is true for things, ideas, beliefs, or dreams we may attempt to hold onto instead of embrace with open arms.

It is amazing how much we attempt to hold on someone or something that energetically is no longer in our lives, and most of the time we are unaware that the people or things are truly gone, or, for that matter, that we are holding on. For years, I tried to hold onto a marriage and a husband who had already left me without actually physically leaving. And the deeper truth was that I had already left him, as well. Though both of us had left a long time before, I held on energetically, which blocked me from moving forward in my life. I also was holding on to what I had stored, as the last vestiges of a life that had been gone for a very long time. Though I didn't know it at the time, I had so much more to release than just the *things* I had kept in two large walk-in storage crates for over two decades. And it was not an accident that I went to Seattle three days earlier than I had originally planned to sort through 50 years of my life. December of '09 to December of 2010, was to be a time of letting go of so many things on multiple levels, and the crates were just a metaphor for years of holding on, not just to the possessions, but also, to the thoughts, feelings, hopes, dreams, wishes, and beliefs unconsciously embedded in the possessions. I needed to release the world those contents represented that no longer existed, and I needed to bring back to myself the parts of me trapped in the memories of the past. Before I could move ahead into the life I had seen in so many visions of my future, and fully occupy the world that was drawing me to it, I had to let go of the life I once lived and the world in which I lived it. But I couldn't do that until I identified what I was trying to hold onto that still had its grip on me. And I clutched at it, as well, despite the pain and sadness the former world held. Until I began working with the subtle energies of what those crates contained, I hadn't realized how much some parts of me still longed for everything to have not changed and wished for the sadness to go away, sadness that could show itself, now and then, behind mask-formed smiles.

A METAPHOR OF A WALK IN THE PARK

The best way I can explain the experience of having parts trapped in the past, is to ask you to imagine that you are leading a group of people through some park, and you have to get to the exit gate before dark, but you need to do that with all people accounted for. All the people, from a number of children, a few teens, and adults at various ages are tied together and must move with you if you are going to reach your goal. You are walking, focused on the gate ahead of you, but you feel a tugging on the rope that binds you to all the others. You look back and notice that one of the young teens stopped to talk with an attractive teen that was standing next to a tree; the two had spent a wonderful summer together sometime in the past and wanted to reminisce. Fully engaged in the conversation, the teen does not notice that the rest of the group has been slowed down.

A child sees a pony ride and tries to get to the pony that looks just like the animal she rode a couple of months before and she throws a tantrum, pulling and screaming at her rope because she does not want to move past the pony, while another child struggles to prevent the other from getting to the pony. One child remembers the joy of riding and the other remembers that a similar ride ended in a nasty fall. Another group member does not want to go to the gate because of a very bad experience at a similar gate many years before and still carries the fear of gates; this adult digs in and refuses to budge one more inch toward the gate you need to find because darkness is approaching. And still another sees a bench that used to be a meeting place for a long departed loved one. This person wants to go sit on the bench and spend the rest of the time remembering the life lived with that person as if time and passing never happened. Yet another sees an amusement park off in the distance and wants to experience the thrill of a wild roller coaster and is attempting to pull the whole group, you included, in that direction, and as might be expected, another group member wants nothing to do with roller coaster rides or thrills that are risky.

If you were very strong, you might be able to pull against your tether and drag all those people, fighting and screaming to the gate, but you would soon discover your muscles and joints hurting from the difficult task. You could drug them or give them some intoxicating substance, making them so weak they can't resist your forward motion, or distract them with whatever each might want, sort of like the tying a carrot on the end of a stick and putting it in front of the horse to make it run after the carrot and go in the direction you want it to go. But your long list of necessary distractions might become a distraction to you making you not find the gate before nightfall.

Until you recognize that everyone in the group is tethered to you, and unless you find out what has caused each one to have objectives that are different from yours, perhaps finding a way to help them let go of the past, release the fears and resistances, and communicate in a way that allows you to create a destination that works for all, perhaps even changing your need to make the gate by nightfall, you will be spending your time being pulled every which way, struggling and fighting instead of enjoying the walk through the park.

Now imagine that there is someone else, in the center of this unruly group that understands the deepest reason you all have been tethered together and what would allow each person to open to his or her highest and best purpose, and that includes you. But in order for this to work, each one will need to surrender to the wisdom of the one who is in the center of the group, there with you all, but is untethered.

Some will be willing to let go of whatever was pulling them in one direction or the other and listen to the one with wisdom, but others will have to be allowed to express what they hoped would be received if they could have made everyone go with them. Those who wanted to recapture something from the past would need to understand how the past is not where life exists and whatever they longed for does not belong to the person or thing to which they attached themselves. The ones who are afraid of the future because of the past would need to express what they fear and be allowed to discover the deeper root causes of whatever happened that caused them to be afraid. If they still carry pain from something in the past, they will need to go back into it, bring truth, love, and wisdom to what happened and release the pain.

When they let go of those things they became attached to, whether it was from pain or longing, and open to what is in their hearts to experience what brought them to the park, they will find that it was no accident that they were tethered to each other. What one needs to experience his or hearts desire is the same for all of these people, and that includes you.

This group of people is a metaphor for the many parts inside you. And the wise untethered one who goes with you wherever you go is your *Unique God Essence,* your Spark of God-Self that exists in each of the parts of you and is who all parts are at their very core really are . . . that is why what each part truly needs, but may not know it, is the same for all. You are a part of the group, but not the part you think you are; the multiple aspects of you are discovering how to be who you are as you take a walk in the park . . . a walk called life.

POLAR BEAR

Not so long ago, I was watching a nature special on television about polar bears and the concerns environmentalists have about their likely extinction. The program provided information about the species and included a segment showing how crews track the majestic animals in their icy habitats. The video camera was photographing a bear running across an ice sheet trying to avoid a helicopter occupied by its pilot, the cameraman, a sharpshooter, and veterinarians, as they kept up a relentless chase across the frozen landscape. The bear zigzagged wildly in a futile attempt to outrun its mechanical predator, but finally, the man with a stun gun was able to zero in on his target and shoot the bear with a tranquilizer pellet. After the hit, the bear continued to run for a few more lumbering steps and then fell, after which the helicopter pilot found a safe place nearby to land. The crew scrambled to complete protocols in marking and checking the health of the gigantic animal, and just before the bear began to regain consciousness, the humans hurried back to safety and continued to film. Before he stood up, the huge creature began to tremble and quake as if he were experiencing electrocution while outstretched, vulnerable, and helpless on the ice. My heart was breaking for what I presumed the bear must have been experiencing, because instead of seeing him as a ferocious creature, he looked like a helpless cub with no one nearby to help him through this terrible experience. I couldn't understand how these people could allow the beautiful giant to suffer like that. I felt such emotional pain watching the screen that I almost turned the channel. But I stayed with it, and I am so grateful that I did.

After the quaking and quivering stopped, the bear seemed to take in a big breath and let it out again, like a heaving sigh; then he stood up, looked around, shook himself as if he were getting out of the ocean and shaking off water, and walked away as if nothing had happened. What I heard next verified what I know happens with clients who enter places deep within through processes such as in the work I do and in the work offered by well-trained body therapists such as Michael, depth psychologists, psychotherapists, counselors, psycho-spiritual therapists, and others who focus on deeply buried trauma.

The announcer explained that the bear had been in a heightened state of fear that produced great amounts of adrenaline coursing through his body when he was running as fast as he could to save his life. But, he was stopped in the middle of his intense drive to find safety. Shaking and quivering was an essential part of his recovery from what had happened to him; it was his body's way of releasing the excess adrenaline and other chemicals from the tranquilizer, as well as his own physiological responses that remained in his body from the failed escape attempt. If he had been able to outrun the helicopter and find a hiding place, he would have collapsed in that safety and breathed through the quivering and releasing process, which would take him into a resting state, just as he did after he awoke from the tranquilizer. And then the announcer added a small but powerful comment that made the whole experience of watching have even deeper meaning for me. He said that humans often block releases in their pets that happen naturally for animals in the wild, and the toxins from the unspent adrenaline, fear, and trauma of life experiences remain in the bodies of pets, poisoning tissues, organs, muscles, and bones, doing long term damage, something that does not happen in the wild. Of course, the same thing happens in humans when they do no release trauma in their own bodies.

THE HUMAN COUNTERPART TO THE POLAR BEAR

What I have done in my own healing process and in the work I do with others is to return to the memories recorded in the tissues to support the release of the pent up energy, the toxins that resulted from unreleased trauma, as well as the beliefs and patterns that form the internal protective structures that inhibit post trauma recovery. This process gives the person the chance to experience his or her version of the polar bear release, and then move on in their lives with organizational structures related to new beliefs and patterns.

Without knowing what they are doing, adults often prevent children from releasing physiological buildup from traumatic experiences, which inhibits emotional release that if allowed to be expressed in a comforting and safe atmosphere could lead to a reevaluation of the mental conclusions and patterning that develop because of those traumas. Children learn very early what emotional or physical releases are and are not acceptable in their familial and social environments. By overriding the child's innate ability to release trauma by inflicting more trauma for releasing the energy or by preventing the release by smothering the child with over-protective responses, parents can deny the child the opportunity to have their polar bear release.

How many of us were told that an animal we dearly loved was taken to a farm where he would be happier, when in fact, he was put down. But something inside told us a worse thing had happened, and even now, we can cry over the traumatic loss of that animal. Despite the good intensions of many parents, the child is not able to let go of the pent up energies or express what their minds concluded from the experience. The intense energy remains inside, only to re-emerge at unexpected times. It would be far better to tell the truth with love and allow space for the child to release the stored energies: to cry, to ask questions, to move through the stages of grief, while offering support for whatever he or she needs. If the child needs comforting, and if the parent has been willing to supply a *port in a storm* for their little one in the past, the child will come to the parent when they need to, not when the parent needs this to happen to ease their own discomfort with their child's response.

It is also not uncommon for some adults to minimize or ridicule their children for what they are feeling and eventually they learn to hold it in and disconnect from knowing that they had the feelings to begin with. If a child is rejected for crying, in time he or she stops crying and then takes on the belief that there is no need to cry, and it doesn't take too much longer for the child to disconnect from knowing crying exists inside. Often, when others stop a child from feeling and expressing, or from trembling and quaking with all that is rushing through their bodies, it is because they can't allow themselves to feel their own feelings, either. To see a child in fear or in pain can remind another of his or her own fear, long ago denied and too painful to remember. So the feelings, the adrenaline and all the other body responses at the chemical and hormone levels remain in the tissues in both the parent and the child compromising their immune systems and potentially, their health. All of this is stored for years or for decades, producing great amounts of stress, often without any awareness that this is happening until illness shows up because of the toll such unexpressed energy takes on the body-mind.

STORED ENERGIES IN MY OWN LIFE

It was clear to me that reconnecting with 50 years of my past had affected me because of what I still was holding onto inside me. And letting go of the external storage units became a metaphor for letting go inside. This was the time to allow the energy to pass through me, by being present with the feelings and allowing all the quivering and quaking that I was never allowed to express—first by my parents and then by me—for all those years. Even though I had worked with so many of the stored memories in the past, many body memories remained, and they needed to be released.

There were times I wished I could just move on with my life and not have to get entangled with any more pain, but what we store within affects us even if we don't believe it does. Even if we do move on without the release, and create what seems like healthy lives, parts of us can remain trapped in the trauma preventing us from being fully present as we move forward. When parts of us metaphorically remain frozen on the ice, still living as if there is a predator ready to do harm, these unhealed experiences and our patterned responses become a part of our unconscious reaction to the world around us. When we send those parts to the inner storage units, not unlike dungeons deep inside, so we can move on, our lives lack authenticity and no matter how successful we may become, we feel as if there is something missing, without knowing what it is. We can also live in terror without knowing why, or we can feel as if a volcano is ready to erupt at any moment even in response to inconsequential events. There is an old Chinese adage that says, *"Once frightened by a snake, a thousand times frightened by a rope."* And many of us spend our lives attempting to avoid our version of the rope.

Our inner wisdom has a way of drawing our attention to what is not healed in us by recreating similar experiences that have the potential to connect the present to some past event that we have stored and buried. Our wise self can do this in many ways, such as by bringing people into our lives that exhibit similar patterns so we can recognize the same patterns in ourselves that still trap us; our wisdom, perhaps, will recreate events that match past events, or give us dreams that help us see what keeps us from being free. Or the wise self can use books, movies, television programs, and world events to let us see what we have avoided seeing and knowing in ourselves. And sometimes, when we don't pay attention to life experiences, to the mirrors others provide for us, our dreams or anything else used to awaken us, something more may be needed to shake us enough to see what we didn't let ourselves see before. That kind of a shaking up took place for me with a very different experience on the ice than the one the polar bear endured.

UNEXPECTED HEAD INJURIES

Late in the evening of December 22, 2009, three days before I began writing the first chapter of *Under the Mask,* I was about to discover another place inside that had kept trauma from the past hidden away, but I had not paid attention to messages to work my way through it when I had been given other reminders. That night, I was walking my dog in the wintery cold of the Colorado Mountains. I had been back for just over a week from the three-phased trip to the Northwest, which included emptying the crates in Seattle, reconnecting with Michael in Bellingham, and visiting with Oregon David for a few days. As Jenny and I descended the stairs from the carriage house, I noticed how much it had snowed during the day covering everything with a blanket of beautiful white, making it a challenge to find a spot where Jenny could take care of her needs.

I was bundled up in what I call my Mountain Mamma clothing, dressed nothing like I do when I am in Florida. I was wearing a huge down-filled, butterscotch man's jacket, which I found far more durable and rustic than most women's jackets, making the men's version more appropriate for my life in the mountains of Colorado. I had on my long underwear and heavy knit pants, with my laced hiking boots and heavy sox. Living in Colorado caused me to let go of having to win any beauty contests, remote as winning something like that would have been even without the mountain mamma clothes. As I had done as a child in Alaska, I still resisted wearing gloves and hats because I have never liked feeling as if I were cocooned, unable to hear or feel what was around me.

Well protected from the cold, I walked with Jenny in her search for a spot where she could relieve herself. But, without any warning, my foot hit a patch of ice under the snow, and in a microsecond, I fell backward, down a slightly inclined part of the road, and hit my head on the ice with a crack that filled my entire head with light, as if at least 50 trillion of the 100 trillion synapses in my brain simultaneously exploded with lightening strikes, and I began to wail loud enough to wake the dead or any hibernating animal in the rock caves above me. But unfortunately, no human being heard my cry. Both my landlady and her friend who acts as caretaker of the main house, were gone, as were the nearest neighbors; the one to the north of me is about a half-mile away and the one south, a quarter mile away, but they seemed to have left for the holidays. The only others who might have heard my cry were the wild animals. All indications pointed to the fact that I was alone, wondering if the fall had caused death-threatening injury to my brain.

Unable to move for a few minutes, I remained nearly motionless on the ice-covered ground holding the back of my head as it began to throb with excruciating pain. I don't ever recall my head hurting so badly. Then, I felt around until I found a place under the snow and ice where there were rocks providing footing to pull myself up. I steadied myself, and was relieved I could walk back to my place and up the stairs to my little carriage house.

I knew I had done damage because of the intensity of the pain, but didn't know how bad it was. An ice pack didn't take away the pulsing throbs, and though I would have liked to take something to ease the pain, I knew not to take any thing with aspirin in it or any blood-thinning painkiller in case I had internal bleeding from a concussion. Lying down was not possible since the throbbing pain increased in any position other than sitting upright. Several times during the night, I thought of calling 911, but decided to hold off until the morning. I continued to put ice packs on my head and neck through the night and into next day, and then I made an appointment with a Conifer doctor for the afternoon of Christmas Eve to be sure the damage wasn't life threatening. After asking a few questions and looking into my eyes and ears, the doctor concluded that I likely had a concussion, but the lack of swelling, as well as the absence of broken vessels in my eyes or leaking cranial fluid in my ears indicated that the head damage was probably not as bad as it might have felt. I was advised to be watchful and get myself to an ER as soon as possible if the pain or dizziness increased. I was sure I'd be okay; besides, driving myself to a hospital on Christmas day didn't sound too inviting.

After the Christmas Eve doctor's appointment, I went home and for some unknown reason decided to listen to the CD the astrologer had redone for me the past summer. When the recording finally arrived sometime in August, I set it aside because I felt out of harmony with the reader. And, I didn't feel drawn to listen to it for the intervening months. However, it became the catalyst for my beginning to write this book, something I mentioned in chapter one. I concluded that I might not have been ready to really take in the deeper meanings until after the crack on my head.

A week later, just before New Years Eve, another snowstorm had blanketed my mountain retreat. I got up in the morning, after having had a good night's sleep—the first since the fall—and was feeling so positive about everything! The continued icing of my head made whatever damage I'd done feel somewhat better. I was pleased that I had begun to write again, and I felt ready to embrace movement without resistance, giving permission, once again, for my body to become healthy. I took Jenny out for a walk, which was the first time since the fall a week earlier. She wanted to stay out a bit longer, so I extended our walk up the road to check the mail. But, on the way back down from the mailbox, despite my caution, I had another fall. I had been so careful, stepping only on the crisp snow, but somehow I caught another ice patch and down I went. The slip and fall happened so very fast; one moment I was upright, and in a microsecond I was on the ground holding the back of my head that I'd hit in the same place as the week before.

For the life of me, I couldn't figure what I was trying to tell myself. Maybe it was...*Don't worry! If you fall down, get back up again.* Or maybe, *Notice that your body is much stronger...bones are healthy; muscles are resilient, so appreciate what your body can do.* I wanted to think there was a positive message in the head banging...but I wondered.

My sister had sent me a pair of cleat shoe coverings following that first accident to avoid such a thing happening again, but I hadn't put them on. I would have done so had I thought I was going for a longer walk, but the decision to check the mail so Jenny could play outside a bit longer was spontaneous. And... I was being careful. All the way up I was fully conscious of every step. I even pulled my parka hood up to my neck, which I am sure helped when I did fall. It happened so fast. I continued icing my head, just in case there was internal bleeding reopened from the first fall.

I had become aware that my child-self was still so afraid of the world out there; she still believed the world was out to get her, even in the form of ice that would make me slip and get hurt. When I did an inner check, I sensed fear about the world was a collective fear, held by many aspects of myself at multiple ages in my life. When this thought came to me I could hear mournful crying coming from so many places inside me, from parts extremely terrified about being in the world. This made perfect sense since one of the things I knew I was being drawn to learn was how to embrace, not just the universe, but also, this place where humans live, here on this Earth...a place that had not seemed particularly kind to me most of my life and wasn't being very kind to many others in the present if we look at all the disruption of life on all levels going on at this time in our history.

Even though my mind had embraced the concept that whatever happens in our lives is what we draw to us, to bring healing to us; fundamentally, part of my heart had never fully accepted that whatever is wicked or painful out there that impacts me is what I have drawn to me because something in me needs to be brought into consciousness for healing. I was aware that more than one aspect of my child self still felt separate from the world and believed it was filled with darkness and pain, as well as wickedness that was out to get her. Though I had worked on this issue so many times, a part of me was convinced if she did something wrong, God would get her, too, and again, I began feeling her fear of a world that would crush her if she took the wrong step. My child-self believed that making a wrong choice or doing a wrong thing would pull her down as surely as gravity does and she would go to hell. Even thinking about ideas that were different from those I was raised to believe caused this child part of me to go into immense terror. There was no question that from the very beginning of my writing the trilogy, I knew that *Under the Mask* would go into ideas that this still-damaged child-self was sure would condemn her to hell, for eternity.

Most of my life I have wanted to feel like I belong in this world; however, because my experience taught me to believe the world has not committed to wisdom, goodness, health, and especially to love, my wish to connect with it seemed inadvisable, if not dangerous. Maybe my wish for connection to the world continues because despite all the cruelty, the evil, and ongoing life threatening danger that abounds, I can, also, see the goodness that exists under the evil, health that lives under the illness, and wisdom that keeps showing up in the middle of ignorance. I have always known the love that has never gone away, in spite of the fact that so many of us have turned our backs on love, if not continually, at least some of the time. At the same time, I see the expansion of people's ability to become more conscious as so many are reaching out in connection, offering help to the downtrodden and suffering people all over the world. Probably, the most disturbing concern I held, had to do with the amount of fear that seems to permeate every level of existence. Fear is what can cause people to turn to the dark side and do what they would never do if they were not afraid, and I knew I feared the fear that could take over the hearts and minds of others, an understanding that reflected back to me that my fear could take over my heart and mind, as well. This, too, was calling out to be healed.

These thoughts were coming to the surface in the first days of 2010 as I was writing the earlier chapters in this book, and preparing to leave for Connecticut and then Florida for the first couple of weeks of January, which meant three plane trips in 10 days. Prior to the trip, there had been so much on the news that seemed to fuel people's fear about flying. I sensed that while some cautions are justified, others seemed to come from the fear of fear, itself, so unfounded, yet, causing people to be afraid of everything in the world. I could see how I'd been drawn into the energy vortex of fear that so many of us have experienced, but mine went beyond terrorist attacks or social uprising; I had been taken in by the fears related to the future of our entire world with all the political, economic, geological, social, and national unrest. Fear of what might happen can be so powerful, especially, when we have our own unreleased fears inside us. It seemed as if my deeper, unconscious dread about my being condemned if I wrote the ideas that would be included in *Under the Mask,* were paralleled by all the fear stirring in the outer world.

***

A couple of days before my January 2010 visit with David and Ben in Connecticut, I did it again! I banged my head, doing what felt like more damage to an already compromised skull. In frustration, I wrote an email to my dear friend from Oregon:

David, I can't believe that I whacked my head again, today...not outside this time, but of all places, in the bathroom. I have been so very thoughtful and careful about walking outside, not just avoiding icy places, but also, during this very icy and snowy time, keeping my focus on my steps, not becoming distracted on my outdoor excursions by contemplations and wonderings, something that happens quite often when I am walking in nature.

I woke up this morning with a fuzzy head feeling, wondering if the cause was a possible mild propane leak from my furnace that is somehow acting on my brain, but the more realistic reason for the my head's condition is that I whacked my head royally on the ice two times. Before this third head-whack, I sent love to my brain, and saw it more clearly than I have ever seen it...with all its electrical levels. It was beautiful. I let my brain and skull know they didn't have to defend against traumas from the past by hardening themselves, but could take on being strong, yet flexible, without having to get hit to recreate flexibility. I really felt like I had a good connection with my head, my brain, my bones, and everything. I even let my body know that it had my permission to become flexible and open to all wisdom and knowledge that was available, and it didn't have to close down out of fear generated by thoughts about the world in my head.

After having that meditative conversation, I went into my bathroom to put a few things away, leaned down, and in the process hit the top of my head on a 2X4 that supports the A-frame part of the ceiling, something I have never done the whole time I have lived here. I just sat down on the toilet and cried. I told whatever part of me had some need to hit me to just stop it! I was so angry. I know so much happens to me in 3s, but I told the one putting my head in harms way that I would not stand for any more head trauma. The weird thing is that the fuzzy feeling went away, almost immediately. I hit the very top of my head...my crown chakra, but instead of feeling like the hit has caused my head to close down, it feels like something has opened. I recall Carlos Castaneda, the famous anthropologist and author, who wrote about his shamanic experiences, described being hit really hard on his back, right between his shoulder blades by his mentor, Don Juan, as a way to help Carlos enter alternate realities through reassembling what he called the *assemblage point* located there. Maybe I have a mentor, from some unseen world, that's been hitting me on the head to reassemble something in me. More later... Love, Sandy

Oregon David responded by asking me to really take in the idea that I can learn important information other ways besides hurting my body. I promised I would, but I'd made that promise before...and still I was drawing harm to me. A few days after all of this happened, I began my trip to Connecticut for a week, and then I returned to Florida.

***

The trip to Connecticut was lovely, though I was very tired most of the time. Despite my three-times damaged head, I seemed to take the change in air pressure in the plane without incident, but I knew I wasn't up to my best. It was good to see David and Ben after two whole years of not seeing them, but because I was not feeling completely okay, I spent a fair amount of time sleeping. Three adults, two children, two cats, and four dogs in a small house made the visit tender, yet exhausting for me and my cracked head. Naptime was something I valued far more than the kids did. I was glad I didn't visit them at Christmas, as was usual, because I am sure a plane trip so soon after that first hit on the head would have been dangerous, but then, maybe I wouldn't have had the second fall or third hit if I had gone...Ah, well.

Despite the rest I had gotten in Connecticut, I began to feel strange sensations on the way to Airport that seemed to get worse while in the air, and by the time the plane landed in Tampa, I was extremely sick.

147

I felt it wouldn't be good to stay with my friend, as I always do when returning home from Colorado, because I was afraid I would get her sick, in case what was going on for me was the flu that at the time was being touted as one that could become a dreaded pandemic, so I checked into a hotel. My original plan was to spend most of the time going through my storage unit in Clearwater, as I had done earlier in Seattle, to get rid of the vast majority of what was left there in 2006, but I was unable to do that. I returned to Colorado in mid January, and planned another trip to Florida the first part of February to take care of what hadn't gotten done during the previous trip. But I became sick again on the plane and spent 9 days in bed, most of the time, unable to move at all without feeling like death was waiting for me in the next room. And, as before, when I was finally well enough to take a plane back to Colorado I returned to my writing location, but ended up spending many hours in bed every day for weeks.

Finally, in late March, three months after the first fall on the ice, I had an appointment with Shar, a most gifted Tibetan cranial therapist in Longmont, Colorado. She is the woman I wrote about in book two who did such magnificent work with me. She reads the subtle messages in the cranial pulses to support releasing trapped *polar bear-like* energies in the body. Not only is it possible to release that pent up energy, but it is also possible to release the deeply embedded psychological and emotional patterns and beliefs that so greatly limit life, as well.

The cranial appointment had been scheduled for 10:45, but when I heard that a snowstorm was headed our way, I called Shar to see if we could make the appointment earlier. She adjusted it to 10:00, for the same day so I could avoid the expected road problems later, and based on the Weather Channel's hour-by-hour weather report, a 45-minute head start could make a difference. I was really looking forward to the work she would do with me, especially because my head had begun hurting quite badly again after my return from my second trip to Florida. For several weeks, I'd been waking up at night after only a couple hours of sleep with a pounding headache, and my shoulders and neck felt like they did after the first fall on the ice just before Christmas.

After waking, I had to get up and move around to ease the pain, and then I'd work on writing for an hour or two before I could go back to sleep for a little while. I was feeling quite exhausted from lack of restful sleep, even though I was spending huge amounts of time in bed. I did make attempts to get out and walk and do physical exercise in the daytime, but the more I did, the more I became completely depleted and had to take a daytime nap; some days I took two or three naps. My life had been thrown as off balance as I was when I fell. The problem seemed to be getting worse instead of better, so I really needed to have this special lady work on my head.

The morning of the appointment, the sky was a beautiful blue...and there was no evidence of any snow on the horizon. As I was exiting Interstate 470 to enter I-70, I was in the left lane with a guardrail on my left and another lane on my right, which was occupied by a 16-wheeler. I was almost exactly in his middle, equal distance between the front and back of the truck, when the driver began to move over into my lane as if he had no idea I was there. The moment I saw the side of his truck getting close enough to smash into me, I leaned on the horn and slammed on the breaks as an adrenalin rush flooded every cell in my body. If he had continued to move over, my breaking would not have been enough to prevent a really terrible accident, likely flipping and rolling me over the exit ramp and onto I-70 below. But hearing my horn, the driver swerved back into his lane, sped up and then pulled ahead of me into the lane I was in, cutting so close it felt like he would surely hit me that next time, as well…but he didn't.

I took in a deep breath...actually a few deep breaths, and tapped the passenger seat next to me, thanking my car for its wonderful breaks and the angels for protecting me from what could have been a fatal accident. I smiled because the day before was the first full day my car really belonged to me; I had just made my very last payment, and despite a near accident, the car was still mine. I realized my body remained revved from the adrenalin so I began making ohm sounds to release the excess energy. The trucker was ahead of me for a while, and I wished him alert driving on his way to wherever he was going. What seemed really important was that despite appearances, I was safe and no accident happened. I let my body know that it didn't have to hold on to fear of what might have, but didn't happen.

***

When I arrived at her Longmont house, Shar opened the door and explained that she was sorry I was entering a difficult energy field. Her last little Lhasa had gone into a critical state the night before and was going to be put down that day, probably during the time she would be working with me. Her other dog had been put down two weeks before; both were very old, and when one passed, the other must have let go of needing to stay around. Shar's husband was extremely distraught, holding his little love on his lap for the last time. When I walked into the living room, I petted the dog's brow and told her she would be just fine and asked her to say hi to Sara for me. Then I assured Shar's husband that once love is born, it never dies, something I didn't just believe might be true, but knew in the deepest places of my heart as a result of my own loss of Sara 13 years before. I felt honored to be there during that painful, yet, meaningful time in their lives.

We went upstairs to the therapy room, and I settled down on the wooden table. As soon as she touched my head and discovered the damage, Shar expressed how sorry she was that she'd not been able to see me earlier. I had tried to make an appointment before going to Florida when I spent all that time in bed, and then, tried again, when I got back but felt too sick to drive. After I began to feel better, Shar was traveling and teaching others what she learned from the last remaining Tibetan Monk who held the knowledge of this ancient healing art. This was the first day she had any openings after she returned, which was many weeks after the original fall.

She placed her hands on my head, checked the pulses, and then told me that the bones in my neck and head had been badly jammed and that the back of my head had a 3-inch crack along the sutures. The resulting compression only allowed only a trickle of cranial fluid into my brain, and blood flow was down to about 30% of what it should have been. She couldn't figure out how I made it for 3 months with this head injury and told me that if I had gone to bed when the headache began the night after the first fall, I would likely have had a stroke. Then she asked

150

if I felt like I had the flu, which is what I had felt for all those weeks, either like I was about to get the flu or was down with it like the two times in Florida. Apparently, the symptoms of the flu are very similar to those that can follow head injuries like the one I had. Since the fall on the ice, my immune system had been badly compromised because my life force was focused on keeping my brain alive. She explained that the flu feelings were related to my body getting very little energy. I'd sensed things were not good, and when I was unable to get to her for help, I tried chiropractic sessions and other forms of body therapy, but nothing relieved the problem for all that time. Not only did I have very little energy to do much of anything, but also, I began to look like an old woman with dusty gray skin and eyes with very little light coming from them.

Shar worked with me for an hour and a half, opening up the flow, but could not bring it back to 100%. Too much at one time, she said, would flood my brain, sort of like getting the bends if a diver comes up too quickly from deep places. This sounded parallel to why it is often difficult for people to deal with emotionally traumatic events from childhood, or for that matter from other times in their lives all at one time…too much could flood the system and cause more damage. So we learn how to handle a little at a time.

Shar left for a short while during the time my head was in traction. When she was out of the room, the women, who come to people's homes to put dogs down, had arrived. These ladies help people connect with and then release their pets to spirit and support them while the people grieve their loss. Then the women take the pet to be cremated and return the ashes, afterward. All during the traction part of the session, I was seeing images of lots of dogs, even my sweet Sara, all coming to welcome Shar's little dog. While Shar and her husband were releasing their dog, my heart was filled with love for them and what they were experiencing. I know Sara was there and my other dogs were there along with many that seemed to be dogs Shar and her husband had over the years.

In the silence of the therapy room, I recalled the passing of my own Sara. Shortly after I had a heart attack, Sara developed congestive heart failure. I did all I knew to help her find healing, but nothing worked. I was heartbroken that she seemed to be slipping away from me. Then late one night, she had a grand mal seizure and I rushed her to the emergency vet hospital. I left her there, and they promised to take care of her and keep me posted. Not long after I returned home, I got a most dreaded call with the news that the love of my life had died. I returned to the hospital and sat with her for quite some time telling her how much I loved her, as her warm body grew cold. The attendant asked if they wanted me to take care of her remains, and I agreed to cremation, with them returning the ashes in a few days. No trip I had ever taken back home felt as painfully lonely as that night I drove back to my apartment, at times, too stunned to cry, and at other times unable to stop the avalanche of sobbing that felt as if it would completely drown me.

When several days had passed without hearing from the clinic, I called and was told they hadn't gotten the ashes back yet. Finally, I drove to the hospital and told them I wanted the ashes immediately. The attendant went into the back and after an apology for the delay, told me that Sara had not, yet, been taken to the crematorium, and that her remains were still in the freezer, but he would make sure they were taken care of that day. Sensing that something was not right, I demanded to see her body. The attendant disappeared into the back again and in a few moments, the doctor came out and told me that a mix up had happened and her body had been placed with a number of animals that were unmarked and were all cremated together; the ashes were already disposed of. To ease my pain, they were going to give me ashes of another animal. I could not stop the wailing tears. It was as if my own child had been murdered and her body desecrated. It took a long time to heal from the pain of this loss, but finally I recovered enough to go back to work.

The first day back in my office after Sara's passing, a client came in to work on issues related to trust. She seemed to be blocked, so she leaned back in her chair and closed her eyes to begin doing inner work. In a moment, she commented that she had the strangest sensation of the sweet smell of puppy breath. Immediately, I knew it was Sara, though I hadn't told her or anyone of my loss. The client closed her eyes again, and almost immediately began to laugh and said she could swear she felt the muzzle of a little dog against her cheek. And as soon as she spoke those words, she began to wail like a small child, in agony. She told me she had not thought of her puppy for decades. She saw herself as a little girl in her back yard playing with a puppy a relative had gotten her for her birthday. This beautiful animal was the only love she had ever known in her childhood. Her father was withdrawn and disconnected, while her mother was cold and angry nearly all the time. The child had fallen in love with the dog that had become her most trusted companion. One day, her mother decided that she had become too attached to the animal and ordered the child's father to take it away. She never saw her puppy again. From that time on, she could never trust anyone in her life. The healing work this woman was able to do was phenomenal. She reconnected with her child self and went to a higher place where she could commune with her sweet dog. A lifetime of agony was healed because of the smell of puppy's breath and the feel of a dog's face against hers that took her to the place in her childhood she needed to go to heal a lifetime of pain.

Sara showed up for a number of other clients over the next few days and I knew my sweet girl was still with me. It seemed as if so many of those who needed support had come for sessions related to dogs in their childhoods. In time, I didn't sense her there so much, as clients came in with other issues, but I always felt if I needed her she would come. Not long afterward, I discovered layers of sadness related to three of my own dogs in childhood. One had gotten sick and my father arranged for someone to come euthanize him. I saw him being shot and then several men tied his feet to a pole; his body hung limp and lifeless as they carried him away. The other two dogs were my huskies. Because I had more control over them than others in my family, my father told me to accompany him to the kennel. After getting them into the car, I sang to them and then coaxed them out of the car and into the cage. When it was time to leave them, I promised I'd be back to get them at the end of the summer, but at the end of summer vacation, instead of driving back home, my father decided to move us to Seattle, and told us our beloved pets would have to stay in Alaska. I still had release work to do with the pain I held inside for those two incidents.

I believe it was no accident that I was there to share in the healing energy of the passing of that lovely little dog. Had I come at 10:45, the time of the original session, I would have come in the middle of the trauma, unquestionably having impact on the process they were all experiencing. For whatever reason, I was also reminded that what we call death is a transformation, and when we are able to release our fears and deep grieving, we can more fully embrace the connection that love creates. Without any doubt, I know that once love is born, it never dies. And I shared that truth with the animals of the past that I loved and grieved.

After Shar returned and released the traction, she completed the cranial work and then helped me up so I could look at my face in the mirror. I was very surprised at what I saw in my reflection; my old lady gray face had life in it again...my eyes were bright and skin looked healthy, something I hadn't seen for 3 months. I had really felt so bad about aging to the extent I had in those months and thought it might be irreversible, but clearly, it was not.

When I left to head back to my place, gray clouds were floating off in the distance, and the snow began to fall as I reached the top of highway 285, which is about 10 minutes from my mountain carriage house. Within a few minutes of getting to my place, the snow was coming down so heavily it was hard to see the trees in the front yard. Driving would have been extremely dangerous.

Earlier that morning, before I left for Longmont, a client called to see if I could work with her in the afternoon. If I had not made that appointment when I did, and because the weather did not look threatening on my drive back, I would likely have gone into Denver instead of driving up into the mountains. I would have run a few errands and maybe have gone shopping. But then, I would have been driving up into the center of the snowstorm instead of watching it from my window. I like it when synchronous events work out like that.

MORE RELEASES

Not long after I began writing book one, I started participating in a traditional Indian sweat lodge ceremony that took place every few weeks in the mountains above Denver. Since that time, I brought my deepest heart prayers with me into the sweat lodge ceremony, as well as my concerns for healing from cancer that I wrote about in books one and two. In every case, my prayers were answered. I recall one of the things I prayed for in the last Inipi sweat lodge ceremony was that I would find the way to trust in and surrender to the God Essence in me and The God Essence of the Universe. Despite the amazing experiences I've had my whole life, when things fell into place perfectly, as they did the day of the appointment with Shar, I still could drop into internal places where I was unable to fully trust. As a result, I spent too much of my life in the unhappy place of distrust just under the surface of trusting.

Everything that happened on the day I went to see Shar was perfectly timed to let me experience the trust I can have in both *Sandy God Essence*, as well as trust in my connection to *Universal God Essence* to keep me safe. I felt even more compelled to complete this last book and speak about what I know in my heart is true. The other thing I was aware of was if that 16 wheeler had flipped me onto I-70 and I had died, I would be wonderfully okay...AND...it would not have been my conscious choice to die at that time. I really did prefer to live to 92 and complete what I know I came here to do.

***

The next morning I took Jenny for a walk in the forest, sat down for a moment on a bench overlooking the little stream that had grown quite big from the snow melt...and I realized that though I could see the events of the day before had taught me deeper levels of trust, I hadn't felt much joy in my life, not that pure beautiful joy that fills every cell and allows a rush of openings. And I became aware that laughter—true laughter that most people lose far too early in their lives—had been missing for as long as I could remember.

In retrospect, maybe I had felt joyful feelings at times in my adult life too, like when the river and sun dance together to melt the ice in a way that allows a magnificent breakthrough. This ice, stream, and sun metaphor seemed to touch something so very true for me. I think because of the previous few days, I had been feeling like the part of the stream that was completely covered with ice...maybe mostly frozen with just a little movement underneath. But I also knew that I had not felt that totally open feeling with life and with all that is in the outer world. I could get there in meditation, but I hadn't translated that open feeling to my lived life, interacting with the outer world. I was aware that something had been blocking my ability to experience the joy, laughter, connection, and openness I wanted in my life. The concussion was just a metaphor for my life, pressed down by decades of stored feelings that had not, yet, been released. I wasn't feeling depressed about this realization, I was just aware of it.

As I sat looking at the water rushing past me under the ice with occasional breakthroughs where the frozen surface opened to the warmth from the sun, I realized that I had lost taking in beauty with awe and delight as I did during special moments when I was a child, and I wanted to reclaim the spontaneous laughter and delight, as well as that feeling of connection and openness with the world.

GRIEVING STORED LOSSES

On April 1, 2010, I went up to Longmont for another session with Shar. With only the half-opening of the back of my head the previous week, we needed to open it further to allow blood and sacral fluid to flow more fully to my brain. The first thing she said to me when she checked my pulses was that my kidneys were quite low. Both had very weak pulses. She said that could happen if a person had kidney stones or some other kidney malfunction, but that it could also happen because of grieving. As soon as she said that word, the whole left side of my torso, from my left hip to my heart, began to shake as if that whole area wanted to cry. I had no idea why because nothing seemed to be making me sad in my life. I wasn't sure what such sadness had to do with the fall on the ice a few months before despite the concussion that left me with spasmodic muscles that had tightened so much that for three months I just hadn't felt like myself. But I wasn't aware of anything going on emotionally, and certainly not related to grief. Shar wondered if, perhaps, my going to Seattle to clear out the storage had stirred something on a very deep level, and my immediate response was that I had gotten through it very well; I seemed to be fine, although, I did have a sense that there would be more work to do with it.

While she worked with the back of my head and the pulses in my scull, I started to ramble, saying whatever thoughts arose, and describing the images that were coming to mind. I am not sure I even remember all that I said, but as I write these words, a deep sadness is happening inside me...this time running up the middle of me rather than the left side. Lots came up during the session, but I left the work that day feeling there was something more that we hadn't touched. This may be what I am touching now.

I recall mentioning to Shar during that session, the second since the fall, that I'd done huge amounts of healing work on my child self, as reflected in the first two books of this trilogy, and with my adult self, some of which came out in book one, but have done very little with my teenage self. That part of me hovered in the background all these years, giving me tiny memories and little pictures of the forgotten teen years... and when I became aware of that young girl, all I could do was feel deep sadness. Teenage Sandy had lost her ability to laugh. She didn't know what her life meant except to study, so that is what she did.

I told Shar about a girl in my 10th grade English class who tapped me on the shoulder one day, Looking directly into my eyes, she said, *"Everyday, you are different, but not just because of your hair."* I used to wear my longer than waist-length hair in many different styles, but she had seen something of far more significance that no one had ever said out loud before. I don't remember how I responded to her comment; it really wasn't a question, though there was a question in her eyes when she said it. Reflecting on that experience so long ago made me wonder if there was something that I had not remembered. I couldn't imagine anything worse than some of the horrors of little Sandy's life, but there was a sense of something really painful that I just could not face from my teen years.

Whatever it was had touched the deep grieving sadness that I had buried on my left side, as if the most important person in my life had died. The grief felt as debilitating as when my precious Sara had died, but I knew this wasn't about Sara.

Following that second post-concussion session with Shar, I had been seeing different images of my teen years. Each one came to me like a partial clip of few feet of film from a full-length movie. There were many, many little film clips giving me clues to whatever it was that caused such deep grief.

During the third session following the fall on the ice, I told Shar about the time I walked out of school when I was in the 8th grade because I didn't know where I was supposed to go for my next class. I had been a hall monitor in my junior high school, meaning that I would remain in the hall until the bell for the next class rang and all the kids were in their classes. Teachers knew that hall monitors would come in a couple of minutes late for their classes. When I looked down the very empty hall, I had no idea where I was supposed to go. Feeling a sense of panic, I walked into the main office to find out where I should be, but before I said anything, I realized I didn't know what name to give the woman at the big desk, so I left the office and walked outside to go home. After walking about a block or so away from school, I realized I had no idea where home was. I remember being so, so scared but even more, so very grief stricken that I didn't know who I was or where my home was. I dropped my head in utter hopelessness and closed my eyes to hold back the tears. I felt so very, very lost.

A moment later, I opened my eyes again, but my shoes were not the ones I had just been wearing, and the books I was carrying had the high school name on them instead of the junior high school name. I opened one of my books and noticed that I had my name written on a piece of paper taped to the title page. I had written my class schedule, the period, the room number, and the time of the class in every one of my books. I ran back into the school to find all the halls were empty of students. I looked at the wall clock and saw the time, which meant I was supposed to be in Algebra class, so I hurried to the room on the second floor and slipped into a noisy classroom.

The blackboard was covered over by roll-up maps and a screen that had been pulled down. There was only one seat left in the classroom, so I sat in it. The teacher didn't notice I had come in late. He walked up to the front of the class, told everyone to take everything off their desks, get out a piece of paper, and put their names on the top. I followed his instructions and carefully wrote out the name that was in my book. Then, he pulled up the maps and screen and told us to work out the problems. I had no clue as to what the numbers and letters on the board meant. I felt desperately afraid. That part of me that was the junior high turned senior high-Sandy must have left and another one who had taken algebra came out to take the test, while the deep grief of the 8th grader, who couldn't remember her name or where her home was and instantly became a year older, was buried on the left side of my body from my hip to my heart. Every now and then, when an event occurred in my adult life that involved getting lost, I experienced inconsolable grief far beyond what the event would have called for because the later experience had tapped into the part of me that lost a year of her life along with her identity.

As Shar continued to work with me, an image of my first boyfriend from that same year I was taking algebra came to mind. Patrick was a junior; I was a freshman. Our relationship was confined to walking home from school together, and sometimes he'd come in for a few minutes before heading for his home. On occasion, we would meet at the Admiral Theater for a Saturday matinee to see a movie together, but I always had to bring one of my siblings along, something that happened even in my senior year when I began dating Jake.

Patrick was a popular boy, which made me wonder why he was interested in me. I was incredibly shy and couldn't go on normal dates because my parents required that a brother or sister accompany me, even if it was to the Saturday movie matinee. I really liked that he liked me, until one day when he decided to sit on the kitchen counter while I began my after-school dishwashing chores. We were talking, but when I turned my head to talk with him, I noticed that he was having an erection. His pleated wool trousers couldn't camouflage the fact that his male libido had activated. From that moment on, though I never spoke to him about it, a part of me hated him. Instead of feeling happy to be around him as I had been previously, I withdrew, becoming more distant. He stopped walking me home and stopped asking me to meet him at the local theater for the matinee.

A little while after that kitchen incident, my brother offered to take me to a Saturday matinee movie; he bought me popcorn and we settled down into seats my brother had picked out. A short time later, Patrick came into the theater with a girl on each arm and sat down a few rows from where my brother and I were seated. I believe my brother wanted me to know what was going on with Patrick without having to tell me. All during the film, some part of me grieved, even though I knew whatever the relationship we had was over. I held onto a sweater he had given me for quite a few weeks, until one day he told me that he was taking a trip and would like to have it back. I told him I'd bring it to school the next day, and I returned his red and black high school sweater, but not before I sewed a strand of my hair into the woven fibers as a way to hold on to something that no longer existed. Until this very writing, I had never told a single person about what I had done.

My focus shifted from the little snippets of memories about teenage Sandy's experiences to feelings about Jake, before he became my husband. During the cranial session, I told Shar about an 8X10, framed photo of Jake taken when he was 17, at the beginning of his first year of college. He had given it to me over Thanksgiving break when we both had returned home from the colleges we attended that were far away from each other. The image of him was so, so beautiful. The portrait captured Jake's essence like nothing I had ever seen. The feelings that flooded through me every time I looked at it were even more profound than the ones I felt the morning we two were standing in the hall outside his chemistry class in high school, when a sunbeam shown directly into his eyes. The light seemed to illuminate something so deep and beautiful in him that my heart was very sure he was the one I would love the rest of my life. Every time I looked into his eyes in that photograph, my heart opened as never before, and I kept falling more deeply in love with the essence that glowed from the eyes of that beautiful 17-year-old man-child.

There were only a few times over the 28 years we were together—5 years as sweethearts and 23 years married—that I was able to see that essence in his eyes in real life rather than in that portrait. After we were married, I remembered Jake playing with our Great Danes on the front lawn. He was so much in touch with his laughter and his little boy innocence while he was wrestling and playing with the dogs that my heart opened completely with joy and love. That same kind of radiance flowed from him when he completed a project that made him extraordinarily proud. And then, I recall how much he enjoyed chocolate cake. On special days, and not so special days, too, I baked him chocolate cake, spread thick chocolate frosting all over, and while it was still warm, I'd cut him a huge piece covered with chocolate ice cream. When I brought it to him, he would get that beautiful look of delight filled with joyful abandonment and devour the cake like a little boy. I called that part of Jake, Chocolate Man; the part of him that was connected to his heart and could connect with mine. As I was sharing this with Shar, I began to feel a deep grieving so intense I felt as if I were going to die.

Between the tears, I told her that just before we separated, when Jake and I were sharing a moment of deep conversation, I told him how much I loved Chocolate Man. I asked if he would let Chocolate Man come out for a while. But in what felt like a wickedly harsh and cold response, Jake turned to me and said, *"I hate chocolate man! I killed him."* He said it with such cruelty that it felt as if he really had murdered the most tender and authentic part of him.

Everything in me went into shock, followed by deep grieving when he told me he had killed the part of him I'd fallen in love with when we were so very young, and the pain returned with the same intensity when I began to tell Shar what had happened more than two decades in the past. He had killed the part of him that came out and connected with me only a few precious times in all the years I had been with him. Though Chocolate man was there when I gave him cake or when he played with our dogs, I could only experience his presence indirectly because he was not connecting with me at those other times. I spent the entire 23 years of our marriage trying to figure out what I needed to do and what I needed not to do that would allow Chocolate Man to come out and interact with me. I tolerated years of emptiness for the hope of one tiny connection with the essence of the man I believed to be my soul mate.

I began to cry mournfully for all the time that went by without ever touching the love I knew could have been there between us, but was so painfully missing. I felt as if what should have been there had died, and I never had a chance to say good-bye.

As that grief moved through me, I was struck with another extremely sad realization, though I was not conscious of it until that moment while working with Shar. Before Jake and I were married, and even afterward, a hidden part of me was terrified of what would happen if Jake ever found out what had happened in my family's house. I was sure he would find me repulsive, something he would need to wash off him if he knew. For all those 28 years, I could not allow myself to fully surrender to him for fear that in my vulnerable openness, the parts of me that I needed to hide would emerge, and he would find out how repulsive I was. The result was that I withheld from Jake access to Sandy Essence as much as he held back Jake Essence from me. That realization opened my whole body to howling cries of grief that felt like they would never stop. What had been stored in me for decades since I was a teenager was finally being released.

It seemed I was grieving the loss of the young man that was captured in that 8X10 college freshman photograph. But also, I was grieving all the years of loneliness, during our marriage and in the years since. I was grieving that I never got to feel my whole body open to blissful joy in my first sexual experience with the man my heart dearly loved. I was grieving the tenderness of teen years, young love, pure feelings of innocence...ah, yes, I was grieving my innocence. I know I did a lot of work with little Sandy with this, but I had never before worked with my teenage self and my young woman self who fell in love and married a man with a huge sexual appetite that I dreaded because of how painful it was to access what I had repressed and stored deep inside me.

I was grieving not only the loss of Chocolate Man, but of my own counterpart, whoever she was back then…that radiant beauty, the part of me—the whole of me—that embraces life, that opens to sensuality, sexuality, and love, the part of me that delights in beauty, and laughs with pure joy. All of that was stolen, and in its place, pain and sadness were stored.

It is amazing what can be touched by going through old things and getting rid of so much, like I did when I went though those storage crates in Seattle…such deep and unexpressed feelings on the inside that I didn't even know were still there until I hit my head and brought all of the grief forward. And letting go of those old things can become a metaphor for letting go of the unexpressed pain and grieving attached to the past that, not just for me, but for so many of us, was stored inside so long ago.

DISCOVERING STORED RESENTMENTS

As I am writing this, now, I recall a line from a song back when I was in my first year of college. I don't remember who sang it, but I do recall the refrain, *"Have some Maderia, my dear; you really have nothing to fear."* It was one my roommate's favorite songs. Though I don't remember all the words, I remember the story. There is this old man who is enchanted with a young 17-year-old girl. So he entices her to his place to look at etchings, or something like that. He keeps offering her Maderia, and she turns him down. When he comes on to her strongly, she finally accepts a glass of the wine, but then remembers her mother's words that drinking would be her ruin, so she drops the glass and runs down the hall…and as she runs she hears him saying that same phrase, *"Have some Maderia, my dear…"* The last verse says she wakes in the morning in the man's bed, with a smile on her face and a gray beard against her ear as he says, *"Have some Maderia, my dear; you really have nothing to fear."*

Everything in my body recoiled from a song that made my room- mate delight. I know I was not seeing some unknown grey haired man in the song when I heard it, I was seeing my father and my teenage self. I have worked with women who have such self-revulsion because their fathers had sex with them when they were teenagers. It was not uncommon that sexual abuse had been in their young childhoods, as well, but there is something about it when it happens later that can make the girl take full responsibility for not running away. I told my teenage self that she didn't need to be ashamed of anything or afraid of my judgment for what had happened to her. But that was not enough.

Despite my reluctance to pursue them, there were lots of other little snippets of memories that would fit a scenario, which included abuse happening beyond my first 11 years in Alaska. It would make sense that if the abuse was still going on after my family left Alaska and I became a teenager, I still would have been doing splitting to forget who I was in the 8th grade the day I forgot my name and couldn't remember where I lived, and it would help make sense of a classmate's comment that she noticed different Sandy's sitting in front of her in 10th grade English. It is possible that ongoing abuse would result in my violently hating a boyfriend for having an erection and be repulsed by a song about an old man seducing a 17-year-old girl.

I do have another memory from that 10th grade English class that seems significant for what it represents. I had read a book titled, *They Were Expendable*, but when the teacher called me to the back of the room to give him a report, I couldn't remember the main characters or a key event that my teacher asked me to describe. I must have answered something right because I didn't fail; I recall the teacher wrote a D on my paper and sent me back to my seat. I remembered the incident, and the name of the book, but not until just a few moments ago when I looked the title up on Amazon did I discover the content of the story that took place during WWII. It was about 4 men who were treated by the military as expendable. Their job was to stay in the line of fire, being shot at, and if possible, shooting back at the enemy, while giving time for the others in their platoon to get out of harms way. When I read this, I was amazed at how this book was a metaphor for my life, and it touched the feeling I had that I, too, was expendable; perhaps that is why I could not remember what I had read. I, also, did not like having to sit so close to a man in the back of the classroom, with all the other students facing forward. Getting a D was devastating, especially when I knew I read the book, but couldn't remember what was in it.

There had been many tears shed during that session with Shar, and the next morning I woke with another very bad sinus and bronchial infection that reminded me of all the times in my young life that I had gotten similar infections that led to pneumonia. I am very sure that all the repressed sadness and grieving that had been expressed in the session with Shar had opened deeply buried toxins that had been trapped in my lung tissues for decades. Something really important opened up. I began sending in love energy during meditations to help teenage Sandy know she would always be safe, and it was her time now to heal.

***

I had gone back to Seattle to empty the storage crates, but ended up touching so many experiences from those years of my life that had not yet been healed; without knowing it, I had stimulated those deeply buried memories. Not long afterward, I returned to Colorado only to slip on the ice and bang my head so hard it closed down the flow of my life force, something that happened on so many occasions in my childhood in order to live through the trauma. While Shar was helping me deal with the blocked energies, accessing the tissues around my cracked skull caused me to open to the memories that I had pushed to the back of my head such a long time ago.

When I re-entered the memories of the very deep grief about Jake and Chocolate Man during a meditation, I realized how I had tried to cling to Jake's God Essence even when he couldn't or wouldn't allow that essence to be free except for only fleeting moments. I had hoped this beautiful part of Jake would allow me to feel safe enough to reveal what seemed so repulsive about me. Deep inside, I believed that Chocolate Man would not reject me, though I was very sure the part of Jake that was his masked self, would have, and certainly, the parts of him he hid behind his mask would not have been able to accept what had happened to me that I hid behind mine. As I embraced and forgave more of my hidden parts and protections, I felt myself forgive all the protective shields Jake had constructed around his essence, and released him from the responsibility of creating safety enough for me to be my undefended self. It felt so expanding, so profound, and so peaceful to get to this level of forgiveness and release like the polar bear.

I was, also, aware that surrendering to my essence would be my way back to experiencing pure beautiful joy and authentic laughter, as well as feeling the dance of the stream and sun inside me. I knew that all of Sandy deserved to feel embraced by life as I learned how to fully embrace life. I was aware that even if I had never before felt pure joy and laughter in this life, my soul memory is that I did feel it sometime on my journey and I wanted to feel it again.

Unbeknownst to me, I was about to reconnect with that vulnerable part of myself: the part of me that could reach out and take in what life offers and knew joy and laughter, but only after I released another layer of tears from another part of me had been buried deep behind my mask since I was 2 years old, and covered over by all the ways I had tried to keep myself safe when I didn't feel safe.

MIND/BODY COMMUNICATION

I had been on a combination cleanse tied together with a weight loss program for about a month and was pleased that weight was coming off as never before. For the first time in all the years I'd been on diets too numerous to recall, I had the full confidence that, this time, I was ready to be regain my healthy, more slender body. All the other times in the past, I approached dieting with hope, which always holds fear within it. With each diet I had ever tried, I feared that it wouldn't work or I feared that it would work, but only for a short time, and then I'd gain it all back and be heavier than before as seemed to always happen. I also feared that if it were to fail again, I'd become even heavier than the 276 pounds that was my highest weight, something I spoke of in greater detail in *The Mask*.

When I made the decision to begin a new program, it was because I knew deep within that this was the right time, and there was neither hope nor fear . . . only confidence. I'd let go of so many of the painful experiences, which caused my body to use weight as protection, and I truly wanted to be strong and healthy, which meant I was finally ready for a life-style change. The focus was not on reaching a goal, but on learning to live differently. I was doing it for the health of my body and for my life, not to impress or please any one else.

As the weight was starting to melt away, I began to feel pain in my arms that, in time, became debilitating. I could no longer use my arms to assist me in getting out of bed in the morning. And, lifting almost anything became difficult. One morning I woke with excruciating pain in my left arm that traveled down to my hand and into my fingers. My first thought was that I was getting the signs of a heart attack. But an internal check with my heart told me that it was fine. And then, I saw images of very inflamed tendons. The pain sent me into a few days of depression; it didn't seem fair that after all the inner work I had done, I would still be facing such debilitating pain. I was falling into that dark place where I held a belief that I would grow old with all the body pain faced by others in my family despite all I had done to heal, and I did not want to repeat those family patterns. It felt as if I was being punished. I'd forgotten that pain isn't judgment; it's a message letting me know there is something buried inside that needs healing.

For a number of days, I sent healing to my tendons. I used images of healing salve applied by loving, nurturing angels and sent in messages of appreciation to my tendons for all they do for me, and it wasn't long before my arms began feeling somewhat better. But I knew the healing was not complete because I had not found the cause of the inflammation other than the general explanation of having lived a lifetime that was filled with stress.

In the middle of all this, Oregon David called because he hadn't heard from me for nearly a week, a bit unusual unless I am feeling down about something. I shared with him what had been taking my attention, and he reminded me of an earlier suggestion he'd made to talk to my body before it breaks down, gets sick, or is forced to find other ways to shout out what it needs; otherwise, I don't listen. He reminded me that asking my body what it needs ahead of time could preempt illness, falls, and all manner of other troubles. David suggested that, maybe, I could draw a figure of a body and then ask each part what it needed and wanted before it turned to pain or illness to get my attention. I have worked with clients this way, but too often, I've forgotten to do this with myself.

That very morning, not long before David had called, I had asked my body if it wanted to go to the Inipi sweat lodge ceremony later in the afternoon. My mind had reasoned that because I was feeling tired from the cleanse and weight reduction program, on top of having the inflamed tendons that had spread that morning to my legs, maybe I shouldn't go. I wasn't sure if my mind would let me hear my body's answer so I used a pendulum . . . and . . . I was given a very positive *yes* answer that I should go.

For those who have not heard of using such things as pendulums, it might help to visualize a chain with a stone attached. The one using the pendulum holds the chain out in front and lets the stone drop. If a person is using such a thing for the first time, the first question can be to ask for it to show a yes, and a no. Generally a *yes* answer is given when the stone swings away and toward the person holding it, and a *no* answer is given when the stone swings to the left and right. My sense of this process is that the body often knows what the mind does not allow itself to know, and when we take the time to ask a question to the body, the body uses the most subtle energy in the fingers to move the chain as a way to communicate with the mind until we learn how to interpret the direct messages we get from the body all the time. Because we have not been trained to listen to our body's voice, a tool can help as we begin to pay attention to our whole self, and it can help when we are in a state of mind that finds it difficult to know without support like this.

As David and I spoke more about this idea of working more lovingly with my body, I realized David was suggesting mind and body being equal partners, rather than one holding power over the other, as far too often exists in the human experience. The idea of partnership can be foreign to a culture that emphasizes mind in decision-making and sees the body as the source of support for the demands of the mind while using body sensations to feel pleasure as a distraction from the concerns of the mind.

In one scenario of inequality, the mind is in control of the body, and it pushes the body by making it work too hard, run too fast, or live too intensely. It sets goals to make the mind feel good about itself, which too often, require so much from the body that it can barely keep up, and then the person might take pills or stimulants to force the body to keep going when all the body really wants to do is to rest. This is the mind over matter model where the mind forces the body to endure all manner of stresses and the body complies because most of our bodies have been taught from a very young age the mind over matter principal that sees the body's responsibility is to be sacrificed for the will of the mind.

In this model, the body, made subservient to the mind, will do the bidding of the mind until it finally breaks, which is often the only way the body may have to communicate to a mind that refuses to see its demands are asking too much. Such a model does not permit the needs of the body to be expressed or honored if it inconveniences the mind. When the mind does not honor the body's needs, the only way the body can communicate is for it to scream and shout through breaking down with illness, disease, accidents, malfunction, pain, weight problems, and more because, then, the mind is forced to take heed of the body's needs.

Because the body's breakdown is such a disturbing experience for the mind, it often goes into panic mode, not knowing how to deal with the symptoms or problems created on the physical plain. The mind often seeks experts to find out how to get the body back into being its servant. I am sure so many people take pain pills so they can go about doing what they want to do, without awareness that the body is still suffering or they take antacids to stop the stomach from trying to communicate that what is being put into it is not good, and then we eat what is hurting us, anyway. The only thing different is that communication of the suffering is being stopped through pharmaceuticals and distractions, but the body still is in unfelt pain and being overtaxed.

It was clear to me that my body/mind had not been in an equal partnership most of my life, but rather most of the time, even after all of my work to change this, my mind ruled my body, and my body's response was, *"I will do whatever you want of me. I will let myself be pushed and pushed and pushed, even beyond what is healthy for me until I break down and cannot do it any more; only then will I be forced to stop serving you."* I could see that within the sacrifice and breakdown is huge body anger, brought on by being treated as inferior, along with a great need to inflict punishment on the mind for disregarding the needs of the body, even when the body also will suffer from the punishment. After all, sacrifice of the body is the accepted pattern, even for the body. And in my own life, when I experienced a heart attack, when I got cancer, and when I began to suffer ongoing internal pain that kept shouting that I was going to die, my mind experienced confusion and panic. Eventually, I got it, that I really needed to listen to the needs of my body. This is a skill that takes time to develop, but it is so worth it.

I've noticed that this same mind over matter concept can be replicated in relationships in which one person dominates the other and the person being dominated acts as if his or her role is to be subservient. Even though our male dominated culture may be changing, historically, men have been the master's of their wives and children. In this system of control in relationship, it is not uncommon for women to find their own particular ways to exert power over the controlling man, and the net result is an ongoing struggle for power in so many relationships, just as the body finds ways to force the mind into doing what the body wants, and internal body/mind wars can ensue, resulting in all sorts of self-sabotage behaviors. Partnership takes time to evolve, whether it is between men and women, between partners, between friends, associates, neighbors, or between the body and the mind.

***

In another scenario, the body rules the mind. The needs and wants of the physical self override the mind, creating just as much disorder as the mind overriding the body. While the mind is ruled by reason—whether it is reasonable or not—the body is ruled by pleasure seeking and pain avoidance, and occasionally, the reverse, especially for bodies that only experience the rush of being alive if they feel pain. Like a dog drawn to lick up sweet tasting antifreeze, despite the fact licking it up will likely kill the animal, the body can be drawn to what it desires to produce pleasure when pleasure is needed or pain when pain is desired. However, pleasure used to avoid pain, contains the pain, just as hope contains fear, and finding pleasure from pain holds the threat of damage to the body and to life.

In the first scenario, with the mind ruling the body, a person may experience the after affects of unconscious thought processes that direct accumulation of excess fat as protection from experiencing pain. The mind may unconsciously reason, *"If I am fat, dangerous people will not find me attractive and hurt me"* or, *"If I am fat, I will not feel attractive and will stop myself from getting in harm's way or reaching out and being rejected."* From my own inner work, I found that my body used the accumulation of fat to prevent stored pain from being felt, caused by memories of both physical and emotional trauma. I suspect that the engorged fat cells and excess water held by traumatized bodies act as a cushion to prevent the arching of electrical currents within the body, caused when the body has been holding pain. Perhaps someday, researchers will find how to test for this hypothesis based on my personal inner work, and work with hundreds of clients.

But in the second scenario, fat may be a side effect of a person identifying with the body's longings to find momentary pleasure in taste rather than eating for health. I have heard overweight people say they simply like the taste of certain foods and their overeating has nothing to do with trauma. But what may remain unnoticed are the unconscious reasons that motivate the desire. The same can be said for bulimic or anorexic behaviors, which are extremely unhealthy and life threatening, but the person may engage in the behaviors in order to experience the fleeting pleasure of being in control, or maintaining some desirable image, or receiving praise. The unconscious mind could also be in charge of the bulimic behavior in what seems like a reasonable way to counter some deep internal pain in the belly that can only be relieved when the energies of binging or purging occur.

So many prominent leaders in all walks of life have fallen from grace because they allowed the immediate desires of their bodies to override their minds. It is possible many have used body pleasure to avoid feeling the pain of loneliness, to keep from feeling unimportant even though they are in important positions, to remind them of their power when deep inside they question their power, or to distract themselves from confronting the issues that block them from loving the ones they are "supposed" to love, but they lack the courage to do so. They feel driven to follow the desires of their bodies to seek relief through actions assumed will bring pleasure, but afterward, will cost them their families and their positions for a fleeting respite from pain, which generally creates more pain, in the process.

However it is important to not trash the experience of pleasure or bliss—occurring when a being with integrated mind/body/spirit experiences energy centers opening and flowing simultaneously—very different from the frantic seeking of pleasure as a way to escape pain or distract us from what is unwanted. The energetic opening into bliss is one of the most beautiful gifts of being in our bodies, equally as beautiful as experiencing the expansive mental satisfaction of some great discovery made, some curiosity satisfied, some act of creativity expressed, or puzzle solved. These are wonderful incentives for our spiritual essence to remain in physical form, despite what seems like an abundance of pain present in our world today. Frantic pleasure seeking to distract from or cover up pain is an inauthentic attempt to duplicate the real experience of bliss with a surge of pheromones in the moment that does not work, long-term.

Advertisements often brainwash people into believing if they just buy, eat, drive, experience, or are identified with a certain product they will be seen as hot, desirable, acceptable, loveable, successful, brilliant, in the *in* crowd, or whatever feels missing and is longed for in their lives. So people spend money that would be better spent elsewhere, overcharge their credit cards, or even damage themselves to experience what the advertisements promise, without including the thoughtful reasoning of the mind to direct their actions. Attempting to satisfy or gratify unrequited longings of the body instead of experiencing the pleasures that naturally come to us when we are in the flow of our lives becomes the focus when there is a lack of partnership between body and mind. A body without the balancing of the mind becomes just as threatening to life as a mind without the balance of the body.

***

After the conversation with David, I focused on each of the organs that had been included in the body cleanse I'd been doing, and began a meditation, asking each organ how it was feeling and what it wanted from me. The overwhelming response from each was a surge of love for finally being recognized and honored for what these hard working parts of me do for my whole body, for my mind, and for *Sandy God Essence*. My whole body/mind/spirit felt fully expressed as one, and I felt myself filled with radiant light and love. It felt as if a partnership was being created much deeper than I had ever felt before. Honoring the message my body/mind gave me earlier, indicating that the Inipi ceremony would be good for me, I readied myself and drove to Pine Top, in the foothills above Morrison, Colorado.

RECONNECTING WITH DADDEL-DEE

When I was a little child of two, I had two older sisters, the oldest was 3 years older and the next was 3 days short of one year older than me. Because my older sister was not able to say my name, she called me Daddel-Dee instead of Sandy. The two of us were very close, sharing everything and watching out for each other. For all of our growing up years, we were each other's best friend, and somewhere along the line as we got older, my sister learned how to say my name. The year she was in the first grade, I waited for her to come home to tell me about school, and when I began my first year in school, I snuck out of my classroom and sat with her in her reading circle, and we ate lunch together. We had an unspoken understanding of each other and always seemed to know what the other was thinking. But we never talked about the things that happened in the night, not even to ourselves. We two remained close until my senior year when she and I no longer shared those special times of walking to and from school. Jake came into my life and my sister began her life in the world of work. But when I was two, something so very important happened between us that came close to taking my life . . . and that became the focus of what happened in the Inipi Sweat Lodge, a few hours after the telephone call with David.

***

The Lakota Sweat Lodge Ceremony is one that has been passed down for centuries, related to sweat-lodge experiences dating back before recorded history and it has changed little in all the years it has been practiced. The beginning of the ceremony takes place outside the lodge, as all participants gather, and each is smudged with the smoke from a pot filled with smoldering sage embers. Everyone joins in a prayer, while those who know the words sing the Lakota songs sung and prayed in the 4 directions, North, South, East, and West, to the sky, and below to the Earth. After the Lakota prayer and songs, the women enter the lodge first, one-by-one getting down on their hands and knees and crawling into the womb of Mother Earth, wearing their long dresses or skirts and cotton tops. The men follow the women. They, too, crawl in on hands and knees to symbolize reentering the womb of Earth Mother with humbled honor. The men wear cut-offs or shorts whenever there are women in the ceremony, and out of respect, there is no nakedness in the Lakota ceremony. Everyone sits in a circle facing the fire pit dug into the ground in the center of the lodge, and over the course of the 4 rounds the pit will be filled with very hot rocks. Sacred water is poured over the rocks producing hot steam that fills the lodge and penetrates deeply into the hearts, minds, and souls of those who have come to pray.

As usual, during the first round that day, everyone sat in silence as the first seven red-hot rocks were dragged in on a pitchfork and were placed in the pit. After the period of silence, another seven rocks were dragged in and the entry flap was closed, cutting off all sources of light but for the rocks. Water was poured on the earth surrounding the rocks and then on the rocks, themselves, leaving us in total darkness with waves of hot steam penetrating our bodies. Participants were asked to mention the names of the animals or spirits that came to them during the prayerful singing of Lakota songs. Many different animals and birds were mentioned, as well as a few of the well know Indian spirits who often are present in the ceremonies.

In past lodge experiences, I usually saw my eagle totem or, on occasion, a mountain lion, but this time I saw a child running with a bear cub, and then I saw the same circle of shamans from all around the world from many different time periods, as well as the angels and spirit beings that often work with me. This was the circle of beings that directed me to change my name back in 1998 to Sandy Sela-Smith, a story I wrote about in book one, *The Mask.* These beings also guided me in many of my major life decisions and supported me in finding my carriage-house cabin in Colorado.

At the end of that first round of prayers, songs, and welcoming the spirits, I felt extremely weak. It was hard to breathe because the steam from the rocks was overwhelming. More large, red rocks were brought in, glowing in the darkness, as we began the second round, during which each of us prayed for ourselves, and sacred water was poured over the crimson rocks producing even greater amounts of steam drenched heat. When it was my turn to pray, I asked to be reconnected with my blissfully joyful self. In all the work I have done in self-healing, this part of me seemed elusive. Early in my life, I had escaped into my head to avoid the memories of the physical pain and devastating emotions that I locked away in my body, along with the meanings I attached to them. Though, in the past, I had done so many levels of healing, some of which was reflected in all three books in *The Meaning of Three*, and though there were times I did feel joyful and happy, the feelings were fleeting, just enough to let me remember such feelings existed. I knew I could experience these feelings much more deeply, and I wanted to feel them, though I couldn't ever recall feeling the deepest levels of joy.

While people were praying during that second round, I kept seeing the image of the little girl and the bear cub I'd seen earlier. I knew she was an Indian child and the cub was her pet, abandoned close after its birth when men on horses had shot its mother. I began to see more of the child's life, which seemed to be wonderfully joyful and care free. She was surrounded by love, not just from her family, but also, from the entire tribe and the many forest animals she considered as her friends. In the vision, I followed the child and cub from the forest back to her village. Something caused me to feel uneasy, though I had no idea why. As I watched them enter a clearing where she lived, I saw that everyone in her tribe had been slaughtered from a brutal attack. She was now like her bear cub, an orphan abandoned in a world that no longer had a place for her. I felt her feelings and knew I had been that child in a very short past life. My intuitive sense was that the shock of the discovery caused the child to die of a broken heart.

***

That vision faded, and I saw an image of myself at about age two. I was outstretched on the floor with a bottle of cola next to me. Though I had heard the story many times over the years, I hadn't worked with it, not from the place of feeling. But I did have a memory of seeing myself on the floor, as if I were watching it from the ceiling.

Just before this had happened, my 3-year old sister had climbed up on a chair and onto the kitchen counter, opened a cupboard, and took out a coke bottle filled with Tincture of Benzoin, a liquid that is lethal if ingested. She climbed back down and asked, *"Wanna coke, Daddel-Dee?"* My oldest sister came into the kitchen about the time my older sister was offering me the coke; and somehow knew what was happening wasn't good. My oldest sister found my mother in another room and told her about the coke. But in the meantime, I had already drunk from the bottle and collapsed on the floor.

My mother ran from the bedroom and found me lying on the kitchen floor, not breathing and blue in color. Her little girl appeared to be dead. She lifted me up off the floor and ran down the street to the doctor's house, which was about a block away, but after telling him what had happened, she realized in her panic she had not removed the bottle, and her other children might be at risk. She left me there and ran back home to be sure no one else had ingested the poisonous liquid.

The immediate thought that came to me following that image in the second round of the Inipi ceremony was that when I had drunk from the bottle and felt death over-taking me so long ago, the tendons in my arms and legs contracted into an extremely tight condition and became horribly inflamed. Feeling death as eminent, most of me left my body and was watching what was happening from above, near the ceiling. Though the doctor had given me some antidote to survive the incident, an aspect of little Daddel-Dee, was still in that locked up tension. Since then, every time I reached out to take something I thought was a gift being offered, I experienced stress, which caused my arms and legs to ache.

From many inner journeys, I have learned that my body had gained weight as a means of protecting me from the extremely great amount of pain it carried from my growing up years, including this near death incident, as well as the pain I had experienced in my relationship with Jake, before and during our marriage. As the weight was beginning to melt away, energies related to unhealed experiences such as this one were coming forward for healing. I am confident that the grieving in working with Shar was coming forward because the storage places in fat cells were diminishing. And, it was time to deal with Daddel-Dee.

Because the sweat lodge was so incredibly hot and I was having a hard time breathing, I decided to leave the lodge after the third round was complete but before the healing pipes were brought in. I lay down for a time during the third round, but when I tried to sit up I became extremely nauseous and dizzy. I felt as if I might pass out. I believed if I stayed, I would throw up or die, or maybe both. I am sure that is what my child self, unable to breathe, must have felt as life was slipping away from her on that kitchen floor so very long ago. Despite how sick I was feeling, when I did a check with my body, it let me know I would be okay. I decided it was important to stay, at least long enough for the pipe ceremony.

During this part of the ceremony, tobacco pipes, called Chenupas are brought into the lodge and passed around as practiced by the Lakota for hundreds of years. When everyone has either held the pipes or puffed on them and passed them on until each pipe has gone full circle, the leader blows smoke from his pipe on anyone who needs healing. Luke, the leader of the ceremony, announces that this smoke represents the breath of God bringing healing to the one who receives it.

On that day, he called one person forward and blew the smoke in the direction of his injury and asked if anyone else needed the healing smoke. I indicated that I would like to ask him to send the smoke both to the tendons in my arms and legs in the present and to my child self in the past to help her breathe again. Both he and his wife, Patty blew four puffs of smoke from the pipe into me, and I felt it enter Daddel-Dee decades earlier. She began to breathe, and tears filled my eyes. I felt my heart smile more deeply than I had ever felt it before.

Patty handed me her pipe wrapped in a cloth and told me it held the little girl's heart. I cradled the pipe in my arms and felt the presence of Daddel-Dee with me, as if time had collapsed into itself and the two of us were truly together. I felt love pouring from my heart into her little two-year-old heart, and I felt her love coming back to me. As this was happening, I heard Patty ask others to breathe into me. I have no idea who was blowing or how much of the healing smoke entered the little girl of so long ago; all I know is that it was enough. I felt like I was radiating light and heat as life filled this child who had been rigidly stiff from tension, so very cold, and blue for decades.

I believe this little one was my child self who held my bliss, my joy, my love of life. She is the child who had not, yet, experienced being raped and abused in so many atrocious ways. The telling of some of those incidents was included in the first two books. I also believe an aspect of my little girl self had been in that in-between place between life and death for decades. In the spiritual realms, where it is possible to go during the ceremonies, time is not a linear experience. I believe I went back in time to bring life to a child who would have died without the intervention. It took my going back into my childhood, carrying with me the breath of all those in the lodge—the people, the spirits of Indians who often come during the ceremonies, the spirit animals, and the shamans from many times and places, to breathe life back into the little girl called Daddel-Dee. Decades before, when an apparently lifeless little body was on his table, the doctor must have thought what he was doing is what brought his little 2-year-old patient back to life. He had no way of knowing that smoke from Inipi pipes decades in the future, carrying the prayers of all of us, is what actually caused the child to breathe again. From the mystical place of shamanic travel, I would say that little Daddel-Dee had a visit from her future self, a woman who had learned enough to travel back in time to rescue her own self, by bringing the breath of God blown from many caring souls to a dying child.

Though I don't know for sure how I know this, I believe my little child-self, and myself in that past life as the child who had made friends with the bear cub, were connected though the shock of unexpected death. I sense that the child in that past life died of the shock when she saw her relatives all murdered, and when I left my body and saw myself on the floor, dead, the shocking experience reconnected the two lives. Though I revived in this life, a part of me remained in shock and tension for all these decades until that amazing ceremony in the sweat lodge, just as an aspect of the child from that past life had been stuck in an in-between place for what may have been centuries.

As I was writing about this experience, I kept seeing images of the child and her bear cub. I knew the child was calling for help. An aspect of her had been trapped between the worlds, and needed to know that it was safe for her to go home. I invited her to come with me to a higher place where she could see what had happened to her family following their deaths. She discovered that the murder of their bodies did not destroy the essence that flowed in each of them, and they continued to live in another reality. She was finally willing to let go of her former home in the clearing of that forest so long ago, a place that had been stuck in death and go to her home in another dimension. She was reunited with the love that had filled her life with bliss, joy, and happiness, as she had lived it in that former incarnation when she played in the forests and connected with the animals. I believe that when this aspect of myself from a past life and the separated part of me, who was Daddel-Dee in my childhood had found each other in the space between the worlds, both were given the opportunity to move beyond the shock of what seemed like death, to rediscover life. Both little girls released the shock and opened to receive life. They returned to me, as I am now, alive and well, ready to open more deeply to the joy of life.

It was no accident that Oregon David had called to check in on me so we could talk just hours before the Inipi ceremony, and through our discussion he reminded me about creating a partnership with my body. That most beautiful connection I had made with my body following our conversation led me to fully accept the message my body had given me earlier about going to the ceremony. And after I got there, my connection to my body allowed me to hear its message to stay through the pipe ceremony, though my reasoning judgment suggested I should leave because of how sick I was feeling. I believe my body was experiencing the dizziness, the nausea, and the feeling that I was about to die from my child-self who had come very near the surface of my awareness during the ceremony to be healed.

During the second round, I had prayed for the return of bliss, joy, and happiness to my life, a prayer that was answered before the sun went down that day. It was answered in the form of a beautiful reconnection with two aspects of myself who carried the wonderful feelings before the shock caused them to believe that the world was no longer a place of joy and they were separate and alone. They lived in that belief until all of us in the Inipi lodge helped reconnect them to life, and to me.

As a sidebar, the word Inipi in Lakota means rebirth. The ceremony of reentering the womb of Mother Earth calls on all the spiritual beings that are needed to transform the participants who pray for changes to happen. And when the ceremony concludes, each person crawls out, which is symbolic of being born again. I crawled out of the lodge with two aspects of myself that had not been connected to me for so long, a child from a past life who had joined a child aspect of myself from this life, and the three of us became one.

Welcome home Daddel-Dee.

SOMETHING STILL IN STORAGE

Despite the healing that happened when I was able to reconnect with the part of me that deeply grieved the loss of Jake, to embrace the part that had felt such hurt that she feared reconnecting with love, to heal the past life rejection of sensual love, along with my reconnection with Daddel-Dee's blissful embrace of life, I had become stuck, unable to make progress in writing for several weeks. It was then that I had a dream that seemed to tear me apart more than most dreams, so much I avoided writing it down for nearly a whole day, which was very unusual for me. But finally, when I began to write about it, I became aware of meanings I had not seen when I first awakened. This helped me unlock another storage unit inside and release what I had held onto for so long.

In the dream, I was in a place I didn't recognize, and was with people I seemed to know, though I didn't know them in my waking life. A man was with me, and it was obvious we were both attracted to each other. I was slender and seemed younger than I am now, but from the context as well as the content of the dream, it was clear I was my current age. The man sat down on the couch where I was seated and began talking with me. He wanted to become a bit more intimate, communicated by touching my shoulder and looking directly in my eyes. I could tell he wanted to kiss me, and he must have noticed I was having similar feelings. But I wasn't comfortable expressing affection where others could see.

He offered to give privacy by going into his bedroom; apparently the house was his. The room was definitely a man's room, with a large king sized bed covered by a chocolate colored bedspread. The room had a sense of masculine strength, but no feminine presence. He said I could be on the window side where I might feel safer and promised he wouldn't do anything I didn't want. I trusted him. We lay down next to each other and talked for what seemed like hours. We were both feeling very drawn to each other, and I felt feelings inside me that I hadn't felt for years . . . many years. I felt as if I were a young woman feeling sensual love for the very first time. He began to kiss me, and we both could feel where this was all leading. Just as I was about to surrender to his love, I pulled away from him. And with tears flowing, I let him know I had to stop.

He wasn't angry that my tears and my message to stop disrupted such a beautiful flow of sensual energy; instead, it was obvious he was concerned about what I was feeling. I told him that I had surgery that changed me, somewhat, and I didn't know if I could have normal sex. I had forgotten all about this while I was in the middle of these really amazing and beautiful body sensations, but when the touching and tenderness was leading us toward sexual intimacy, the realization of a possible problem struck me, and I began to sob. I told him that it wasn't just that I thought sex might hurt my body, but that he would find me unattractive, maybe even repulsive. He tried to assure me that he was fine with however the operation might have altered my original appearance. He told me that the surgery was a part of my history and that was okay with him because it was one of the many things that were part of the evolution of who I am now. But I couldn't feel his words, likely because I wasn't fine with my own body. I felt what was done to me surgically was a post-trauma expression of what had been done to me as a child . . . only now, the damage could be seen.

As I was writing this portion of the dream, I recalled that when the stitches were being removed from my vulva after the first operation for cancer, the resident doctor's clippers pulled tissue that hurt, and then she said *oops,* an expression that didn't feel good to hear. I asked what was wrong and she said she shouldn't have removed that one stitch. Then she said that it really didn't matter. Everything would be fine, it was just that cosmetically it wouldn't look as good as it would have if she hadn't removed the stitch and had given the tissue more time to connect while healing.

What I felt had been communicated in the young doctor's tone was, *"No big deal, you're not going to be having sex anyway; you are too old and nobody would want an old overweight lady anyway, so my mistake is not so bad."* She didn't say those words, but that was the feeling I got from her intonation. And the truth was, I had figured I would probably never be in love or be sexually involved with a lover again in this lifetime, so maybe she was right that a little loose skin was no big deal. But another part of me was very disturbed by what I interpreted as her cavalier attitude, and that part of me appeared in my dream.

Going back to the dream, the man for whom I felt such a strong attraction was very loving and kind to me, doing what he could to console me and assure me that we could get through this, but I was unmoved. His words didn't seem to help. My heart was broken. And the dream shifted to another scene, as dreams often do.

I was in a doctor's office that looked like a lab of some sort. The physician was a very old man with white hair, looking somewhat like Albert Einstein. He was wearing glasses and had on a white doctor's coat. We must have been talking for some time before I became aware of him. Then he told me he knew I still held concern about residual cancer. But before I could even respond to his comment he asked me if I had continued with the sun treatment. I had no idea what he meant by those two comments because I wasn't aware of holding any concern for cancer residue, nor did I know what the sun treatment was. And I woke without being able to talk to him about his comments.

On waking, my stomach was in knots and I was near tears. I felt that familiar aching hole in my solar plexus and got up immediately. I walked over to my computer, and began playing a game called *Jungle Jewels* that I can play for free from a multiple-game website; I've considered it to be my number one addiction. I played for over an hour, but the knots in my stomach didn't dissipate, and I was close to tears the whole time I was playing. As long as I could focus on the game, I didn't notice the pain that felt as if it were consuming me. I also noticed that despite the fact I was aware it was only a game, the tension around scoring a higher number than the game before caused a tight feeling in my stomach that was strong enough to counter the worst of the ache that came with the knots.

It was easy to see how people can get caught up in any kind of addition that causes the body to be filled with adrenaline and respond with tightness similar to energies of fear or sadness, anger, or pain inside us that we don't want to address. Like two waves in the ocean coming from different directions and crashing into each other creating a flat place in the water, the body responses from the "addiction" coming together with the body responses from an unaddressed emotion can create a flat place inside, at least for a time. But, despite the flat place I was creating by the challenge of the game, the pain was still there each time I finished a 5-minute contest. I stopped the game to do housework and then turned on the TV to watch a program I'd recorded earlier. But after an hour or so, I returned to the Jungle Jewels game and became absorbed in it for several more hours. I had attempted to create a series of distractions by becoming absorbed in the moment to avoid feeling the pain in my emotional body that had been screaming out all day that something was wrong. At the end of what felt like a completely wasted day, I could no longer block feeling the inner pain awakened by the dream; I knew I had to process what I had dreamed.

There is a great difference between being in the moment by focusing on an addiction used as a distraction and being in the moment to experience authentic life in the here and now, the only true place where life exists. I'd been doing the former, and in the end, like the result of any addiction, using the game all day felt terrible.

There is no question that the dream was bringing up unhealed issues around the two surgeries I had for cancer between 2008 and 2009 and my sexuality. Because I had started bleeding vaginally a few months following the first operation, the surgeon thought I was presenting symptoms that indicated I had uterine cancer, and he was sure removal of all my internal female organs would be necessary. He told me there was also a possibility he would need to perform a complete vulvectomy this time because the results from the previous surgery indicated that the edges of the tissue he removed were not clear. This meant they had not gotten it all. However, the second operation revealed no cancer anywhere and not one of my organs was removed because none of the tissue exhibited any signs of cancer. The resident doctor told me that the surgeon had removed one cyst, which was benign, but did not remove a second cyst that was non-threatening. I have no idea why I didn't ask for the reason that second cyst appeared to be benign, but I didn't. So maybe that is what the old man in the dream was telling me, that all this time I've continued to carry a concern for the cyst that was left.

Regarding the other comment about sun therapy, I know I had been spending too much time in my little place, absorbed in writing or working with clients or students. I hadn't gone outside enough just to take in fresh air and sunshine. The dream helped me remember the need to get natural vitamin D from the sun, and to allow my body to reconnect with walking in the beautiful natural setting that surrounds me when I am in Colorado, and the ocean when I am in Florida.

Another possible reason for this dream was that I started losing weight, which for the first time in years led me to believe that I might actually attain a healthy, slender body, just like the image of myself in the dream. Perhaps a part of me saw a possibility of reclaiming my feeling attractive, sensual, and sexual again, and opening to having a love relationship in my life. However, hope almost always stirs fear, and my unspoken fear was that the surgery had ruined me, making a love relationship impossible. So, I dreamed of the man who wanted to be sexual and the woman who grieved because of a belief that she could not experience a sexual relationship or would be rejected if she tried.

While the sensual part of me truly wanted to experience the joy of surrender, an ashamed part of me felt I would be unacceptable, which brought excruciating pain regarding my deeply held sense of being unacceptable because of my childhood. This part of me held the belief that if I became slender and felt attractive, as the woman in the dream felt, and had the potential to experience in waking life, I was too damaged to be able to enjoy it and too repulsive for any man who might be attracted to me to remain attracted when he really got to know me and my past.

The dream told me that because my body was in the process of loosing excess weight, there was an inner war going on about what this would mean. One part of me connected becoming slender to consider being in love, but another part feared the pain she believed would accompany being in love and resisted the idea.

My wish for a future in which I could feel a sensual, attractive aspect of myself stirred beliefs that had been stored within me for most of my life, and the need to empty the storage units in Seattle was just a metaphoric reminder of what still needed releasing within me. I had to re-enter the dream and bring healing to the parts of myself still stuck in the pain of the operation, which was connected to the pain from childhood, causing me to shut down my sensual feelings.

Despite all the healing I had done up to this time, I was not yet ready to deal with what was coming up for me . . . but I knew that the storage place inside that held this pain would be opened and be released, as well . . . when the time was right.

A LONG BREAK

For two months following the realization I had come to about what still needed healing, my writing was completely blocked. Something was wrong inside, but I was unable to go inside to deal with the cause. After about two months of nothing, I decided to go back through the first chapters to edit my work as a way of getting me back into the pulse of book three. I stopped with what I had thought was the end of this chapter saying I would open and release whatever was disturbing me when the time was right. Without knowing something important was about to happen with regard to the content of the previous pages I'd written two months earlier, I prepared for the drive to Longmont for another session with Shar, the Tibetan Cranial therapist, who had been a great catalyst for my healing process.

During that same time period of non-writing, I was taking care of Rachael my 18-year-old cat. She had been experiencing a great many health problems that began when she developed a growth at the nap of her neck. After that was removed, the focus shifted to rebuilding her immune system, and then, she developed inoperable cancer in her mouth. Most of the time, I was by her side taking her to the vet several times a week and giving her a plethora of medications. I had cut back on outside activities so I wouldn't be away from her too long, but somehow, I knew I needed to see Shar again. And after that session, I wrote to Oregon David.

Hi David, I am aware that it has been a while since I've written. I didn't intend to be silent . . . it just happened. Much of my time has been caring for Rachael. She gets 12 shots a day and several medications by mouth. And in between, I clean up the food mess she makes. Her tongue does not work well with the tumor in her mouth so she attacks her food and ends up splashing most of it everywhere as she tries to swallow it. She has been having a hard time drinking, so I give her water, as well as an under the skin saline water drip twice a day. It is not unlike taking care of a sick child or old person. She is a little of both.

And though that has been my focus, I am not upset with it. It seems like an honor to support her in her wish to live. She is purring so much and appreciating the TLC she has been getting. I don't know if I am fooling myself, but I think this new homeopathic medication in her shots seems to be improving her health. She has been trying to drink and seems successful at times. And today she worked at eating dry food, her favorite indoor cat pellets. She is not failing, and she is moving around much better . . . so I am by her side.

The other thing that has been going on has been something I just couldn't identify . . . until today. Last week, I began to have vaginal bleeding again, and much more than before. I felt as if I were having a menstrual period like I did when I was a teenager when it was really painful. I know the medical profession considers that something like that means cancer in a post-menopausal woman, but I did an inner check and got a very strong negative answer to my body having cancer. Along with the menstrual difficulties, I also had back pain around my kidneys. I thought that maybe I had an infection, but there was no indication of anything like that . . . except the fact that I couldn't move much. At first, I thought I had strained my back muscles while carrying Rachael up and down the steps in her big carrier to take her to the vet. After a few days of distress, I was unable to stand erect. I was bent over like my father used to be . . . and I really disliked the reminder of him, though it caused me to feel compassion for the pain he must have felt in his later years.

While all this was going on with Rachael and my back, I felt a strong inner push to get back to my writing. It had been quite some time since I was really writing, so I decided to go back to the beginning and do editing. It was then that I edited the section that I felt was unfinished, but didn't know how to complete it. The writing involved the abuse during my teen years, something I only felt in my cells, though I had no memories to support my sense of invasion during that time. But for some reason, I couldn't move on with it.

Two months ago, I had my last session with Shar, the Tibetan Cranial Therapist, and when I called to schedule an appointment a month ago, I found that she was headed out for her teaching in Europe; today was the first day she had an opening after her return. I scheduled the appointment without knowing if I would need one by today or not. And, I did.

After she took my cranial pulses, she noted that she sensed there was still residual grief going on for me, but not about anything going on in my life now; it was something unresolved in the past, and she sensed that it was not coming from the little child, but from my teenage self. It was then that I told her about the distress I felt about believing there was abuse in my teen years, but I didn't have any images. I told her about that song my roommate in college thought was so great that I hated, the one about an old man that was attracted to a 17 year old girl . . . and the last stanza of the song says the old man got the girl drunk and had his way with her and the song indicated that the girl liked it.

I was so incensed about that song when I was, myself 17, and then I began seeing other images of my father. I hated a photo that someone took at Christmas, when my oldest sister was, maybe 16 or 17. She had gotten a sweater as her present, and was trying it on. The photo shows my sister putting on the sweater and shows an image of my father reflected in the mirror, with his jacket partially covering his face as if he is trying to shield himself from seeing my sister with her shirt off and the sweater only partially on. Even when I was a kid, I hated that picture, though I didn't know why. Now I know my hatred for it was because that whole thing was a performance, the height of sham. The man who saw his daughters naked, who raped them from the time they were little children was pretending to be the innocent man who was protecting himself from seeing something that was taboo. He had a smirk on his face that turned my stomach. Everything was so, damned fake as the whole family was pretending that no one knew what he was doing, and I am very sure that deep inside, everyone knew.

Then my thoughts shifted, and I told Shar I remembered the first time Jake and I went on a weekend together. It was with the church youth group after graduation from High School. There were many kids and a number of adults that caravanned from Seattle to the Oregon coast. My little sister and I went in Jake's car. The first evening, Jake asked if I wanted to drive down on the sand to watch the sunset, and while we sat there talking, he put his arm around me and then in a very quick move, his other hand went down my shirt and grabbed my breast. I had no clue what he was doing at first, and was in shock. I began to cry and told him I needed to leave. I spent a long time walking on the beach all by myself and purposely stayed away very late. I wanted him to know how much he had upset me. In retrospect, I can see now there was manipulation in my wanting to scare him because of what he did to me. It wasn't until my work with Shar today that everything fell into place.

My father had stolen my innocence when I was a little child, and I split off the part of me who knew it so I could maintain some semblance of innocence, but then he stole it again when I was a teenager. There was a long break in his violations between Alaska and Seattle, but when he did it again in my teen years, I did another major split. Part of me knew that he had done it again, but blamed herself for not stopping it . . . and another part of me held on to her innocence, by dissociating and not remembering what happened. The Sandy who believed she could hold on to her innocence even though her father had stolen it, thought Jake was attempting to steal it, just as my father had. My 17-year-old self could not believe that Jake was just a younger version of my father. But at least I was able to tell Jake, *"No,"* and a couple of years later, when he tried to rape me, I stopped him, something I was unable to do with my father.

For some reason, my mind then jumped to my older sister. She was the strong one, the bull headed kid that did what she wanted to do, and as far as I know, didn't let anyone manipulate her, not even my dad. Several psychics have told me that they don't believe this sister was sexually abused by my dad as others of us were. I started telling Shar about the time this sister decided to find out why she was scolded and told not to play around wall plugs. When she was about four, she went into the playroom, pushed furniture against the door to block anyone from coming in, and then, took a safety pin and pushed it into the wall socket. The electricity burnt her hand and flipped her across the room . . . but she found out for herself. A couple years or so after that, when we were at a restaurant, my mother ordered milk, along with our meals, for all the kids. My sister was the first to take a drink and complained that the milk was spoiled. My mother became angry with her and demanded that she drink it because *"Restaurants don't serve spoiled milk."* She drank it all, but with defiance on her face. Then my brother took a sip and complained that it tasted bad. My mom tasted his milk, and then told the rest of us to not drink it because it was spoiled. But my older sister had already drunk all of hers. She told me that it was at that moment she decided no adult would ever make her do what she didn't think was okay for her to do, and no adult would tell her she couldn't do what she wanted to do. She became her own person from that time on.

I had a very strong sense that this sister did not allow our father to abuse her. She likely stood up to him with that kind of defiance that caused him to know she would have screamed; she would have put up a huge fight . . . and then, she would have told on him. For years, I have believed that my oldest sister and I must have been weak because we didn't stand up as she did. Even today, she has a great intolerance and disgust for anyone she believes is weak when they should have been strong, and an almost sacrificial rescuing impulse for those she sees as weak because they could not have been strong, and I believe she thought we were weak. But like the rest of the family, she denied that anything bad happened, so she finds ways to express the disgust and the codependent rescuing in other ways.

I also believe that I took in what I believed was her camouflaged judgment of me, and a part of me judged me as harshly as I believe she did. The part of me that didn't want to know anything bad happened judged the part of me that knew bad things did happen. And there was another part of me that believed the abuse happened because I was weak. While I was sharing all this with Shar, my whole back began to experience uncontrollable spasms, quivering as it was releasing so much pain . . . pain around my sister even more than around my father. I think the reason I hated that photo of my dad pretending to cover his face at Christmas, is that I was also pretending. There was a part of me that knew . . . because I hated the picture, and that part had to act in the family drama that said nothing bad is happening in our family. I am sure much of this conflict was stored in my back, which made me feel as if I had no backbone to stand up for myself as I believe my sister stood up for herself.

That is what got released today. The deep pain in my back is gone and the symptoms that felt like a painful menstrual period are gone, and there is no more blood coming out of me anymore. It is amazing what our bodies can do when they are reliving something in the past. My back muscles are sore from what moved through them, but I can stand tall now.

I know I have more work to do with the girl who holds herself responsible for not stopping what my father did to me in Seattle. I have a feeling it was only one or two times, but enough to make me feel like I was old enough to say no, like my one sister did, but I didn't. As I write more about this, I will be able to set her free from that self-judgment. Love, Sandy

David responded to my email in another . . .

Hi again, after reading your powerful note. It must be difficult to keep unwrapping things when you thought, at some level, that all was already unwrapped. I think we over value having everything "complete" so we cover things up instead of healing them. We want to be finished, as if that has so much value. It's probably better for us to embrace the processes and embrace the idea that part of our good ongoing work is to continue work without feeling like its "supposed" to be finished. It is like housecleaning or dusting. It never gets done and that's okay. Or even like exercise. It's an ongoing process that we embrace. So unwrapping the onion forever is okay, not a flaw or mistake, or weakness. Embracing the working process says we want and need to work right up to the very end, and maybe beyond. We can even leave work for the next life. Labeling the undone work as bad has to slow down our healing because we can't even admit it is there to do. Wanting to be finished is such a problem. It takes us out of here and now, where there is always much to do. Embracing the working right here, right now is more mindful.

I send healing angels to help the teenage girl and the *"you"* in the present to unite, make peace, and heal. Love, David

In retrospect, I believe my father began his involvement with a woman who had two young daughters around the time he raped me again as a teenager. Perhaps, he was attempting to get what he needed from a familiar source before he moved on to the other girls in what was to become his new family, which included girls who were a younger version of our family. He had a child with this woman—a little boy—and soon, my father's focus was on that family instead of his first family. About that same time, he started calling my brother *number one son*, as detective Charlie Chan said when referring to his son in films. Charlie was one of my father's favorite film characters. The reference insinuated that if there was a number one son, there must be a number two son. Looking back, I interpret this as his pathological attempt to disclose without disclosing, thereby, seeing us all as fools for not deciphering his reference. When he used that phrase toward my brother, he had the same smirk that was in the Christmas photo that I hated.

***

When I decided to go through the storage units in Seattle to release so much of what I had held onto for so long, I had no idea how deeply that experience in the outer world would impact my inner world. The many scattered and shattered events that I held inside me in my internal storage had blocked me from embracing life. The internal work that followed my emptying the crates and releasing what I had been stored in them, finally led me to significant events that needed to be accessed and released. My own version of polar bear experiences finally re-connected me with many parts that had been separated for decades. And, they are now back home in the heart of my heart, rather than being stuck someplace in the past, locked away and unnoticed like the many boxes that had been in storage in Seattle. These releases allowed the events to become only memories of the past, no longer held deep within, covering over and separating me from who I truly am.

We do not possess anything; what exists in our lives remains until it is time for it to no longer be in our lives. Attempting to hold on to what was in the past can rob us of our experience in the present and prevents movement into a healthy future. Letting go of what used to be in our lives, even when those things are painful, can be one of the hardest things for any of us to do, and yet, it can be one of the most liberating.

Chapter Seven
MICHAEL'S MESSAGE
A LESSON IN TURNING WITHIN
Releasing the Pattern of the Same Story
Attachment/Separation/Re-attachment/Separation...
And...finally, Connection

As long as we live from the mask or what is behind the mask, disconnected from our authentic self, the stories that define our lives involve such dramas as unfulfilling or unfulfilled attachments, frightened clinging, debilitating longing, painful separation, desperate escape, angry resistance and any other agonizing story line. The stories repeat themselves over and over again causing us to experience lives consisting only of patterns, neither spontaneous nor unique, which leave us feeling disconnected and empty. Without knowing why, we feel as if we are playing a role that is not who we are.

hen I scheduled my trip to the Northwest in the winter of 2009, the objective was to have body therapy sessions with the man I called *Saint Michael* in chapter one, the master Rolpher from Bellingham, even though I didn't know why I had been given an inner directive to make the appointments. However, instead of the work with Michael taking center stage, I separated from its significance while the experiences around the Seattle storage crates and the trip to see Oregon David grew to take more of my attention. Even after I returned to my carriage house in Colorado and began writing again, my focus remained on memories and emotions that had been stirred up from behind my mask. I became immersed in what was required for releasing the agony of past attachments and the pain of separation that were a part of the memories I had stored. I'd also been drawn to consider experiences encountered during my trip to Oregon around feelings about myself, as well as thoughts and feelings connected to my relationship with David and the curious set of circumstances that involved my great grandmother, Sarah. And, though I had been inner-focused to heal childhood trauma, I neglected the simple message to turn within to consciously reconnect with *Sandy God Essence*.

However, after finishing the previous chapter that brought stored experiences from the past into my conscious awareness, it was time to address the next segment of the three-part trip and turn to the time I spent in Bellingham and with Michael, a chapter I knew belonged right here where it is in *Under the Mask*, but I just couldn't make any progress. After weeks of writer's block that turned into months, the thought occurred to me that I should delete this portion of the outline that I saw just after I began writing on Christmas Day of 2009. If I could eliminate all references to my work with Michael, and delete this chapter, I thought I could move on. Deleting a part of the trip to the Northwest that contained what appeared to be nothing more than reconnection with Michael seemed like the rational thing to do, especially because there seemed to be nothing to add to what I had written in the first chapter. As far as I could tell, nothing dramatic happened during those days in Bellingham, with the very mild exception of the tear that fell down my cheek when Michael mentioned that parts of me were likely getting reacquainted with him. No memories flooded in from my past, and no polar bear releases occurred, as was usual in my past work with him. Deleting my trip to Bellingham seemed like a viable answer to my writer's block, but to do that, I would delete a third of the three-part trip and would erase the very reason for having made that trip, in the first place. This neither made sense nor felt right, but I didn't know how else to get past being so stuck.

When it was clear that deleting was not possible, I shifted from feeling very stuck in my writing to feeling disconnected from any purpose in this third book, which sent me back to editing my earlier writing, again. I began writing lengthy filler sections to give me the false feeling of accomplishment. As much as I tried to figure out the importance of my Bellingham experience, I couldn't remember much of this part of the trip that seemed basically uneventful and much less important than what had emerged from the reflective experiences that grew from emptying the storage units. Much later, I learned how this not remembering anything significant was reflective of a pattern, not just mine, but also, a very common human pattern of forgetting what gives meaning and provides fulfilling direction to our lives because of our focus on all the trauma and drama we live with far too much of the time.

Nearly a year had passed before I came to an understanding of the importance of my time in Bellingham, as well as the significance of forgetting the importance of that time. December of 2010, while on a trip to the opposite end of the country, I recognized a lifetime pattern of deleting things I didn't know how to integrate. I became aware that I had thought of doing the same thing while writing book two when I got stuck in *Behind the Mask* and considered deleting all references to *the worst of the worst* because I couldn't find the way to say what I had avoided knowing most of my life. I knew I was avoiding writing about it even though it was so very important to what was hidden behind my mask.

And, of course, deleting what I didn't want to know was a replication of a pattern called dissociation—deleting traumatic events from conscious memory and storing them deep in the dark dungeons of the unconscious, along with the parts of self that experienced the trauma—something I did from the time I was a tiny child. This pattern repeated itself in my adult life, too, when I "erased" the memory of my boyfriend's attempted rape of me when I was 19, and then, I married him when I was 21, no longer consciously aware of that very painful event two years before, a story I wrote about in *The Mask*. The pattern reappeared when I deleted knowing that my husband was having an affair that lasted for a number

195

of years, but instead of letting myself know that I knew, I attempted to live as if no betrayal was happening.

Not so unlike computers and other devices that hold memory, when we delete something from our conscious memory, and no longer have easy access to it, what we delete is not really gone. Well-trained people—computer experts, depth psychologists, excellent body therapists, hypnotherapists, and more—who know how to go deeper into memory systems can find how to support information retrieval. The pattern of deleting what I didn't know how to fully understand is not a pattern that is isolated to me, but also, was a family pattern, one that allowed all of us to survive what would otherwise have seemed unsurvivable. This pattern is present in many other family systems, in our culture, and in our species. We focus on what we believe will advance us, while dismissing, ignoring, or forgetting what we've come to believe will hurt us if we remember it; however, the side effects of the buried information continue to create dysfunctional patterns that disrupt or even cost us our lives.

***

Over the years, perhaps, one of the most pervasive client answers to my therapeutic question, *"Can you tell me what it was like to be a little child growing up in your household?"* has been, *"I had a wonderful family; everyone said it was like living in Leave it to Beaver or Father Knows Best. I was a happy child and knew my parents loved me very much."* But after more investigation when clients begin to open to deeper places, they often disclose exceedingly painful memories of being beaten, ignored, disregarded, disrespected, verbally abused, or physically abused. Somehow, parental arguments, alcoholic raging, intolerance for normal childhood behavior, even sexual abuse denied by the offending parent and ignored by the non-offending parent were experiences in clients childhoods but often deleted from conscious memory. And, the most common excuse for parents behaving badly has been, *"They did the best they could,"* often said with compassion for parents, while a part of the client is in pain that has been hidden away in the unconscious, still in agony for all that happened. Many people hold on tightly to a wished for image of their family of origin and dismiss the actual experience of growing up. To admit the damage would feel like a betrayal of their version of the perfect parents, as they project onto their own moms and dads the images of June and Ward Cleaver or Jim and Margaret Anderson. Deleting what does not fit is so very common.

***

Instead of completely deleting Michael's message of turning within from my conscious mind, I remembered only part of it; I recalled turning within to find parts still living in the inner dungeons to bring healing to them, and I remembered experiencing parts of me who were deeply affected in the reunion with Michael, but I forgot about turning within to connect with *Sandy God Essence* and in the process forgot about the hotel and all that was there for me that I unknowingly chose not to take in.

My inner life and writing had been caught in the magnetic pull of the stories that seemed to prove the truth of separation and attachment. I had become entangled in the tornadic, energy vortexes that stories create, just as we humans seem to do most of the time, and I didn't notice the subtle, yet compelling message to *turn within* to find *Sandy God Essence* connection, a message which holds the deepest of meanings, not just for me, but also, for humanity. It took months for me to see what needed to be reconnected within me before the rest of the story that belonged in this chapter could unfold and be told.

Before I was ready to move on, I had to accept the reality of my being stuck, tolerate the frustration of not being able to move forward in completing book three in 2010 as I had planned until what I was not seeing could be seen and understood by both my head and my heart.

DISCOVERING THE RECONNECTION
TO THE REST OF THE STORY

A few weeks prior to my Northwest trip, I did an Internet search and found a number of places that were possibilities for me to stay while in Bellingham, Washington, but I decided to reserve a room at a bayside hotel, called the Chrysalis, because it was within a few blocks of Michael's house where he practices his Rolfing therapy. I wanted a hotel that would be close-by, so after my appointments, I wouldn't have to drive too far, especially at that time of the year, when the weather could be so unpredictable and could become as treacherous as it had in December of '96, right after my father died the last time I had appointments with Michael, almost 13 years to the day before the 2009 appointments. What could be better than a near-by hotel where I could unwind in a room with a fireplace, a gigantic soaking tub, and view of the expansive bay just outside the windows? The Chrysalis seemed to be a place where I could deeply relax following what had the potential to be intense body therapy sessions! The other reason for booking the hotel was that I wanted to consider the facilities in preparation for workshops I hoped to provide in that area someday after this third book was finished.

For all the years I'd worked with Michael in the mid 1980s, I had to drive an hour-and-a-half before returning home and retreating into my apartment where I could finally unwind, and I just couldn't do that to myself this time. So not only did the hotel solve this problem, I liked the name, *Chrysalis*, which seemed perfect for what I wanted in both circumstances—my current inner work, as well as work with participants in future workshops—providing a place to wrap up in a cocoon of comfort and allow transformational changes to be made inside. I just didn't know it would take close to a year for those changes to incubate and then burst open to what I finally came to understand as being the significance of the time spent with the man I've called *Saint Michael.*

During the months of being stuck in my writing, I'd forgotten the fleeting feeling of awe I experienced the first time I walked into the elegant, *Chrysalis Inn and Spa,* situated on Bellingham Bay, the waterway leading to the San Juan Islands, the Strait of Juan De Fuca, and the Pacific Ocean. I had forgotten the hotel's slate floor entry that provided a powerful sense of foundational strength for the natural cherry wood interior and the beams that supported the cathedral ceilings, which loomed three stories above my head. I had, also, forgotten the sweeping spiral staircase that seemed to invite me to walk to my second floor room instead of taking the elevator.

Walking into the lobby of the hotel caused me to feel a sense of grounded peace and an assurance that I had really picked the right place for all that was to happen, not just then, but for the future, as well. It was the sense of awe and peace I'd forgotten, and forgetting became a metaphor for what was to follow.

From the Internet website, I understood every room in the hotel had a view of the bay, and mine was no exception. The experience of walking into my room was far more moving than what I'd seen in the photographs. When I opened the door and entered my elegant room, my body was flooded with expansive joy; I felt as if I were being embraced by my surroundings, just as the beautiful space was being embraced by the immensity of the energies of the ocean and sky. In that moment of entering what was to be my personal space while in Bellingham, I had felt connection with everything; however, my mind was not consciously aware of the profound significance of the feelings. Moments after entering the room and taking in the sweeping view, both inside and out, I returned to my car to get my suitcase and other items, including a number of the boxes I had taken from the storage units. Almost immediately, I began focusing on logistics of getting settled, opening a couple of the boxes salvaged from storage filled with the stuff I intended to sort, as well as making a few calls to get needed hotel information for workshops. I did this all before leaving for my appointment with Michael, and I never again reconnected to the feeling of awe I experienced the first moment I entered the hotel lobby and a few minutes later when I opened the door to my room.

I believe I'd forgotten what being in that hotel had to offer, as well as the deeper message that came to me during the time Michael worked with me because I had gone into another pattern. My time was wrapped up in a mental checklist of doing and deciding what to keep and what to throw away instead of turning within, relaxing by the fire, soaking in the large tub, and gazing at the night sky filled with stars, or tuning into the sounds and vibration of ocean waves crashing into the shore just below my window.

Sorting through the boxes that held my past was something that didn't need to be done at that time, but out of habit, I did it, not just before my appointments, but afterward, as well, far into the night. The driving force to take care of the chore was more about pushing myself to complete a task than about dealing with something rising up from inside that needed to be healed, at that particular time. Compulsively working, not allowing myself any rest until a job was done, was a pattern I'd followed so often over the years. And the damage of that pattern was that there was almost never a time when there were not chores to do or jobs that needed to be completed, meaning that there was seldom time to turn within. When I did take time off from work, to just relax, my mind busied itself with what to do when the rest period was over. And, resting was neither resting, nor turning within. I had not yet become conscious of the pattern enough to be able to discern when pushing myself to complete a task was necessary and when giving myself peace and calming rest was more important.

My felt sense is that those of us who obsessively work can hold on to the pattern as a way to avoid turning within. We hold unconscious fear of discovering what we've buried behind the mask. Our conscious self, which has identified with being the mask, may be terrified of finding our *Unique God Essence for* fear it will ask us to release the patterns that the masked self believes are the only things that that can provide protection from a dangerous world. The decades I spent in healing what was behind my mask had allowed many profoundly beautiful experiences while turning within, but writing and being blocked in writing allowed me to see far more clearly that when a part of me that has identified with the mask feels threatened, that part will find a way to resist that inward focus. The months of being stuck between writing the first six chapters and writing this one needed to be played out before I could see what the Universe was reflecting back to me.

When I became more conscious of my pattern related to forgetting what I had experienced in Bellingham, I could see that most of the time, I hadn't really stopped to *smell the roses* in my life from the deepest meaning of that saying. My pattern was to notice metaphoric roses, and at times, to even smell them, but seldom did I actually linger long enough to allow my body to let go of the chaos of the outer world and its related tensions and stresses and be with whatever were *the roses* that lined my path. To slow down, and just be with what was in my life could mean that when I was off-guard and vulnerable, unexpected information might come forward. Having this happen was more difficult to anticipate, even unconsciously, than when I more intentionally approached what was hidden within. And, on this trip, I hadn't slowed down enough to take in the aroma and sensations of soothing bath oil while soaking in the immense Jacuzzi tub or to absorb the ambiance of the fire casting light and shadows across the ceiling and walls creating a feeling of vibrant energy dancing to the pulse of silent music. I had only *noticed* these things, more as observations than experiences, while doing what seemed like necessary work. I spent too many years of my life multitasking to do what my mind decided needed to get done or thought I should be doing rather than opening my heart and giving my body the gift of being one with lovely, loving, calming, peaceful, and relaxing experiences when the opportunities arose, and this time proved to be no different. What I didn't know was that I was resisting really being with the roses because there was an inner resistance among the various "I" parts within me to be one with anything.

The pattern of being driven to accomplish something, leaving no room for pure and gentle relaxation was actually a distraction from living my authentic life. I pushed to accomplish what was on my list rather than allowing myself to be motivated by my heart's desire to accomplish those things I was born to do. When I finally recognized how much I had allowed to pass me by while staying at the Chrysalis, I knew that someday, not only would I would return to this beautiful hotel by the bay and open to experiencing what I had only observed, but also, I knew I would take the lesson I'd learned and give myself permission to become more attuned to roses in all the other forms they take in my life. Forgetting the gentle good things was a way my unconscious could prevent my consciousness from noticing that there were still difficult experiences that needed to be brought forward for healing and releasing.

***

As I mentioned in the first chapter, Michael's gentle touch caused me to turn inward, something that few of us know about, and even those who know about inward focus don't do as often as would be beneficial. Instead of turning within and allowing life to flow from the *Unique God Essence* inside us, many humans spend most of their lives identifying with the mask, which is focused outward, looking for ways to act or roles to play that help them present what they believe will be the most effective image to send to the outer world. Most of us search for the right things to say and do, or we struggle to find a way to fit in with those we believe will make us feel acceptable; some of us try to find a way to change what is outside, by intimidating, manipulating, and controlling everyone and everything, to make the world fit with us. These, and many other potential responses to the outer world are attempts to feel safe in what appears to be a very unsafe world, secure in a world that feels increasingly insecure, loved in a world that too often does not seem to know how to love, and important in a world that, too easily, can dismisses us as being insignificant. But, in the end, these ways fail to provide our needs because they are disconnected from who we really are.

In order to feel safe, secure, and loved, we need to trust in the truth that safety, security, and love, coming from within our God Essence, will unconditionally be there despite outer circumstances, and will remain in spite of what we might say or do. If feeling safe, secure, and loved are dependent upon someone or something from the outside, we do not feel safe, even in moments of apparent safety; we cannot experience security during times when temporary conditions create impressions that everything is secure, and we do not feel loved in the moments that love is offered to us…because any of these things can be gone in a microsecond. Just knowing this truth about the outer circumstances being experienced as temporary disintegrates the feelings of safety, security, and love based on external sources. Because these basic human needs can only be experienced inside us, the source of those feelings must come from within us, as well.

Awareness of the basic human needs of finding safety, security, significance, and love, and satisfying the more complex need to experience personal growth, as well as the deeply embedded need to experience fulfillment in contributing to advancement of ourselves, and then others—our loved ones, our community, our culture and our nation, and, for some, to contribute to the advancement of our species or the whole universe—has been understood and expressed throughout time by many philosophers who have studied what it is to be human. And, even if we are unaware of it, the focus of much of our lives is on attempting to fulfill these needs. However, we cannot *experience* fulfillment when we are disconnected from *either* the world *or* from our authentic selves. And if we are disconnected from our authentic self, automatically, we are disconnected from the world.

Unfortunately, we live in a culture, which almost exclusively focuses on the outside instead of on our inner being, and without inner connection, our focus on the external world becomes attachment or separation rather than connection. And, true connection can happen only from the place of our internal *Unique God Essence*. What nearly all of us have forgotten, at least some of the time, is that when we connect to our inner self—to the *Unique God Essence*, the ineffable something that pulses in each of us—we automatically experience connection to *Universal God Essence* that is never separate from our unique essence, though it may feel that way if our consciousness is connected to our mask or what is behind our mask instead of to our internal being. In the same miraculous moment of connection, we experience the most blissful union of *Unique God Essence* with *Universal God Essence*. Most of us have moments scattered throughout our lives when we feel this union, but few of us experience it on any regular basis and even fewer of us live from this place of exquisite union for extended periods of time.

Only when our consciousness experiences authentic connection to our inner being, can we feel *connection* to the outer world, which is, like us, made up of billions of expressions of God Essence, so many of which are living unconscious of their inner God Essences. When we turn inward and connect with our true selves, we discover that safety, security, significance, love, growth, and contribution exist within and flow naturally in us and from us to all of the other aspects of God Essence. Without inner connection, outer world contact is fear-based, which we experience as dependent or co-dependent attachment to other people or things, or as pathological or existential separation, if not repulsion… but not connection. Such fear can also cause our consciousness to attach to our masks as our identity, which then causes us to resist becoming consciously aware of turning within to experience connection to inner God Essence. Consciousness, when attached to the mask, fears inner connection will melt the mask and the self will die, which is a partial truth. When the mask melts away and all the beliefs about the self based on the mask are found to be lies, it can feel like a terrifying death, just as expressed in the Jefferson Airplane words as quoted in the first chapter and later reflected in the story of *The Serious Man.*

Instead of knowing safety, security, significance, and love within us, it is not uncommon for humans to be in continual search for what we hope will create those things. In that disconnected, mask-attached state, we depend on our mask or on other people, like ourselves, who are also in a desperate search for something they don't experience, hoping they will find it in us because they, too, are disconnected from their own Essence within. And, we can experience an entire lifetime feeling separate, isolated, and alone, not connected to either the outer world or to ourselves. Our relationships become a reflection of one if not all of the three parts of the codependent triangle, where we take positions of rescuer, victim, or persecutor in an effort to control another person we experience as separate from us, but someone we need to behave in a particular way for us to feel okay. In order to feel good, we attempt to delete from our conscious awareness anything that reminds us that we are desperately holding onto someone or something as a facsimile of true connection, and so often, we call that desperate attachment *love.*

Even though the deepest truth is that we are all connected, we are eternally safe and secure, always loved, and never alone, we can feel as if we are alone, unsafe, insecure, and separate from everyone and everything. Like rivers that are not separate from raindrops or from oceans, our authentically unique being is not separated from the pulse of other unique beings, which are an inseparable aspect of Universal

Being. However, from a limited perspective, raindrops can appear to be separate from each other, and separate from rivers that may seem separate and different from the Ocean. In truth, water in all its forms is one united substance, moving and flowing in, around, above, below, and through every thing that exists, including us. This sense of connection is what I could have experienced if I had allowed myself to sit quietly in my window seat watching the waves wash in from the Pacific Ocean, and my body would have been reminded of its connection to all that is. But instead, I unpacked boxes and sorted things.

From a limited perspective, the spark that ignites and creates the pulse of life in us may seem separate from the spark in other people and separate from the spark that ignites the pulse of the universe. Even if we are not aware of it, the light inherent in the spark is the same continuous light, flowing in, around, above, below, and through everything that exists…even us. When we connect with the spark in us, we experience connection to the origin of the spark and to all that has come from that Universal Spark, or what I've come to identify as *Universal God Essence*.

Recently, I went to a leadership conference for the 21st century where one of the speakers, I believe it was Dr. Bruce Lipton, stated, *"Each of us is not just a drop in the ocean but each is a drop that contains the ocean."* I realized he was saying the same thing, only using a different metaphoric image. When I consider this idea, I am reminded of Jesus' statement, *"Father, let them know that they are in me, even as I am in you."* Like water or a spark, God Essence is not separate from or outside all the billions of billions of aspects of *Unique God Essences* that make up itself. It just looks that way… from a limited perspective.

***

My religious upbringing taught me that I was separate from God, and that God was up in heaven, far away, though he could look down and see everything I ever did. I believed I needed to find my way back to him if I were to experience salvation, but I believed that what had happened to me made me unacceptable to the *God of our Fathers*. When I began to embrace the thought of non-separation, that we are all one and in One, I rejected the teachings of separation, without noticing

I had not dealt with the *experience* of separation, something that felt very real, because I had not yet clearly understood the significance of uniqueness in relationship to oneness. Confusion arises when there is not a distinction made between uniqueness and separation, in that being a unique expression of God means that I am not exactly like any other being in the universe, yet I contain the same essence that fills everything else in creation, making us all a part of the One. However, being separate, as I was taught in my childhood, means that God is not in me. And it was this distinction I had to experience during the time I was blocked in my writing. What I did not know was that the writing process, as well as the periods of blocked time in writing, created the pathway for me to more deeply understand this distinction.

Many experiences and stories arose between December of 2009 when I went to the Northwest for that three part trip, and December 2010 when I took a trip to the Southeast, which helped me to understand uniqueness, separation, and connection far more deeply than ever before.

Without knowing why I was taking the 2010 East Coast trip, except for the fact that I had created a pattern of visiting friends in Florida and Connecticut in the winter, usually around Christmastime, I made reservations, and began the trip that was to allow me to complete this chapter and finish *Under the Mask*. A year has passed since I went on that trip to the Northwest and reconnected with Michael who encouraged me to turn within. As much as I believed I had learned what I had written earlier about connection to God Essence, a part of me was still trapped in a pattern of feeling separated from myself created another experience of separation. And then a deeper pattern arouse that needed my attention so I could know what it is that creates the illusion of separation and erases the experience of connection.

**OH WHAT A TANGLED WEB WE WEAVE
WHEN FIRST WE PRACTICE TO DECEIVE**
Sir Walter Scott

Normally, when I return to Florida to reconnect with my place of residence and my friends, there is so much I have to do. Generally,

I spend most of my time with two friends, Esther, and Terry, often neglecting other people I would like to have contacted, and I've never seemed to have the time to deal with what I'd placed in storage there in 2006, despite the fact that for at least three of the years, I had intended to empty that space. In August of 2010, I had traveled to the Tampa Bay area for a very short, three-day trip to see a number of medical doctors for check ups as follow up from the cancer problems that arose in 2008 and 2009. Because my two friends live so far apart, and my doctors were very close to Esther's place, and because I didn't want to have to spend my extremely limited time traveling between houses, or disappoint Terry if she knew I was in town and only saw her for lunch while I was there, I decided not to tell her I was in town. Much of the very short time there, I felt guilty about withholding, but seemed to have gotten over it, until I began the process of booking my next trip in December of 2010.

Before making arrangements, I checked with Terry to see when she would have time off from work. She had four days off in a row the first week of December and based on her schedule, I checked with Esther to find out if she would be available for the days following my stay with Terry. However, when I checked the airlines for the first day Terry had time off, the flights were too expensive, so I let my friend know I'd be coming a day later, and then scheduled my flight, which actually came in very late at night the second day she had off. She would have two days off the following week, the exact days that Esther had pre-existing plans, so I told Terry we could plan for the days before I went to Esther's and those two other days the next week to do something together. Even though I was not consciously aware of what I was doing, deeper inside, I felt this would be a way to make up for my not being there earlier for all the days she had off, and my guilty mind thought this would make up for not telling Terry I was in Florida back in August.

Feeling disappointed that she would be off when I wasn't there, Terry changed her schedule, giving her an additional day after I arrived, so we could still spend close to the original amount of time together. I know how difficult it is for her to make work changes and didn't want to disappoint her by telling her I had planned to spend that time with

Esther, so I emailed Esther that I would be at her place a day later, without explaining why. Because I hadn't told Esther I'd be spending time with Terry at the beginning, Esther assumed that I would be flying in the same day I would arrive at her place, and I said nothing to give her any other impression. I'd thought Esther might feel slighted if she knew I had shortened the visit with her because of Terry's schedule and didn't want to deal with any possible hurt feelings from either of my dear friends.

I was definitely caught in codependent behaviors, trying to take care of what I thought would be hurt feelings of my friends and as a result was caught in deception.

Before my departure from Denver, I got a call from Terry, telling me that she had a medical emergency and wouldn't be able to pick me up at the airport because she was not feeling well. I decided to rent a car instead of taking the shuttle to Terry's house, especially because it wasn't clear if I would be staying with her if she had to go into the hospital, but when I landed, I found out that she had already paid for the shuttle. Terry told me that a family emergency required that her daughters fly out during the time we were to spend together, which meant Terry would be taking care of her grandchildren some of the time, and she would need to pick them up from school and drop them off at various activities. It looked like our plan to spend time together was placed on hold.

Despite the extra responsibilities, we had time to go shopping, get our nails done, and even go to a movie. Because Terry's movie experiences were always child-oriented, she wanted to see a "grown up" film, so we went to *Burlesque.* On the way out, Terry commented that it was too bad Esther couldn't have come with us, because that was the kind of film she would have liked. In that moment, I realized complications might arise from withholding information about my being in Florida without telling Esther I was there if she wanted to see the film I'd already seen.

While I was at Terry's house, Esther called my cell, leaving a message that asked about my plans while I'd be at her house, so she could work them into her schedule. Normally, I would have returned her call, but I was afraid she might ask too many questions if we talked on the phone. Instead, I sent an email message answering all her questions. At the end of our visit, Terry drove me to the airport so I could pick up a car rental for the rest of the time I would be in Florida. In that earlier email, I had told Esther when I thought I'd be picking up the rental car and driving to her house, not a lie, but also, not the complete truth, because I had withheld information. However, Esther had not gotten my email message from earlier in the week and was concerned because from her perspective, she had not gotten any response from me, something that was unusual. So she left another message the night before telling me she was concerned. But the message was delayed in getting to me by my phone service until I was at the car rental office. After I had picked up the car and began the drive from the airport to North Pinellas County, where Esther lives, she called, again. I didn't know what to tell her, so I didn't answer my cell. I needed to decide if I would tell Esther that I was already in Florida, or continue with the impression that I had just arrived.

When I finally listened to her most recent message, she said if I didn't return her call by 5 p.m., she would call the police to see if they could find out what had happened to me. I realized I could simply tell her the truth, but I struggled with how to explain that I had been there and had not called her. So I called and told her I was on my way, without explanation about where I was, only telling her that I had sent an email and had only just then gotten her calls, which was true. I did tell her that I had come in earlier to help Terry out because of a family situation, but made it sound more like I had just come in that morning to help Terry. Esther had gotten a new computer and was having difficulty getting on line, so she hadn't gotten the message I had written earlier in the week, something I found out on that short call. If this is sounding like some inane plot in a soap opera, it is probably because it was very much like that.

Not long after I arrived at her home, Esther and I headed for a Thai dinner and the *Potter* film, which was one of our traditions since the Potter films first came out, and just before the movie started, she asked what time I had left Colorado. For the first time in this whole experience, I actually lied to her. I said 8 a.m. When I was looking for flights before I booked one, I saw there was a direct flight at that time, so my mind calculated that I could have left at 8, arrived at 11:15 or so and would have had time to help out Terry as I had mentioned. My withholding had turned into manipulation and manipulation had turned into a lie.

I do not do lying very well...I could have told her the truth, but I was caught in a pattern of trying to take care of other people's feelings and after the first deception didn't know how to make everything right. I felt my whole body contract and I was glad that the lights went down in the theater so Esther wouldn't notice the expression on my face.

After the movie, I wanted to tell her, but as soon as we got home, she turned on the news, read the paper, and then went to bed. But as she looked at the paper, and upcoming films, she said she wanted to go to *Burlesque*, and asked if I'd be interested. I told her I had already seen it. She was disappointed, and then asked me with whom I had seen it. And, I lied again. I told her I saw it by myself. I believe it was at dinner that Esther commented about my nails being done, something I rarely did since living in the mountains. And of course her comment was another reminder to me that I had spent time with Terry without being honest with Esther. It was as if each of her questions and comments provided an opening for me to tell the truth, but once I got caught in lying, I didn't know how to get out of it and "save face" or maybe more appropriately, "save mask." Esther gave me a goodnight hug before she went to bed, but I couldn't feel it. She may as well have been a total stranger. Before going to bed, I checked on the internet to see when Burlesque had begun and was relieved to find out that it had already been in theaters for a week, which meant that I could have seen it in Colorado before I had left for Florida. Again, my lie was leading to more covert covering of my tracks.

210

For the first time, I felt deep compassion for my x-husband, Jake, for having an affair and then not knowing how to tell me, until the lies grew so big and the distance between us grew so great that we ended up separating and then divorcing. We never got the chance to find out if divorce was what we really wanted…it was a natural result of the distance, and both of us experienced broken hearts. I knew I was not going to allow lies to create that kind of separation between Esther and me. Our friendship meant so much to me, and I didn't want to recreate that very painful pattern I lived out with Jake so many years before.

But husband Jake was not the only one who kept secrets and didn't tell the truth. As our marriage was falling apart, I met a man at a high school reunion. My husband did not want to go, so I went without him and met a man, also named Jake. We really hadn't known each other in school, but had both been in the school concert choir, and we had both participated in the same local talent contest when in our early teens. We told each other that we were not interested in initiating an intimate relationship because I was married, though struggling with the idea of divorce, and he had just come out of a very painful breakup. But in reality, he was seeking to end the pain, and I was looking for a way to not suffer from a husband who had grown cold and distant from his lies. For a while we met at various restaurants for lunch, and then he invited me for breakfast at his house. We began seeing each other whenever I could steal away for a while. It was only a matter of time before the relationship became intimate.

Not long afterward, husband Jake and I separated and I moved into an apartment. We agreed that the separation was to help us find a way to make our relationship work and began marriage counseling. The truth was, by that time, I didn't want the relationship to work; what I had hoped would happen is that Jake would gain connection with the therapist so when I left, he would have someone to help him. But I couldn't bear to tell him the truth. I thought it would crush him to know my intentions, and he would reject any support from a therapist.

For a time, I was seeing both Jakes, lying to both about my intentions by withholding or outright saying things that were untrue. I loved both men in very different ways and didn't want to hurt either, but the choices I made could not have done anything else but hurt them both, as well as hurt me. I was so torn within myself I couldn't feel anything for either of them but fear…fear I would be found out and rejected by both. I couldn't let go of my husband and didn't want to lose my boyfriend who offered me hope that my life could be love filled. What happened in this troubling double relationship cannot be explained in any ordinary way.

I can't tell you how many times husband Jake would call, and during our conversation, I would see call waiting with boyfriend Jake on the other line or the other way around. Husband Jake would call, telling me he would like to go to a movie, and the next day boyfriend Jake would ask if I wanted to go to the same movie. It was like the two had some kind of radar that let them know what the other was thinking.

One morning, boyfriend Jake called to ask if I would be free to take a drive up north to Canada, the same place that my estranged husband and I had gone the weekend before. And one really freaky time, boyfriend and I took a back road drive to a small tourist town between Seattle and Bellingham. The scenery was beautiful and we found a quiet little out of the way restaurant on the river, where I felt safe for the first time in a long time. I felt at peace there where there was no chance I'd run into anyone I knew. The next day, my husband called to ask if I would like to take a boat ride on the inland waters north of Seattle. Boating on the river was beautiful and peaceful, allowing me to disconnect from the many levels of stress in my life. About lunchtime, he suggested we stop at a restaurant, so he tied up on the dock of the same restaurant I had been the day before with the other Jake. We sat at a table next to the one boyfriend Jake and I had taken the day before. Where I was seated, I could see the other table, now empty, an experience that was so painful and eerie that any peace I had felt earlier, vanished.

That period was such a horrible time in my life. I don't lie very well. It eats me up inside, and I swore I would never do that again, but I was lying again. On some strange level, I was playing out the same general story with different characters and different details. Instead of lovers, the pattern had come up between friends. I knew I had to tell the truth despite the possibility that Esther might be so hurt that I had lied to her she would end our friendship.

After the hug I couldn't feel, I lay in my bedroom feeling so badly disconnected from my friend. I didn't sleep well that night, and when I heard Esther moving around upstairs, the next morning, I knew I would have to tell her what had happened. But there was no time that morning. I felt the time would have to be right. I didn't want to say something when there would be no time to really talk and work it out, and it was really hard to find the time.

I recalled that one time I did ask husband Jake if he loved me and then asked him for reassurance again because I had something very difficult I needed to tell him. It must have not been the best time, because his response was, *"If you just pretend that everything is okay today, and then pretend again tomorrow and the next day, maybe in time it will be okay."* Then he left for work. Another time, I wrote a long letter to him telling him everything, and asked him to read it so we could talk. Just as he took the letter, the phone rang. Without reading it, he placed the letter on the dresser and answered the phone. A project from work had gone badly, so he went downstairs to talk to the lead worker for a time. Instead of coming back upstairs to our bedroom, he remained downstairs, watched television way into the night, and never read what I had written. After a number of days of it sitting on the dresser, I put the letter away to find the right time…and there never seemed to be a right time. I suspect that there would never have been a right time for husband Jake to tell me about his affair, nor would there have been a right time for me to tell him about mine. Neither of us was really open to telling or to hearing. But the same was not true for Esther and me.

Esther came home from work to have lunch, and as we sat down, she asked a simple question, *"Sandy, can you tell me what is wrong?"* Before she asked the question, I had already decided to tell her about my lies, and was so relieved that she had brought up the subject. Instead of avoiding the conversation as Jake had done, I told her about my feeling torn, and that I had lied to her, something I had never done in our friendship, before. I apologized, and then let her know I would never do that again.

Esther said she asked me that question because she'd imagined she had done something that upset me but had no idea what it was. She was so kind and told me my reducing my time with her and spending more time with Terry would not have upset her. I felt so relieved, as the feelings of being torn melted away with the truth. Because of similar feelings inside me about being torn between two people, I had projected my interpretations of Jake and Jake onto Esther and Terry and then responded with old patterns instead of recognizing the differences in both the relationships and the circumstances. Though in some cases, projections are based on parallel stories or subtleties that match in two different situations, in other cases, such projections do not fit, but we fall into our own patterns based on the earlier behaviors, anyway. I was treating Esther as if she were a part of a Sandy, Terry, and Esther triangle like Jake, Jake, and me. And that did not fit. When we were able to talk this out, Esther acknowledged that she honored my support of Terry, certainly an attitude that was not present in either of the two Jakes' thinking. With all the lies gone and the truth told, I became far more animated, and Esther pointed out that for the first time in my visit with her, I was, *"really there."* Not only did I have myself back, I had our friendship back. It was such a gift.

In retrospect, I can see that the lies I told Esther were "white lies" but were nonetheless lies, and even people who can easily tell untruths, the lie creates two energy forces. One of the forces constructs a barrier between the self and the other that in turn creates distance between two people. This barrier is formed out of an unconscious intention to keep the other person from getting close enough to detect the lie. And the other energy force impacts the internal self, separating the mind that created the lie from the God Essence that knows the lie, as well as the emotions that may have very mixed feelings about lying. Even if the person who has lied has no idea that these forces are in play, he or she is experiencing separation, by way of a loss of integrity by disconnecting from wholeness within, which automatically results in a loss of connection with the other.

Whenever disconnection within the self or between self and other is experienced, there is a sense of discomfort that can create many different physiological responses. I felt mine as a hole in my stomach and chest, which threw my whole body/mind energy system out of balance, something that was nearly impossible for me to tolerate. Others have reported feeling racing thoughts that at times created a sensation of spinning out of control, resulting in feelings of anger, often projected outward onto the one to whom they told the lie. And some have said it causes them to feel empty, which resulted in turning to their addiction of choice to fill the emptiness. I am sure there are hundreds of other physiological responses to being out of integrity, and if the person forces him or herself to get used to the feeling, eventually the disorder from the loss of integrity becomes the new normal and lying can become habitual, appearing to not have any effect, when in fact, the pattern of lying has been gigantically damaging within the self and between the self and others; they have lost the ability to be close without knowledge that such a loss has happened. It is possible they may solve the problem of feeling distant by self-talk that says closeness is not needed or wanted.

I suspect that huge numbers of people who experience distance in their significant relationships and in their friendships had first told a lie or had been told a lie...even if it was a little one...and in time, what was once close falls away and trust fades. I was pleased that the lie I told was not a gigantic one that would have done huge damage, but left unaddressed, a little lie has the potential to grow into a big problem. All I needed was to see the pattern of feeling torn, and then see the pattern of lying to repair the inner tearing I felt, which in fact, can't be repaired with another lie.

***

Later that evening, after the time of "confession," Esther and I went out with two of her close friends for dinner, both of whom I had met before. But this was the first time I felt free to be me, perhaps because of all that I had learned about being present and allowing my true self to be seen, coupled with the reestablishment of my internal integrity and my connection with Esther. The women were talking about relationships and the problems they had with men controlling them, when for the first time, I began to share something from my own life related to an experience I had with my former husband. Unless someone was very close to me, I seldom if ever shared anything personal with other people about myself, despite the fact that I've written so much that is exceedingly personal.

I talked about something I did that, along with many other things, led to the crumbling of my marriage. It is not always easy to pinpoint the choices that lead to our entering our personal version of Robert Frost's *Yellow Wood* that will eventually take us to the two roads that diverge, calling us to choose which road to take. There are usually so many little choices that set us on a course with gigantic redirections built into them…down the road. For me, I believe my decision to Take I-90 East to Bellevue instead of I-5 North to go home to my husband and the life I had lived for 20 years, as I wrote about in the first chapter, went back to a call I received 10 years earlier. The principal of the high school where I had taught for the previous 10 years called to ask me if I would be open to go to Washington, D.C. for a fully paid week with a student of my choice to participate in a privately funded government education program. I remember it as if I had received the call yesterday. I responded with great excitement saying I would be pleased to go as a representative of the school.

When I hung up the phone, I began to squeal while jumping up and down with childlike delight. I felt as if I had won some grand prize, even though I had never entered a contest. Jake's immediate response was to tell me to stop acting like a child, and then he asked me what all the commotion was about. I told him, but he didn't show any enthusiasm for the opportunity that had been given to me. He was not particularly happy that I would be gone for an entire week and wanted to be sure it would not cost us anything.

Except for one trip to Kentucky when my husband was in the service, I had never traveled beyond the Northwest and West coast, and had never seen the world outside of my family, my marriage, and the schools I attended and the one in which I taught. As a political science and history major in undergraduate school and a history teacher, the nation's capital was, for me, like entering another world, as wonderful as Disneyland would be for a child who had only been on the school playground. While on that trip, I experienced being in the same room with senators and representatives that I had only known by way of the nightly news. When I was in Washington, I met people from all over the country and even from other countries. I saw the president and sat in the hall of the Supreme Court where the justices passed on the most important rulings in American history, and for the very first time in my life, as a part of the program, I was able to see a live Broadway style performance. In one short week, my world expanded from a small classroom and home to the entire world. However, I carried the small world into the big one.

Because it was supposed to be an all-expenses paid trip, Jake saw no reason for me to have any spending money, so I left for Washington with very little money, and without credit cards, something that was not a part of our lives at that time. Evenings, when there was free time, and a few afternoons when there was nothing in the teachers' schedule there was time for independent excursions, but I remained in my hotel room because I had no money to participate with the other teachers. I felt left out and disconnected from the others during that time and disconnected from Jake who never called me the entire week. When I called him, he seemed impatient with my interruption of his work, and when I returned home, he seemed uninterested in my experiences, cutting me off short when I tried to share any of the exciting things that happened.

Because I was the only social studies teacher in the small private high school, I was asked to participate in the program the following year, and of course, I said, yes. But I decided to do something I had never done before. I found a way to secret away money so that I would not have to go to this great wonderland again with no money of my own. Every time I went to the grocery store, I wrote a check for $5.00 over the amount on the ticket, and placed the bill in an envelope that I hid on a bookshelf. Over the course of the year, I had well over $200 in the envelope, an amount that seemed like a fortune; I felt so liberated when I went to Washington that second year. I bought souvenirs for family and friends and treated myself to lunch during free time. I didn't spend all of the money, so it became the beginning of the secret savings for the following year.

When I was in Washington, D.C., I was in a very separate world, not needing to deceive anyone, but when I was home, every time I returned from the store with a $5 bill that needed to be hidden in the envelope, I felt the discomfort of being out of integrity. In time, I got used to the feeling, without having any knowledge of what it was doing to me.

Though I had no idea what was actually happening in my marriage as a result of these first trips to Washington, I did know that I was not feeling good about being so controlled by Jake. I was afraid that if I asked for money, I would be told I didn't need it like the first year, and deeper inside I resented that he was the one who decided what I could or couldn't have, despite the fact that I was earning money as a teacher.

Seeing this greatly expanded world let me know that there was so much more I could do in my life, a thought I had never considered before. I became a volunteer for Washington State's local programs that produced similar educational opportunities for students to study their city and state governments, and I worked on the planning committee for a Pacific Rim economic conference that included students and their teachers from Alaska to California and even Hawaii, as well as economic leaders from many of the nations that touched the Pacific Ocean. In time, my involvement with state officials led to becoming a speechwriter for several public officials who needed guidance in what to say to students when these politicians were invited to give presentations, including the governor of our state at that time. This led to my becoming more involved in politics and as a result, I was asked to run for state legislator in my district.

The more I lived in the greater world, the more Jake resented my involvement outside our business and home, but I no longer could live with the limitations of being fully subservient to him. Our communication was never good, but it became even worse. Several years later, on the way home from work one evening, I told Jake I wanted to have a chance to discover what I really wanted to do in the world as he had the chance to do a number of years before when he left the job he had since he graduated from the university. At that time, he wanted the chance to explore creating his own business and for three years we lived off my income while he found his way. Instead of seeing the parallels between my needs and his, he became extremely angry and told me that I was destroying any chance we had to really make our business work. I had left teaching a few years before and worked beside him in building the business that was his dream, but it wasn't my dream. He refused to discuss it any more.

Though I no longer was teaching, the Washington DC foundation hired me to be the coordinator for Washington State, which meant I was in the national capitol about 4 weeks a year, and directly involved in the planning and implementation of local and state programs, while still working with Jake in our business. I am sure he felt betrayed by the changes I was making in my life, which clearly impacted our personal and business lives, as well.

Long before all this happened with me, Jake already had developed a relationship with a woman he met at his previous employment not long after we were married, and the relationship continued for many years. He used the time I was gone to connect with her, which then caused him to distance even more from me. We created complicated and painful patterns as a result of our inability to communicate. A great amount of that story was included in *The Mask*.

***

What was wonderful about telling this story to Esther's friends is that I no longer had anything attached to it, and I could speak it from the place of seeing, not just the dysfunction of it all, but also, what might be called the dark humor in it. The next day, both of Esther's friends commented to her about how much they enjoyed having dinner with me, because it seemed that for the first time, I was really involved with our conversation, not just there as Esther's mostly silent friend. One of them even said that the more I spoke, the prettier I seemed to get. I also recall that one of the women had spoken directly to me at the beginning of dinner, saying that I seemed to look really healthy and happy, and that I had a glow about me she had never seen before.

As I look back on those comments, it occurred to me that what they were seeing was not my mask but my *Sandy God Essence*. In the past, I could access *Universal God Essence* when I worked with clients and students, who expressed a feeling of connection with me, but this was the first time I really got the importance of experiencing Unique *Sandy God Essence* with people who were not extremely close to me on a personal level. I felt comfortable sharing with others the wonderful mixture of me as a person experiencing me as *Unique God Essence,* both flowing in and supported by *Universal God Essence.* There is a profound sensuality in the glowing presence of the authentic self...and I was in a place to feel it inside me for the first time while with people I didn't know too well in my personal life. The awareness of the glowing of my God Essence was made more meaningful because just a short time before I had the opposite experience of feeling separated so profoundly from the radiance within me. What a gift! Now that I know it...I know it in my body, in my cells, and I found I could authentically enjoy the presence of other people at a level I had not known before.

Above all else, I believe each of us came into this world to *consciously* experience our *Unique God Essence* in connection with *Universal God Essence* from within our human bodies, which creates the pathway to experience connection with everyone and everything else around us. Without this flow in consciousness, we interpret most, if not all external energies as separate and potentially threatening. As a result we create a consciousness of separation that plays out, too often, for the rest of our lives. And this becomes the makings for all the stories that on the surface may seem so very different, but underneath, they are the same story, repeated over and over again. I needed to experience this in my body, first hand, to be able to complete this chapter and to complete the chapters that follow. It took that trip to the Northwest in December of 2009, the trip to the Southeast in December of 2010, and all the synchronous experiences in between for me to become fully conscious, both in my mind and body of the importance of turning within and the gift of living from my *Unique God Essence.*

I am not under the illusion that from this point on I will fully live from *Sandy God Essence*, but what I do know is that when an estranged part of me is in charge of my consciousness and I am not living from this place of authenticity, because of what happened between the two Christmases of 2009 and 2010, finding my way back to connection will be much less of a struggle.

If we are willing to turn within to make the connection with our Unique God Essence, the being that we really are, we can transform our lives by setting ourselves free of what would otherwise have kept us trapped in unfulfilling, painful, and often predictable, repeated stories. We experience our unique authenticity, and we feel connected within ourselves and to those important to us, as well as to everyone and everything else in the universe; what we do matches who we are. We are in integrity, and we feel fulfilled in our lives.

Chapter Eight
SYNCHRONICITY
A LESSON IN DISCOVERING INFINITE CONNECTIONS
The Unfolding of Extraordinary Experiences with Oregon David

When we begin a healing journey, Universal God Essence conspires with our Unique God Essence to bring to our consciousness whatever we need to release our identity with the masks we wear, to bring healing to what we have hidden behind the masks, and finally, to live in the radiant essence that existed for too long under the masks, setting us free to experience being who we have always been that somewhere along the way, we forgot.

The third part of the trip to the Northwest in December of 2009 involved my traveling to Oregon to my visit with my very dear friend of over 20 years, the man I've called Oregon David. Before I received the call from Jake letting me know I needed to decide what to do with the storage crates, I had thought of visiting David and then taking Amtrak's Cascade train up the coast to Bellingham to work with Michael. But, when I had to include unloading all that was in storage in Seattle, everything worked best for both David and me to make the Portland part of the trip when everything else was finished.

After leaving Bellingham, I stayed with my eldest sister for a day and then took the southbound train, which gave me time to reflect on my concerns related to David seeing me, still heavy. In *The Mask,* I wrote about the pain of going from Slender to Fat Sandy, something that was a defensive move made by my body as a way to protect me from so many fears I held onto my entire life about what being in a slender body, if not just being in a body, meant. Those fears not only made my body fat, but also, created the sense of separation between me and my God Essence, as well as between me and the rest of the world. Despite how much I wanted to lose weight my entire adult life, after months of heroic efforts I would lose weight, but not long afterward, the loss was followed by a period of weight gain. Without understanding what was really happening inside me, I struggled with the physical and emotional pain and shame of constant failure; but my body could not allow the protection to be released as long as I held fear of being in a body.

Despite the many years of healing, as well as the years of teaching principles of connection with *Universal God Essence,* I struggled with periods of time when I felt disconnected from my own God Essence. In retrospect, I could see that this happened when I dropped into fear. Though I had no idea a significant healing would grow in these two areas of separation as a result of my visit with David.

***

In an earlier trip to the Northwest, September of 2008, David had come to a place where he expressed his acceptance of Fat Sandy just as she was, if that is how I decided to present myself for the rest of my life, though he seemed to say it with an underlying sadness, because such a choice would likely reduce the amount of time I had on the planet, and that would be difficult for him. David had wanted to be as supportive as possible and had been for years, but had come to the conclusion that something in me wanted to remain overweight. However, I didn't want to stay Fat Sandy even if he could accept me that way. I wanted something different for myself, but just didn't know how to create it.

In *The Mask,* I wrote about the painful struggle I went through ten years before in the fall of 2000, when I felt torn between going to see David and not seeing him during another three-part trip to the Northwest, that time, centered around my taking a first level Cranial Sacral training class from the Upledger Institute being offered in Seattle. After the training was complete, a part of me wanted to experience being with this wonderful man for whom my heart felt great love in the three-dimensional world and not just via email or phone, and another part of me felt so ashamed that my weight had increased to its all time high of 276 pounds; this part of me didn't want David to see me like that. Projecting my own self-rejection onto him, I presumed he would reject me as painfully as I had rejected myself. But after a very caring phone conversation that began with my telling him I was too exhausted to travel from Seattle to Portland, I finally admitted to David that I was ashamed to have him see me as I was. He told me he was really looking forward to my visit and asked me to consider taking a day of rest and then come for the visit. I set aside my shame and pride; the result was, perhaps one of the most meaningful visits I'd ever experienced. My ability to receive his love and acceptance let me open to the ability to receive love coming from the hearts of others, especially when I returned to Seattle to go the funeral of my former mother-in-law. I reconnected with many people I hadn't seen for over fifteen years and felt their love as never before.

During the next decade, David visited me more often than I visited him. My focus over that time was on completing graduate school, studying to get licensed, and developing my practice that took most of my time, and I did less traveling to the Northwest. The shift to Colorado and beginning this trilogy, followed by health issues I wrote about in books one and two got in the way, as well. His work, on the other hand, brought him to Florida, and later, to Colorado and as much as possible, we scheduled time to see each other. Though there were times that a year or more would pass without us actually seeing each other, a week seldom went by when we were not emailing or talking with each other.

One of the great gifts of our relationship was that we could talk about almost anything. Our conversations included far reaching subjects about the universe as well as the deep recesses within us, and what it means to be the human. Both of us have hermit tendencies, but we've been able to be there for each other at times of our most painful losses and our most exciting successes. We speculated about how the universe works in relation to ourselves and how we create our own universe by drawing to us reflections of ourselves.

One of the profound realizations, which came to us from a series of discussions, had to do with the consciousness of the world. I recall telling him about the great disappointment I felt when I had to release the belief that human transformation could very well be just around the corner. Because of the circles in which I had my deepest connections, it seemed to me that consciousness was taking such great strides in opening and expanding, but then I found myself in a situation where I was observing, very close-up, unconscious and even cruel responses in fellow human beings that greatly saddened me.

With so many dark things happening in the world, I realized it might take lifetimes, if not eons for humanity to release the destructive fear and anger patterns growing out of unconsciousness. Knowing that I am a part of this universe and humanity, it broke my heart to realize that I, too, may have many more lifetimes…or eons of lifetimes…to fully learn the lessons that I have not learned. There were times I thought I was so close to experiencing enlightenment, but then I'd discover another inner dungeon and realize how much work I still had to do. David and I could talk about things like this.

Most any subject, personal and transpersonal could be a part of a discussion, but, one subject that was difficult for me had to do with my weight so, most of the time, we did not discuss it, although, David always encouraged me to find ways to walk and to exercise.

In the fall of 2006, after getting the carriage house in Colorado as a place to write, I felt encouraged to walk more, and in time was able to drop a few pounds, but not really much to speak of. With my focus on writing since this trilogy began in the fall of 2007, I didn't spend much of my time concerned about my weight though the two operations for cancer in 2008 and early 2009, did shift my attention to my body. The entire Colorado experience brought my attention to the fact that from the time I was a tiny child to the present, I had not really connected to being here on this planet or being in my body, something I knew needed to be healed, though I was not sure what path the healing would take. I sensed that the in-between period, those six weeks from the time the second book was finished and the third one began contained the seeds for that healing, and the events that followed in the year between the two Christmases of 2009 and 2010 allowed those seeds to grow; my intuition was not wrong.

***

Following the meaningful discoveries related to letting go of what I had in storage and the significant message to turn within, this third part of the trip to the Northwest contained another message, which was to notice the interconnectivity of everything, which included my connection with my whole self and with all that exists. A series of events that had no causal relationship having to do with my Great Grandmother Sarah helped me to more deeply trust that something much bigger than me was at work in my life.

About 100 years ago, Carl Jung, the father of depth psychology, identified *synchronicity* as the unexplainable flow of events that exist that normally would be considered unrelated, but when taken together lead to significant shifts in consciousness. Jung pointed out that synchronicity suggests an organizing principle beyond causality creating interconnection. Without a doubt, Jung would have called the three Sarah related incidents—finding Sarah's photo while I was in Bellingham, walking near Sarah's grave a few days later in Portland, and getting the message from my distant cousin when I returned to Colorado later that same afternoon stating he had found Sarah's grave in Portland very near where I had been walking—synchronous events. Certainly, what I learned about Sarah, as related to me, was important in my growth, but the lesson was to expand beyond Sarah into the deepest places in my life.

The deeper lesson was to take the understandings from my head about connection and experience them in my body, but I had to reconnect to my body before I could do that and then to experience the interconnection, not as a thought but as a feeling. My time with David in that December 2009 visit allowed me to experience what was needed for this to happen.

***

David met me at the train station and we had a wonderful time in those days before Christmas as I mentioned earlier. But what I had not remembered when I wrote the first chapter in this book was what happened the first night I was there. The bedroom, where I had slept in past visits, was one that a couple had shared for some time, but had left shortly before my arrival. The main concern in the past was the bed was a Futon that could absorb the coldness from the floor and David had found a way for the bed to be raised up on six large, heavy duty plastic cartons that fit perfectly along the support boards under the Futon to allow airspace between the floor and bed; it helped the one sleeping there to be warmer. When it was time to turn in for the night, I sat down on the side of the bed and heard a crack. One of the cartons had split apart. I was devastated. But when I made an attempt to rectify the situation by taking the cracked carton from near the head of the bed where I had been seated and exchange it for one at the foot of the bed, I found that not one, but five of the cartons were already broken. I knew I had only broken one, but my heart felt great shame in having to tell David about what happened. My fear was that he would think I broke all five. I switched the one I had broken at the top right for the only unbroken one at the bottom left. That first night, I found if I very carefully slid onto the bed and scooted into the middle without placing all my weight onto any one of the cracked cartons, the bed could support me.

Despite my feelings of shame, I had to tell David what happened, as soon as possible, especially because he was going to have other guests stay with him soon after I left, and the problem needed to be solved before they arrived. I garnered the courage to tell him about the problem the next day and he created a temporary fix, which would work as long as I balanced my weight more evenly when getting in and out of the bed. He told me that the couple that had stayed there earlier most likely had broken the other four cartons without saying anything about it, but he would figure out another way to give support to the bed.

Because David was so gracious in his response, I let the embarrassing situation slip out of my thoughts and enjoyed the rest of my stay in Portland. But the fact that I'd forgotten what had happened for nearly a year, just as I'd forgotten the significance of the message to turn within, was an indication that this event, too, held a very important message, one that I was to discover between the two Christmases.

***

As you know from reading what I wrote earlier in this book, David brought me to the airport after my stay with him; I returned to Colorado, and a few days later, slipped and fell on the ice, cracking my head open and then, before the new year, hit my head again. Lots of other things happened in the days and weeks that followed, including the Christmas Eve astrology reading, the call from the three Davids, and beginning writing this book on Christmas Day of 2009. These experiences and the events that were related to them led to the healing of many aspects of myself: my 2-year-old self, who nearly died from accepting and drinking what seemed to be something good that was given to her with love; the lost little junior high girl who didn't know her name and couldn't find her way home; the young teen who sewed her hair into a sweater as a way to remain attached when the connection she thought she had was lost; my teenage age self who had found what she believed was the light in Jake's eyes and then lost it when she was his wife; the girl who believed she had lost her innocence; and my post operation self who believed she had lost her sensuality.

A lifetime of experiences written about in this book, as well as in the first two books of the trilogy had caused me to disconnect, not only from the world but from fully experiencing *Sandy God Essence*. Throughout my healing process, as well as what I became aware of as a result of my writing, I've discovered that despite what I had come to know as true, I had a difficult time feeling what is true.

My head has known for a very long time that I belong here in this world, doing what I have been doing my whole life, which is to grow in conscious awareness that I am an amazing spark of God, a unique being containing *Sandy God Essence*, come to learn the truth of who I am and to teach who we are to any who is ready to open to his or her own truth. But, fear, created by myriad events of my childhood and young adult years, caused my body to energetically separate from my head. As a result, many of the patterns I developed cut me off from experiencing the things my head had come to know were true. More than anything, I wanted to be able to experience the *knowing-feeling* of trusting being in the safety, the security, and the love of God Essence within in connection with *Universal God Essence* and know in my cells, that I am eternally one within the One, like Bruce Lipton stated that, *"Each of us is not just a drop in the ocean but each is a drop that contains the ocean."* This was the message I sent to the God of the Universe and then I moved on to other things, not noticing that the Universe had already begun conspiring to support my request.

BILL AND BRAZIL
MAKING CONNECTIONS TO SEE THE FULL STORY

Bill, my Atlanta friend, sent an email asking if I wanted a session exchange, something the two of us had done ever since the early '90s. We both were trained in the Shamanic Alchemical Hypnotherapy process and began to do sessions with each other as a way of honing our work, as well as working with our own issues with a like-minded person for whom we felt deep respect and trust. For any reader who is familiar with book one and two of the trilogy, you will recognize the profound work Bill did with me to help me navigate the deep places behind my mask, which brought about significant healing and transformation in my life.

Because he sent the email, I assumed Bill was dealing with an issue that he wanted to resolve, so I returned his email with a response letting him know I was available. After a short conversation, we discovered that neither of us was aware of any special need for doing inner work at the time. But, before hanging up, I mentioned that there was one small situation that might bear looking into if he had a moment. I had been invited to participate in a sacred circle in Brazil, where shamans and healers were gathering for a sacred ceremony using *Ayahuasca*, which is a powerful medicine made by Amazonians who use a number of Brazilian forest plants that create a substance for use in ceremonies often held in their churches to support participants along their spiritual journeys. This was not the first time I had been invited; however, this was the first time I considered participating.

***

I came of age in the 1960s, when the hippie generation was dancing in the streets of San Francisco with flowers in their hair calling for peace and love in a world that was far from being peaceful or loving. But I didn't participate in the drug culture of the time. In my entire life, I had never smoked a cigarette, much less a joint. I had never taken any illegal substances of any kind, and for that matter, very few legal substances. Once, I tasted beer and smelled hard liquor, and if I thought about it for any amount of time, I could probably count the glasses of wine I had ever consumed. Alcohol and drugs were not attractive to me in any way.

In the 90s, while attending a conference of shamans from all around the world, I had been invited to participate in a ceremony deep in the rain forest of Brazil, and after thoughtful consideration had passed on doing it. But there was something about this more recent invitation, coming at this time in my life, which caused me to rethink the whole question of abstinence for the sake of abstinence.

I began to think of all the possible reasons for accepting this unusual invitation as well as the reasons for politely declining it. Each positive response led to a negative and each negative response made me look, again, at the positive. It was very important to me that the decision I made, be one based on love rather than fear, and Bill's offer to support me in my own discovery in the decision-making process was a gift I didn't want to pass up.

Bill had participated in activities of the 60s culture and told me about two kinds of hallucinations. One is when you see something that is not there, and the other is when you don't see something that is there. And in both cases, what is or isn't there may have more to do with what we are programmed to see and not see than anything else.

It is common knowledge that dogs can hear sounds we can't hear because our ears are programmed to hear a smaller range of sound when compared to our four legged friends. Human senses are set to function within a range of frequencies that most effectively support us in maneuvering through our three-dimensional world. Can you imagine how confusing it would be if we could hear the sounds of ants walking on the floor, hear the blood flowing in our veins and hear the opening and closing of all the valves in our bodies? Can you imagine how disconcerting it might be to see all the electromagnetic waves bouncing around from our television sets, computers, cell phones, and microwave ovens, and see all the vibrations coming off everything, living and what we identify as inanimate? And it might be difficult to be able to smell as keenly as a dog can smell, especially in some settings. But all the images, sounds, and smells are there, all the time, whether or not we can see, hear, or smell them.

There have been theorists who have suggested that around us are myriad dimensions of existence, which we cannot experience, likely because many of us are not prepared to handle them, or they would prevent us from fully appreciating our own three-dimensional world. When a person ingests natural hallucinogens, or even artificial ones, his or her brain is reconfigured to be able to experience other dimensions and sense the things we normally don't sense. A problem that can arise for the one ingesting the medicine is when he or she does not know how to differentiate between the non-three-dimensional messages the senses are experiencing from the three-dimensional messages that are appropriate to the world in which the body exists.

If we were to look in a mirror and see a blemish from the perspective of one of our cells, it might be one of the most terrifying experiences of our lives. In that tiny, almost invisible blemish, the cell would experience what would seem to us like a mile high mound of rancid puss erupting like a volcano carrying the bodies of dead cells that were called up to attack the infection, and that one cell would see huge monster-germs murdering live human cells. The observing cell might see the rage pouring out of the surrounding tissues that have turned a deep and menacing red. And in fear, the *"you"* in the cell would scream out in terror for the horror that was displayed right there in front of you.

Bill explained in any spiritually led medicine ceremony that whatever a participant needs to see, he or she would see it from a perspective that has the potential to teach something important, if the person remains open to learn. When drugs are abused, the visions can be damaging, especially when the user is attempting to escape the very things that are confronting them in their visions.

***

Because of the shattering terror of my childhood, remaining here in the three-dimensional world was not something I sought. I didn't need any hallucinogen or medicine to support my wish to let go. As a result, I easily slipped into a trance state and visited other realities and dimensions while my physical body was experiencing what I wanted to escape, something I wrote about in book one of this trilogy. Part of the abuse in my young years involved drugs to put me to sleep or cause me to become cooperative when everything in me wanted to stop what was happening. As a result, my entire system was extremely resistant to ingesting anything that would cause me to lose control of my own processes. In all the years I had experienced trance states and shamanic journeys, I had done so without the assistance of drugs or plants. But I heard from those who have taken journeys using both the natural and the artificial methods, that it is possible to be projected into other dimensions and alternate realities far more expansive when supported by medicine from plants. For the first time, I seemed ready to at least listen to what might exist beyond the dimensions I had already discovered in my childhood travels, and later in the healing journeys I took for myself and with clients, simply by releasing attachment to three-dimensional reality.

I likened all of this to persons living in a mansion, but only knowing the room in which they lived. For all their lives, they believed that all there was to the mansion was that one room until one day one of the people discovered a door could be opened to a hallway with many more rooms attached. The explorer might return to the room and tell the others about the hall and the many doors that opened to many more rooms. Some would be curious and go through the doorway to visit these other rooms, as did the first, but others in the room might have too much fear to leave the one room they knew, to go into other rooms that would be totally new. They might have to change their ideas about what a room is and what rooms contain when they investigate all that is beyond their room.

Someone else might investigate further and discover a passageway that leads from one floor to another, and on a higher floor, there might be huge ballrooms, very tall ceilings with chandeliers, gold-framed paintings on the walls, and stained glass windows far taller than anything on the first floor and, certainly, very different from the one room where the people had lived all their lives. For those who stay in the small room and refuse to investigate what is outside the door, talking about a hall and a passageway might be challenging, if not terrifying.

But imagine what might go through the minds of all the people if one of them discovered a stairway that leads to another space above the ballroom floor where there is another passageway that leads to a heliport and a helicopter that can fly above the mansion and take passengers to an airport far away. The airport has jets that can fly anyone who is not afraid to a base that has a rocket ship that can take the traveler to the moon…and beyond to other planets. But what if there was a way to travel beyond the other planets to another galaxy on the other side of the universe…and on the other side of the universe there is a portal leading to other dimensions and universes?

In the many years I took spontaneous, unassisted shamanic journeys, I had found dimensions that contained rivers of souls, trapped in the agony of terror, and I found beautiful planets adorned with the most amazing gardens and healing ponds. One planet, in particular, was lighted by a huge array of geometric-shaped moons that bathed every thing in shimmering light. Even though I don't know how to map the places that I have been to allow people in three-dimensional reality to understand how to get there in a three-dimensional way, I know the places I traveled are real, not just figments of my imagination. But like the metaphoric travelers from the mansion might not be able to convince those who never leave the one room that there are passageways, chandeliers, stained glass windows, helicopters, rocket ships, other galaxies, and alternate universes, I, too, have had a difficult time communicating what I learned through my shamanic travels.

ANOTHER DISCOVERY OF ALTERNATE UNIVERSES

Many years ago, I had a dream. In the dream, I was in high school and it was lunchtime. I was seated at a table and noticed a huge floor-to-ceiling screen upon which images were being projected. Fascinated by what I was seeing, I didn't notice that I was the only student in the lunchroom who saw the screen. The other students were all eating their lunches, involved in conversations and completely unaware of what I was seeing, when something funny happened on the screen, causing me to laugh out loud. But because no one else saw what I saw, they looked at me like I was a bit odd, and I felt very ashamed.

Then I noticed a heat spot on the screen, as if the film had stopped moving long enough for the projection bulb to burn a hole in the film. The fire that was consuming the film and the hole that was forming from the flames were being projected onto the screen, so it looked like the screen was burning and a hole was forming on the screen. As I continued to watch, I noticed that instead of being a projection, there was an actual hole being burnt in the screen. I walked up to the place where a fairly large hole had opened, and I peered through. Instead of seeing the rest of the lunchroom, on the other side, I saw a huge field of grass rippling and waiving in the breeze and far beyond the field was a forest. I became so curious that I climbed through the hole, which by that time had gotten large enough for me to step through.

Totally forgetting about the lunchroom and my fellow students, I began to walk in the field. I could feel the breeze on my skin and the warmth of the sun. As I walked through the field of grass, I became aware of a hole in the field of grass. It occurred to me that the whole scene I had been peering into from the lunchroom had opened to another scene that was, in reality, a projection on another screen, but I was able to actually enter that other scene and walk in it as if it were three-dimensional, not just a two-dimensional image on a screen, and this strange world in which I was walking felt as real as the lunchroom had felt. Then, to my surprise, when I peered through the hole in the field, I saw a scene of a beautiful countryside that seemed to draw me into it. So I climbed through the hole in the field of grass and began to walk in the countryside.

I could smell the richness of the black earth and the sweet aroma of a vast array of flowers. This place felt so very real, as real as anyplace I had ever been in my entire life. But then I saw another hole appear. Just like the other ones, it opened to another scene, and that one had a hole that led to another scene, and another…on and on.

I was fascinated by what I was seeing, until a moment of awareness flooded my thoughts. I could see the possibility that these screens and holes in screens that lead to new scenes might go on forever, and then I became afraid that I would lose connection with my fellow students, the lunchroom and my school. So instead of continuing the journey through the holes in the worlds, I quickly moved back through the scenes that had become screens with holes in them. Just as I was about to climb through the hole back into the lunchroom, I realized that the lunchroom was just like all the other places I had entered. And in a far corner of the lunchroom I saw what I had not noticed before; there was a small hole on the opposite side of the screen being burnt into the back of the lunchroom scene. I woke feeling very confused.

A dream that made no sense to me all those many years ago, finally began to make sense. Because of the extreme abuse of my childhood, I had been catapulted into other realities and dimensions, much like my dreaming self, going through holes in screens to enter scenes that others could not see.

***

I became aware of Bill's voice telling me that we live in a world of illusion that this three-dimensional world seems to be a hard fixed state, but it is not. Certainly, this was not a new thought, but somehow it hit me in a way that was new. Bill asked me if I could articulate my thoughts about possibly participating in this experience I was resisting. Even though I had considered the financial cost as being a negative, I was well aware of the fact that the Universe has always supported my decisions to spend money on something that I was being called to do, even when it was a large amount. So, if I would be in alignment with all aspects of me to go, the money would be provided.

As I moved through my pros and cons list in my head, I sensed that one of the biggest reasons I had for not going was the judgment of society, whatever that means. I was afraid that my credibility as a therapist doing the deep work that I do would be tarnished. Since I had never taken any kind of drugs or ceremonial medicines, I felt I could stand tall in the experiences I had, and not give ground for others to reject my discoveries because they could be too easily dismissed as drug-induced hallucinations.

I explained that part of me held on to my innocence of never having taken drugs, and resisted participating in the medicine circle, not unlike a virgin woman who holds on to her virginity for no other reason than the fact that she is a virgin. If I took a hallucination-inducing substance, I believed I would be tainted like nearly everyone else; I would no longer be *innocent* in the eyes of those around me, and certainly no longer innocent in my own eyes.

Bill suggested that the only reason I could be so affected by social criticism is if I had my own inner critic that was in agreement with society. I knew it was important to release judgment if I wanted to be free to make a decision about the invitation from a place of love, not fear.

When I inquired as to what part of me was judging all of this, I saw an image of a woman in a cotton dress, high color and long sleeves, a woman who looked like she was from the Midwest sometime in the 1800s. I was very sure she was "me," in a past life, but I also saw an image of my 22-year-old, teacher Sandy-self wearing a gray suit, that I wore when I was a 35-year-old businesswoman. Both the past life me, and the Sandy that seemed to be a mix of my 22 and 35-year-old self in this life, seemed to have a very narrow interpretation of what was right and wrong, and both prided themselves in having always chosen what was right.

As soon as I said those words, I was very aware of how I had not always done what I believed was right. As a result, I had separated from the Sandy who had done what she believed she needed to do to keep Jake from leaving her. And though she had not technically had sex with Jake before they were married, she had allowed him to see her naked and let him touch her, something she made herself not feel or remember because she had believed it was so bad.

Bill suggested the possibility that I had been programmed in religious puritanical thought, something that had not just come from my mother, but seemed to have come from that past life on the Midwestern prairie. Bill talked to the Sandy of this life and the young woman of the past life, explaining that sex is a woman's power but religious rulers, nearly always men, put rules on it and had stolen the right of choice around sexuality from women. These men created the rules to manipulate women's sexuality for their own power. He suggested that *promiscuity*--a word often attached to sexual freedom--was not always something bad, but could actually be an expression of a woman's power. Though I could agree with him that sexual freedom was not bad in and of itself but was bad when judged by the rules, I could see also it could be damaging to the woman or to others when a woman used her power in a harmful way. I could see how she could be manipulated into being promiscuous as much as being manipulated into not being promiscuous by rules that control her choice.

Bill said something I had heard before, but never really understood, that orgasm is communion with God; it is the ultimate in letting go of the self. His words touched a child part inside me, who broke into tears. She told Bill that she would not allow herself let go and feel any sexual feeling because that is what her abusers wanted. They tried to make her feel so they could feel. If she allowed herself to feel her body and let go in surrender, the invading man would steal her energy; he would be able to feel because she did, and she vowed never to let any man steal her energy.

So my child self held tight onto her control to stop all sexual feelings to keep herself from being stolen. All of my life, she locked up my feelings and blocked my ability to surrender into what Bill called communion with God.

Bill asked if I would be willing to introduce this little child to my innocent self, but as I drifted from the wounded child back through my life, I was not able to find innocence. The moment I was born, I felt guilt and shame for coming into this world. I was a girl and my mother did not want another girl. I was a child and my father did not want children. Even though I didn't have words, I knew that my coming when I did had caused my mother to feel hurt and angry. When I was old enough to understand my mother's words, I knew that my coming when I did meant that my sister, 3 days short of a year older, wouldn't be able to celebrate her first birthday. I felt the mistake…and became *mistake incarnate*, something my mother reminded me of nearly every year of my life on my birthday.

When I connected to my little child self, I saw her as a 2-year-old, who wanted more than anything to run with delight through an open field, chasing butterflies and playing with the wind as it danced in the tall grass. But the child's shame and guilt kept her from being free. Bill asked her if she could see the light that is my true self within her, within me, and she could. For the first time, this aspect of myself saw the spark of god, the *Sandy God Essence* that is in me, that is the real me.

As a little unwanted child, I had to cover up my God Essence with what felt like a layer of cement that prevented me from moving too much, a confining layer that assured I would be nearly invisible to my family so I wouldn't disturb them. If they didn't notice me, they might not throw me away. I grew up with that energetic layer of cement holding me in, not allowing the light that I am to be seen. In time, I became a confined person encased in cement and wearing the mask and from that place was unable to see my inner being, the light of *Sandy God Essence*. When I graduated from college, and turned 21, I married Jake, who I am sure also had his version of a layer of cement covering his God Essence, the part of him I called Chocolate man. I am sure that most of his life, he had no idea that such a part of him existed.

***

By way of explanation of what follows, what I am writing is not intended to give you a sweeping view of Jungian philosophy, but to offer a window into some of what makes up who we are. Alchemical Hypnotherapy, based on Jungian psychology, operates on the premise that every one of us possesses all the ways of being, but most of us tend to live from a select set of patterns that are dominant qualities, and a set of recessive qualities that are more present in our subconscious, the ones we access when we are under stress. Even if we are adults, we have a child-self in us, as well as a wise old man or woman, and if we are male, we have an inner feminine and the woman has an inner masculine. Each of us has an inner mother, connected to the eternal mother pattern, and an inner father connected to the eternal father pattern. This is why people who were not well parented, can grow up to be much more effective parents than they had if they access the wisdom of the ideal eternal parent energy. And we all have inner mates. This is the aspect of us that is connected to the eternal pattern of the lover, the romantic that loves us unconditionally.

I met my inner mate many years ago, and wrote about meeting him in book one. His name is Jon-Luke, and every now and then, I've been aware of his presence in the form of my protector, the one who loves me without judgment of my appearance, my age, my weight, or any other quality so often judged by our culture and is often the cause for rejection in this three-dimensional world, judgment, not just by others out there, but by ourselves, as well. I didn't know that an inner-mate existed until I was in my 40s. As a result, younger aspects of myself had no idea that Jon-Luke existed on the inner planes of my being.

Bill asked if my 22 to 35-year-old-self would be willing to meet the age-appropriate Jon-Luke, who immediately said, "Yes!" He came forward, as if on cue and my young-woman-self immediately recognized him. She threw her arms around her long lost friend, her buddy and her confidante, the one person in the universe she could trust with anything. Feeling his love caused the cement layer to crack and fall to the ground, and in that moment, my young self realized she had made a very big mistake to have married the man to whom I promised my life *until death do us part.*

I was well aware that being around someone who does not have such a layer might disturb people who are too afraid to let go of their protective layers. It is too painful to become aware of how confined we are when we find someone who is not covered over. I knew that as long as he believed he needed to wear his cement layer, Jake would not be happy with my true self shining into his world, as he expressed so clearly when I was joyously happy because of the invitation to Washington, D.C. In that moment, this young aspect of myself knew that she could not remain in the marriage and live.

My inner mate threw his arm around my young self's waist and said, *"Lets get out of here!"* and I felt as if I were my young self experiencing the power of my inner mate. The two of us started running through an enchanted field filled with the most aromatic flowers. I was with my best buddy again and nothing else mattered. I sensed that he was the one who wanted to play when we were both two years old, chasing butterflies and squealing with delight at all the wonders that were around us.

Bill asked if I would be willing to look at this man, not as a childhood playmate, or even the young man who was my best buddy, but as the *Adonis* that he is. It was as if a veil was lifted from my eyes, and my best friend became the man of my dreams. I was in total shock. I had never seen him before as the one to whom all of my being could open, and I felt it with such an amazing rush of energy; I knew I was in love… for the first time in my life it was safe to surrender to a man, to feel all my feelings, the amazing sensual, sexual feelings. It was safe to be in communion with God, and I knew that Jon-Luke would not steal my energy for himself. He didn't need mine; he had his own.

I saw the two of us in a lover's bed, surrounded by flower petals and soft light. We were holding each other, face-to-face, looking into each other's eyes; and I felt totally safe. I had never known it was possible to be fully me, nothing hidden, and be so fully open, vulnerable and so close to a man. He could see me with all my flaws and love me unconditionally, and I could see him exactly as he is, accept him, and love him unconditionally, as well. What a gift! My best friend was my lover. Bill reminded me that my inner mate does not need my energy; his only wish is my openness.

Because my rigid interpretation of what it meant to be a woman came from my mother, Bill asked if I would be willing to open the door to the room where my mother's inner mate had been confined. I saw her gasp, and in an instant she was lost in his arms, loving him with a love like she had wished she could have found in my father, but it was never there. And then I saw the amazing sight of inner mates coming to be with my grandparents, great grandparents, going back as far as I could see …on both sides of my family, men and women alike, finding and surrendering in love to their inner mates, knowing for the first time what it meant to experience unconditional love. The energy was so, so profoundly beautiful. I felt as if I were a small child experiencing fireworks exploding around the magical Disneyland Castle for the very first time.

This was such a magnificently transforming experience. I know that I carry the energies of my ancestors in my DNA, and as a result of the work I did with Bill, I was changing the energy of my own DNA.

Almost immediately after this life-altering experience with my inner mate, I knew I still had to work with the Mid Western woman from the 1800s, me in a past life, who stood tall and stiff backed, feeling self-righteous pride in the fact that she was a virgin, and would remain a virgin all of her life. No matter what question Bill asked her, she remained steadfast in her belief that because she had not succumbed to sex, she was somehow superior to the vast majority of people who had given in to their sexual impulses. She was the most rigid of all the aspects of myself with whom I have ever worked, and I was not sure how I would break her insistence that she was superior to Bill, to me, and all the others who tried to connect with her.

Finally, I asked her if she was happy with how she lived her life. The more I looked at her, the more she began to age. She turned from a proud young woman who felt secure in the fact that she had total control over her life to a withered old woman, all dried up like a prune with little life left in her, yet, she was still feeling proud of her decision to remain abstinent. Bill asked her what she thought of Jesus having a love relationship with Mary Magdalene, and then asked her if she believed she was superior to Jesus because he had a sexual relationship with the woman he loved. This woman from the past-life became very confused. She didn't know how to take this all in. At first, she wanted to reject Bill's comment about Jesus and Mary as a lie, until Jesus told her that it was true. Hearing his words seemed to open the virgin's eyes to see what she never allowed herself to see before. She began to look around to see all that she had missed in life. In the middle of all the violence, the pain, and agony of life, there were moments of love, even in the animal kingdom. She saw the wonder of love and lovemaking, everywhere. I began to cry.

This woman had been taught by her bitter mother that men were evil, that sex was evil, and she best never, ever give in to the wicked urges of the world. To win her mother's love, this past life self accepted her mother's world-view; however, her angry mother didn't love her daughter any more because of the alignment of the two on this issue. Her mother was incapable of loving the "me" that I was in that past life because she hated herself. As self-righteous as her mother was, the woman had to have had sex to give birth to a daughter; so mother had violated her own rules of abstinence. She had blamed sex for resulting in a child, and blamed the child for her young husband leaving her, a thought that turned her into a bitter woman. She passed her bitterness onto her daughter, and I carried those beliefs into this life. Instead of celebrating her womanhood, this former self condemned it and lived her whole life shutting down and turning away from one of the most magnificent gifts of life. For the first time, I was able to see how this unhealed energy pattern in me had drawn to me the mother I had in this life who demonstrated some of the same attitudes as did that bitter mother and myself as the daughter 150 years or more ago.

My past-life self began to look around at everything in nature, and for the first time saw that by maintaining that rigidity to prove to her mother that she was worthy, she had lost connection with a glorious part of life. She had so effectively separated herself from living, that she had spent her entire life not being alive. She began to cry with tears of deep remorse. I held her in my arms and let her know that I am her in a future life, and that she and I, together, could learn the goodness of surrender...of completely letting go...to experience communion with our inner God Essence and surrender to another person who experienced his own God Essence and could honor and love mine.

As Bill and I finished our work, I realized that though I have had profound experiences with *Sandy God Essence* and had many times I felt embraced by the arms of the angels, and merged into the light of Spirit, I had never *completely* surrendered. It was in that moment that I decided that I would take the leap into the void by surrendering to a process that could carry me, perhaps deeper than I have ever gone, past the passageways that lead to upper floors, past the airfields out into the Universe and into other dimensions, allowing all aspects of myself to go wherever the Universe, which I hold within, would take me. More than anything, I wanted to be able to experience complete surrender by releasing any remaining false identity so that all of who I am could merge with *Sandy God Essence*, the mystical magical, mysterious me that has been patiently waiting for me to choose union with my true being.

Not long after the call with Bill, I registered for the trip to Brazil and began making plans to participate in something I had never thought I would do.

***

The experience I had in Brazil touched the deepest places that I had not been able to access before, at least not to the level I did on that ceremonial night. My intention was to bring forward and release the belief I held my whole life that there is no place for me here, a belief that had become embedded in my DNA during gestation, coming from my father's energy that wrapped around and permeated his sperm that said, "*I do not want children'* and my mother's energy, which was wrapped around and saturated her egg that said, *"I do not want another girl, I want the boy I've been waiting for my entire life."* The energy field that surrounded fetus Sandy had a message that became deeply embedded in her DNA; the message was, *"If you come, you are not wanted by your father and if you are a girl neither of us want you...there is no place for you here."* I was another girl, the third "mistake," born three days before my older sister turned a year old...and every year of my life, I was reminded that I ruined my sister's first birthday. This was a message that my coming even disrupted my siblings...so, *"There is no place for you here, you unwanted and disrupting third child."* My unconscious response to not being wanted was to not want to be here, to not want to be in a body and to not want to experience all the joy and wonder of being in a body. A corollary of that belief was that because I was not wanted, I didn't have a place her in this world, I didn't belong anywhere.

Over the years, I processed this belief of not belonging any place in this world, but something never felt completed. This core issue of not being wanted had separated an unknown aspect of me from my *Sandy God Essence*...and though I worked with many parts of myself that held this belief, there was something that still gnawed at my solar plexus every time I even thought about stepping into what seemed like it might be my place in the world.

When I first began to form what I wanted to have as my ceremonial focus, I decided that I wanted to be able to fully surrender to *Sandy God Essence* in such a way that I could come from this magnificent place all the time, or at least as much as would be humanly possible. But prior to the ceremony, as my friend Oregon David, who had decided to travel with me and attend the ceremony, talked about both of our intentions for our spiritual journeys, I came to see that I was skirting the issue of my place in the world and using one goal to create another. If I could surrender to *Sandy God Essence*, I believed I would be able to love and be loved, and, therefore, feel that I belonged. But what I really wanted was to release the belief that made me live as if there is no place for me, even when there has been ample proof in my life that there has always been a place.

I was sure the body pain I lived with nearly my whole life had been, in part, the result a war between two parts of me. One part of me longed to reach out to people with whom I wanted to feel a sense of connection, of belonging, and to whom I wanted to surrender in total safety, but the other part resisted reaching out to anyone for fear all people out there would be like my parents who were supposed to love me and embrace me as belonging to them, but didn't. This part of me feared any surrender would be met with others pushing me away, too. The internal war between reaching out and holding back had created a huge amount of body pain in my tendons and muscles that hadn't responded to any medication I'd ever taken or hadn't found full healing from all the internal work I had done over the years. All these things—body pain, not feeling wanted, fear of taking my place, and my conscious self not fully surrendering to *Sandy God Essence* within me—felt intricately entangled, and though I didn't know how it could happen, I wanted it to all find healing.

Dusk had turned to night and the only light in a very large ceremonial lodge was coming from candles. The shaman and his apprentices entered the lodge; they were dressed in their ceremonial regalia, necklaces made of panther's teeth, feathered headdresses. They wore bones in their noses and had markings on their bodies. They sat in front of a semicircle of participants, at first in total silence, and then they began chanting. As the ceremony commenced, each person went forward and was offered a cup of the tea made from Amazonian plants. When it was my turn, I kneeled down in front of the altar and accepted the cup from the hands of the shaman. I had expected it to taste like the muddy herbal medicines I had taken in China when I had gotten deathly sick with meningitis, but it was not so very thick and it had an almost delicate taste to it. I understood that the shaman and his apprentices had spent 4 days and nights preparing the plants, boiling them and praying over them before they were ready to conduct the ceremony. Their prayers invited the plant spirits to become exactly what the participants needed for their soul journeys. I returned to the mat I had been sitting on, on the floor, feeling no special changes in my consciousness, so I watched as the rest of the participants took the cup and drank their portion of tea.

In time, I closed my eyes and began to see images of beautiful plants swirling around within me, and I gave permission for the branches and vines to expand throughout my body and into the connections in my brain to do whatever they needed to bring healing. Seeing these images was very similar to most of my unassisted meditative healing journey images. As I began this visualization, which entwined the energies of the physical plants embedded in the tea and internal plant energy I carry within me, I sensed that various parts of my body were sending screaming messages of pain to the entwined plant energies to come bring relief, and in moments after pain rose up, it dissipated in place after place, throughout my whole body.

Then I saw light gray images, silhouetted against a dark grey back drop, of many past life figures I've worked with over the years in meditation, in various therapy sessions, and in dreams. I gave these figures permission to release any beliefs that remained embedded in them and, therefore, in my soul's DNA, and carried into this life, especially beliefs related to my being a mistake or not belonging as reflected by the way I lived or died in those past life stories. This all seemed significant, and, yet, there still seemed to be something missing.

The past life images faded and I became aware of the sounds of what they called people "getting healed" around me; I was pleased to notice that I was not being triggered by the sounds of gagging and throwing up, which is a usual part of this kind of ceremony. The belief is when the body is ready to release the toxins related to unhealed experiences and beliefs, it voids the poisons by vomiting. I had always gotten empathetically sick in the past when anyone got sick and threw up. My immediate thought was that over the years of healing and developing healthy boundaries, I had moved away from taking on others' energies by becoming sick to help them release their sickness. I had come to a place where other people's processes and responses were not being absorbed by me. It felt like an affirmation that was important to acknowledge in this grounded reflection of my personal growth.

As the night wore on, I was not feeling any particular body sensation and wondered if I ought to participate in a second ceremonial drink of the medicine, so I asked my body if it wanted me to take in more medicine-tea. I received a resounding, yes. So I went forward. Again, I waited for what seemed like quite some time and had no sensation. Closing my eyes brought me no imaging at all, and after a while, I decided to observe the ceremonies of others, sending love to them for whatever they might need.

In time, I became aware that I needed to use the restroom, so I got up, and as quietly as I could, walked past others who were obviously deeply involved in their processes and stepped into the bathroom. After sitting down, but before releasing anything, I became extremely nauseous, so I quickly stood up, turned around and lifted the seat, squatted down to prepare for my stomach to release...

I was aware that my head was beyond dizzy; I felt extremely light headed, my heart was beating so fast, and I felt impossibly weak; the feeling was very similar to what I had experienced many years before when I had a system wide infection that nearly took my life. Back then, I had become weak, extremely sick, and was not able to lift my head from a pillow to even turn over without feeling like I was dying. I was in my 30s at the time and told my husband that I was afraid something was very wrong. He recommended that I just stay in bed until I felt better, and he went off to work. But the truth was that I was not sure I would be alive when he returned. When he walked out that morning, I remember feeling so sad that he was more concerned about getting to work than noticing what was happening to me, but dismissed that thought and tried to sleep.

When he returned home, Jake saw how sick I was and helped me into the bathroom so I could bathe, while he called to get an appointment with my doctor. He returned to the bathroom and helped me out of the tub, but when I stepped out, I collapsed on the floor, was unconscious, and voided completely all over the floor, messing myself up in the process. He had heard somewhere that it was not unusual for people to release urine and feces when they die. When I was not responsive, lying on the floor in my waste, he thought I had died. But a few minutes later,

I revived, though I was extremely weak, and he helped wash me off and dressed me, because I couldn't do anything myself.

The trip to the doctor's office felt life threatening; every turn in the road caused nausea so immense I thought I would die, and every stop felt like my head would explode. The doctor saw me almost immediately, and then called my husband into the exam room to tell him to get me to the hospital immediately. He later told my husband that I was likely just a few hours away from death from full septic shock, as my body organs had begun to shut down. It took a week in the hospital with IVs dripping, oxygen flowing, and many other procedures given to restore me to health.

That night at the ceremony, I believe, I was dealing with another kind of septic shock, which seemed to have affected my body very much like the physical experience when I was in my 30s, While in the bathroom that first night of the ceremony, feeling like death was calling me, just like before, I'd become very light headed and then passed out. Based on the position in which I found myself when I revived, I must have fallen backward from the squatting position in front of the toilet, and ended up with my back and head against the wall and my feet spread apart on either side of the toilet. I don't know how long I was there, but sometime later, I was aware of a whole series of hallucinations that finally caused me to recognize that this is what others reported when they were seeing visions. On waking, I had no idea where I was and couldn't make any sense of what I was seeing. Slowly I became aware of the floor, the toilet and being very wet. I had vomited down my jacket and I was laying in a great amount of urine that had soaked into my under clothing and covered the floor under and beside me. For a moment, I remembered that there had been a candle on the floor, which I must have knocked over when I fell, but I forgot to do anything about the candle.

It took me a few minutes to orient myself, and pull myself up, remove all my clothing but my dress. Though I was still very weak, I began to clean up the mess I had made on the floor. After washing my face and rinsing my mouth, I very shakily walked out into the foyer and sat down on a bench near the exit to regroup, but that didn't seem to be enough.

I decided it would be good to go out into the fresh air, but in a few minutes became aware that the cold air didn't alleviate the feeling that I was very near death. I sat down for about 20 minutes when I began to experience that familiar overwhelming feeling of nausea. So, I walked toward a tree, held onto it for support, and began to vomit again. The same thing happened as occurred in the bathroom earlier and many years before in my bathroom at home. I fell without knowing that I had fallen. I awakened sometime later by magnificent colors and images in a long series of scenes that ended with seeing a psychedelically painted Volkswagen, which finally sent the message to my conscious mind that this was not a part of my familiar reality. Though my eyes were open, I opened my eyes in another way, which allowed me to see my three-dimensional surroundings; although in that moment, I had no idea where I was or how I got there. And then it all came back despite the sensation that I way lying on the ground in a field of snow next to the tree and realized I had gone through another monumental experience.

My whole body was very cold; I knew I needed to get up and return to the building before the cold penetrated too deeply enough to freeze me to death, but I couldn't get up until I talked to the young wife who lay near death in her home on the bathroom floor 30 years before. I remembered, that horrible day so long ago when I was all by myself going in and out of consciousness as I lay dying in my bed. And I remembered my thoughts that my husband didn't care for me or love me enough to notice that I was near death. I had been so afraid of knowing the truth back then that I pushed it aside and had remembered only that he picked me up and washed me off after I had collapsed getting out of the tub. I told my young-wife-self that it was okay to accept knowing the truth that I was not loved the way I deserved to be loved, and I invited her to let go of her resistance to knowing the truth. She believed that because he did not love her, she didn't belong anywhere. I invited her to join me in 2010. I asked all parts of me who had accepted the lie that I did not belong, and that I had no value and no worth because I was a mistake—a thought that I took to mean there was no place for me in this world—to release the lie and accept the truth. Intrinsically entwined with the truth that there *was, is, and always will be a place for me*, was another truth that those I wanted so desperately to love me—first my parents and then my husband—were incapable of loving me because they had long before lost the ability to love themselves. Being with them felt like being so very cold, just as in my vision of waking up in a field of snow. *My not getting their love was not about me, about my worthiness of being loved, or my having a rightful place in this world; it was about their own wounding.*

I returned to the building and after sitting in the foyer for another few minutes, I knew I could not lie down again. Everything inside was telling me that if I did lay myself down, I would not get back up again, so I stood in the kitchen area, leaning against the counter. My brain felt so very swollen inside, much like it felt the night I fell on the ice just before Christmas, just 4 months before when I hit my head so hard that I had a 3 inch-crack in my skull. I waited a couple of days before going to the doctor, who after checking things out, told me that had I gone to bed right after that fall, I might have died from internal bleeding following the concussion. Somehow, I felt similar energies that ceremonial night in Brazil, and like that night in Colorado, I knew I needed to remain standing after the two fainting incidents, rather than return to the group room and lie back down on my mat. Though I didn't feel as if I had, I might have hit my head again in the two falls and aggravated the concussion.

One of the apprentices noticed I had been gone a long time and came out to see if I was okay. I told him that though I wasn't doing well, I really was okay. I was grateful, so grateful, for his loving support and his response of letting me use my best judgment of where I needed to be. I wanted to return to the main room, but again, I received the strong message not to lie down. After a long time of standing, I moved into the dining room and sat at the table for another long period of time, though I don't know how long. Time seemed to have lost meaning.

Then two people came in to get me for what they called the *Olympia healing ceremony*, which was earlier described as a powerful healing process where people are invited to disrobe, as much as they feel comfortable, and receive a special healing blessing from the shamans. My first thought was, *I couldn't take off my dress*. I had nothing on underneath because of the bathroom experience, and I was alert enough to know still-self-conscious Fat Sandy would be too devastated to be naked in front of a room full of people. The two who had come to get me both said it didn't matter; I could receive the blessing fully clothed. As they walked me into the large room, they assured me again that I didn't have to take anything off and asked me to sit on a pillow in front of the Shaman. I felt as if I had been transported back in time about a thousand years as his deep dark eyes and black hair shimmered in the candlelight and his dark brown skin glowed. He looked into my eyes as if he could see everything in me and still loved me. I had no idea what was happening, or why I had been selected to sit in a place that looked like it had been prepared just for me. I sat down and began to receive the most beautiful energy I had ever felt directed towards me in my entire life. I was being touched on my head, my shoulders, and back with gigantic feathers and was welcomed with healing energy, sounds, and sensations that penetrated into my very DNA. The Shaman and his apprentices began to dance around me, while drumming, rattling, and singing, as had been practiced in ancient rituals. The foot stomping of the dance was so intense I could feel the vibration in my bones. It was as if their dance was sending a vibration into the Earth, and the Earth was responding with a connecting resonation, and I felt as if I was both the stomping energy and the Earth receiving the vibration.

As they circled around me, the Shaman and apprentices created a vortex of energy that grounded me onto the Earth in a way I had never felt before. Chanting in a language I did not know, but somehow my body seemed to know, created a resonance with my soul; each person seemed to be sending in the message that I belonged...I have a place, and in that moment, the place I belonged was in the center of the circle, receiving love and healing from six beautiful, powerful beings. The Shaman filled his mouth with holy water and began another ritual of spraying me with the water, as if washing off all that was not true, and I felt my heart shields crumble; the false message that I was not wanted, and, therefore, did not belong, a message I carried since before my birth, which seemed to have been confirmed when I took my first breath in this lifetime, melted away.

I could feel the truth in my body, in my cells, in my DNA, that I belonged…something that was confirmed in the most beautiful hugs all six shamans and apprentices gave me, hugs my infant self was finally able to feel and receive from a place of truth. What an amazing journey! My eyes fill with tears even now as I write this and I feel the truth resonating in my being. Something I had long since known in my head became engraved in my heart, in my cells, and in my DNA. The message to an infant saying, *"We don't want you; there is no place for you here"* dissolved when met with the truth on Earth Day, 2010, a message that I belong because I am here.

What an amazing transformation that had been, and what a blessing that it took place on such an auspicious day that shouted to me that I belong on the Earth. I was finally able to take into my heart, my body, my cells, my DNA… the messages I have been hearing all my life from people who have known me and loved me, that they are glad I came into their lives, that I am valuable, worthwhile, and worthy of love. My head knew the truth of these words, and my heart could take in only a little of the truth, but because of that amazing experience, my heart and body finally were able to receive the truth that came to me as I sat on a pillow in front of a shaman, in a special place that had been prepared especially for me. I had been the only one who was specially called out to experience the Olympia healing energy, all by myself. What an amazing counterbalance to the message I received prior to my coming into this world and at my birth! I didn't know why I was selected for the special ritual, but I suspect the Shaman's God Essence must have been listening to mine and together they conspired to create this healing.

Though I had not spoken my intention to anyone but Oregon David, I felt as if the Shaman and his apprentices had heard the words of my soul and had given me what I needed to experience, just like Bill said would happen. From the beginning of the ceremony until this very moment writing about that experience, whenever I look inward, I see my life force embedded in a profusion of green branches, vines, and leaves flowing throughout my body aligning with my own life force bringing healing with every intention.

When I awoke the next morning, I knew my body could not take in any more. I was feeling both very strong, and extremely fragile. I had to respect the need my body had to process and regain its strength from this monumental transformation. I had lived my entire life with a low-grade infection in my energy field, and I believe as I began to consider taking my books and my teachings out into the world on a much grander scale, fear of the world and my not being wanted by it caused the infection to burst into an energetically septic state that came to the surface when I prepared my intention for the ceremony. I knew I had to give my body rest and the time to absorb all that had happened without pushing it into another experience.

David had had his own version of an explosively monumental experience that had impacted him as deeply as I had been impacted and both of us knew we needed to be with the changes rather than introduce more. I was unable to eat anything the next day and into the following day. Feeling just on the edge of nausea and fainting, I had a very strong sense that a third collapse might be the final one, so I had to be very attentive to my body's needs. By the end of the third day, the pounding headache had dissipated and I was able to hear without feeling as if I were deep under water, and the swooshing dizziness faded. I was finally able walk without feeling as if I might fall over from weakness. I was ready to return home.

***

Not long after that experience in Brazil, I began to see other connections to that feeling of coming back from death. When I tried to end the horror that defined my life as a little girl of eight by breathing in the car fumes, something I wrote about in *Behind the Mask,* I had felt the same symptoms as before being hospitalized when I was in my 30's and these were the same symptoms following the powerful medicine ceremony in early 2010. It took a few more weeks for me to discover a deeper level of healing that needed to happen for me to fully embrace being alive in my body on this planet.

***

I had been thinking about a conversation Oregon David and I had after our time together in Brazil, regarding the deep sadness we both seemed to feel often because we sensed that 49 out of 50 people in the world would not want to embrace the understandings both of us believe are so crucial to the future of humankind. We both had a tendency to focus on the 49, trying to figure out how to convince them of the goodness of the truths we teach, and in the process, too often, we neglected the 1 out of 49 who are or would be interested.

Our discussion was in my thoughts as I went to the Inipi Sweat Lodge one Saturday afternoon soon after my return from Brazil. I am sure it was the hottest the lodge had ever been, and despite the intensity of the heat, it was okay that I stayed the entire 3.5 hours; I had given myself permission to leave at any time my body gave me the signal. Like at the last lodge ceremony, I sensed the presence of all those shamans and spirit guides from many different times in human history and from many cultures. They had come to support whatever I needed, though I didn't really have a focus as I usually had when I participated in such ceremonies. Whenever these ancient holy spirit-beings appear in my visions, I know something very important is going to happen.

Even before we began the prayers in the second round, I saw a vision of veils being torn down allowing so many people to see lives they had lived in the past in which they had experienced the other side of what they have experienced in this life...perpetrators were seeing themselves as victims and victims were seeing themselves as perpetrators. Rich people were seeing lives they lived as a part of the great downtrodden masses, and the downtrodden were seeing lives when they were wealthy. Slaves were seeing themselves as slave owners and law enforcement people were seeing themselves as criminals in past lives. I was seeing that fathers who raped their daughters saw themselves as daughters who were raped, and daughters saw themselves as rapists in past lives. This concept had been familiar to me, as I had written in *Behind the Mask,* when I worked with my own past life as a military officer who used his power and position to viciously and destructively kick a man who was a subordinate in that life, and I was in shock when I discovered he was my father in this life.

I believe the sweat lodge vision was showing me a profound opening of human consciousness in our world. I felt compelled to tell the others gathered in the lodge what I was seeing and what I concluded about what I saw. I believed I was seeing the final result of this expanded awareness in many people, which ended judgment of self and others and caused rage to melt away. All of those whose veils were torn away finally understood how we are all interconnected, even through lifetimes, far too often by negative patterns, resulting in living stories of pain and suffering. My vision showed me that what these people discovered in the tearing of the veils was they didn't need to play out those negative dramas any more. When those patterns were released, for the first time in lifetimes, they could live freely and experience life from wholeness. It was profoundly moving to see this and express it to the others, and somehow, I knew this was to be a part of what I would be teaching in the future to whatever people would be open to hear.

During the prayer time, I prayed for my own ability to release the residues of what keeps me back from becoming my whole self in this world and I prayed to be able to focus on the ones who are ready instead of those who are not. And also, I prayed that I would remain open to those who might tap on the door of conscious expansion. I said thanks to the lodge energies, the grandfathers, grandmothers, spirits, and shamans for answering every prayer I had ever prayed in the lodge. The prayers and the lodge experience felt profoundly cleansing on so many levels and seemed so appropriate on the heels of the Brazil experience that let me know in my body that I belonged here on the earth.

The day following the lodge experience, a client called to share with me an experience she had regarding awareness gained during an inner journey the day before, apparently, about the same time I was in the lodge. She had been struggling with a relationship that was not working and had considering ending it. In her vision, she saw a whole string of past lives with this person, each one filled with struggle, where her partner had consistently chosen to live his life from the dark side. She looked into her own dark side tendencies and embraced those parts of her who felt so estranged from the light, and decided she no longer needed this man to reflect to her what she had not faced inside herself because she was now willing to face it and deal with what she was holding internally. She decided to leave him. I was deeply moved by the synchronicity of her work and mine.

***

The following week, I had in my schedule to go to Longmont to see Shar for a balancing session, to see a dentist to get my teeth cleaned, and on the way back to stop off at Whole Foods in Boulder to get another week's supply of Organic food. For the first time in my life, I found new pleasure in making healthy meals for myself. And I was actually cooking. Before, I had no interest in cooking unless I was doing it for someone else to enjoy.

But what I hadn't planned was a deeply moving experience coming from the Tibetan Cranial session. Like with the Sweat Lodge, I had no agenda. As a matter of fact, I had been feeling really quite good, and very balanced and only decided to see about a session because it seemed a shame to drive all the way to Longmont for the dental appointment and not work with Shar.

During the first half of the session, Shar indicated how balanced my energy was, and as she continued to check the more subtle and deeply buried connective pulses, we talked about our experiences with the cleanse process and food balancing we had both been doing. In the relatively short time I had been back from Brazil, I lost 35 pounds, and I planned to continue the balanced eating as I had been doing.

But then, about half way through the session, Shar asked me if something was happening to me around my heart. She sensed that there was something very old going on. I was surprised because I was not aware of anything. I really had been feeling so happy...though I hadn't written anything for *Under the Mask* for quite a while. With all that had happened in the previous weeks, it didn't occur to me to ask what might be blocking my progress.

When she asked about my heart, and what might be disturbing it, I began thinking about a trip to Seattle that was coming up for my mother's 94th birthday, and I mentioned it to Shar, but added that

I didn't think it was causing disturbance. She asked how I felt about going, and without giving a feeling response, I told her that every time I have ever gone home, I had always gained 10 pounds, almost exactly, but when I returned to wherever I was living, I would lose what I had gained over the next week or so. I told her I didn't want to do that ever again, especially not since I had experienced such great success with the cleansing program I had begun. Then she asked me again, how I felt about going. And I couldn't answer. I just lay there on the Tibetan table in confusion. When she asked if maybe there was someplace I'd rather go, I said that I wasn't sure I really wanted to take the trip, but the truth was, I didn't know where else I could go.

After a period of silence, I told Shar I kept seeing images of my mother's face and I felt sad. I told her about the conversation I had with Oregon David...how both of us tended to focus on the 49 instead of the 1, and that I felt going home was like not just focusing on the 49, but also, entering the energy vortex of the 49, which always made my heart ache. I felt as if I could not be me when I entered that vortex. She asked me why not, and as before, I couldn't answer.

And then I began talking about my mother, saying I no longer hold any hope that she will change. For some reason, I completely shifted the conversation to the early 1990s when the Florida therapist I was working with suggested that I reconnect with music and singing by visiting a few of the huge local churches that have big bands and lots of congregational singing in the service. I followed his suggestion, but going to those churches literally made me so sad I couldn't stop crying, so I had to leave the churches. Shar asked why I cried, and I told her I thought it was because churches with music used to be the one place I felt at home, but I no longer felt at home in that energy...I didn't have a home with my family, and I didn't have a home anymore in churches.

Even though so many churches professed to be places of love, what I so often felt underneath the love was huge amounts of fear and painful judgment. Tears began to well up, as I confessed to Shar that no place has ever really felt like home to me my whole life. I believed the sadness I've felt under my laughter and joy has been related to feeling like I don't have a home. I was also aware of another truth for me: when I react to something in pain, in fear, or anger, or any of the other dark energies, what I see in others is in myself, as well. So my sadness was not just about love being missing in churches or in my mother's home, it was love missing in me, too. And my awareness of fear and judgment in church members was evidence that I still held fear and judgment of them. As long as I was not connected to love, but attached to fear and judgment, I would never be able to feel at home, anywhere.

I sensed that my trip to Brazil let me know I belonged on the Earth, and the next layer that needed to be healed rose up, which was the belief that even if I do belong on the Earth, I have no home here. And I remembered an old religious country song that said, *"This world is not my home I'm just a passing through. My treasures are laid up somewhere beyond the blue. The angels beckon me from heaven's open door. And I can't feel at home in this world anymore."* The problem was that a very sad part of me didn't feel at home in this world, but didn't believe she was wanted in the next world, beyond the blue, either.

Shar noticed that my child self was very present as tears streamed down my cheeks, and she asked if the tears had words. At first, there were no words, only deep mournful sadness, which was so painful I thought my heart would stop. I felt I was an infant without words; all that came to me was an image of my mother's face that would not let me connect with her heart. She looked *at* me, but not *into* me and everything in me wanted, needed, to have her look into my eyes and see me and let me look into her eyes so I could see her...but she wouldn't, or maybe couldn't do that. The feeling was as if I were being locked outside, and not allowed to come in. I've worked with this experience several times in the past, but this time was different. I felt myself as the infant trying so hard to find the passageway to connect with my mother's soul. If I could only see into the place where she could love me, I would be able to feel safe with her. But she just couldn't let me in.

The other gift she couldn't give me was the assurance that, in fact, I was inside this new little body, that this little body contained me... and the assurance that everything I was feeling in the tiny body was it welcoming me and telling my spirit-self this was where I belonged. This new body was giving me information about this physical world, and once I knew that the body was mine, connected to me, related to me, and interacting with me, my awareness could become one with it. But I never got that gift from my mother because she didn't know how to gaze into my eyes and see my spirit in my eyes. So, not only did I not feel her welcome on my first day in this world as Sandy, I did not feel my body's welcome. My soul felt as if it didn't have a home in my body or in the arms of my mother. It didn't take long for me to discover that the very idea of home either in my parents' house or in my body was that home was an unsafe place that would threaten my very existence in this world.

As I was re-experiencing my first day on this planet, and the deep pain of having been born into the darkness of the 49, I saw an image that was a part of one of my very first alchemical hypnotherapy sessions back in the early 90s when I was in training to be a clinical hypnotherapist. During that session, I had spontaneously gone back to my nearly 8-year-old child-self who had decided she no longer wanted to live. Her life experience told her that the pain of being in that family and in my body would not end, and it would keep getting worse and worse. That is when I put my head under a blanket and breathed in the exhaust fumes from the family car, believing that if I did that, I would go to sleep and never wake up, something my mother told my older sister when my sibling had been breathing in fumes from an idling car near our house.

While in that asphyxiated state, I had left my body and was on my way back home to Spirit, but I seemed to have come upon an energy field that blocked my ability to get through it. I could see to the other side, but somehow the field was configured so I could not pass through it. I called out to God that I wanted to come home, but it felt like he didn't hear me. I began to beat on the energy field with my fists and my request became a howling, tearful pleading to be let me in, and then the pleading turned into a wailing cry filled with terrified anguish, begging for entry. I was sure the ones on the other side must have heard me, but for some horrible reason, none were responding. It was as if all the wicked darkness of the world was at my heels, threatening to devour me, and the blocking energy field was not shifting to allow me the safety of returning to my true eternal home.

Apparently, there was something about all this that I had not, yet, healed, because all the feelings as well as the terror had come back again, as if it were the first time. And then I found myself on the pavement along side the Alaska highway, again, just after my mother found me unconscious in the back seat, but this time, instead of observing this whole scene from above as I had before, I was the child, laying on the blanket, feeling the awakening and experiencing the realization that I had not been able to *go to sleep and not wake up*. I had not been able to break through the energy field and go home...to the only place in the universe that I knew had a place for me, which I believed meant that even that place that I thought was my true spiritual home didn't want me, either. A huge part of the sadness I've carried all my life had to do with the belief that I have no home, not even with the One. I shared with Shar that I had never felt like I had a home, I had never felt at home anywhere I'd ever lived, my whole life.

My awareness returned to the child who first believed she was truly homeless. She is the part of me who was still wailing in desperation pleading for the energy field to release and let her come home. I reached out to her and told her that her home was with me in my heart. I let her know that she would forever be welcome there. Something gigantic shifted in me. I felt the presence of the child in my heart as a release so deep when the energy represented by this little part of me let go and melted into my heart.

I was telling all this to Shar when a wave of intense energy washed through the part of me still on the blanket, alongside the highway. My body was writhing with nausea and I began to heave as if I were vomiting. And then I began to wail...crying out words that had been locked inside me since I was that little girl, so long ago. The words slipped out in a child's voice between sobs, *"I don't want to wake up...I don't want to wake up...I don't want to wake up"* and I kept repeating the phrase over and over again; each time the words became more intense and filled with the agony of my child-self, until there was no energy left for the protest.

Only moments before, I had brought home the part of me that split off and attempted to leave but had felt blocked by the energy wall, and for decades had experienced life from the part of me feeling the pain and agony beating against the energy field that would not let her die to this life. But now, I was experiencing the part of me who woke up on the blanket. While every cell in my body joined in the cry, I began to hear something else in those words. I realized they also represented the words of not wanting to wake up from the dream, from the mass-induced hypnotic state that eons ago caused us to believe we are the roles we play, the masks we wear…and for the first time since I began walking this path toward consciousness, I understood how painful it is for the 49 to wake up to discover who they really are. I realized how terrifying waking up had been to my barely awakened self in the world of 49.

In order for my child self to find a way to fit in with my family and at least superficially feel like I had a home, I had to allow my conscious awareness of my true self to go to sleep. I had asphyxiated my own being; I sacrificed my knowing who I really am to live in the dream—or more accurately, the nightmare—of my family, for that matter the nightmarish dream of most the human species, the 49 out of 50 who are living in not knowing. I finally understood why it was so difficult for me to return to my family and to the people I used to know who are still asleep and might do anything to keep from waking up. As long as a terrified part of me remained separated from my awakened self, I would be triggered by those around me who were still asleep or on the verge of waking, but resisting it.

In that moment, I invited the other two little Sandy parts of me: the newborn who was in agony for having been born and the 8-year-old who had been lamenting waking up for decades, to come into my heart and join with the other aspect of my 8-year-old self who had pleaded to go home and finally found her home in my heart. I let all three of them know that together, we could build a home where they would always know they were welcome and safe. I let them look into my eyes and see *Sandy God Essence* in me and they could see me looking into them and seeing that same essence in them, too. We could see the essence in each other because it is the same essence. And, we could see it in others because, though each person is unique, the substance of the essence is the same. My infant self finally had a home to come home to and for the first time in decades knew that she had a home in her body. I could see how that home would expand outward into the world where I could reach out to other people, who are the 1 in the 50, and the 2 in 50 and the 3 in 50...or, perhaps someday, to all 50 when they have eyes to see, ears to hear, and hearts to open to the open arms of another. I was filled with such peace, following the moment these three parts of me had finally come home.

I believe that because of the work I had done in Brazil where I had been able to experience feeling as if I had no place and then feeling my place created in the Olympia Ceremony, what did not match the truth of my belonging was able to come forward into consciousness for healing.

As I reflected more deeply into this experience, I also realized that the energy field that kept me from entering my true home with *Universal God Essence* was not created by God to keep me out, it was a shield at the top of my Crown Chakra, created by *Sandy God Essence* to keep me in where I belonged, but as a child, I didn't know it yet.

While driving from Shar's, back to my mountain cabin, I was thinking about so many clients that were like I had been most of my life, engaged in self-sacrifice behaviors in their marriages and with families. But as they healed, they could see the damage these behaviors caused not only them, but their families, as well; however, it was not uncommon for the family to use guilt or shame to get them back to the old patterns that the spouses, families, and others had come to depend upon. It can feel like such a loss to step away from the 49 when our families are included in that group, and it can feel also feel so painful to return to the family when they still choose to not want to wake up. I am glad I woke up and have chosen to continue to find any other aspects of myself that may still sleep, so they can wake up, and know they are home, too. Because of that phenomenal work with Shar, I was no longer afraid to go to my mother's birthday party.

REFLECTIONS IN A POND

After Oregon David and I left Brazil and returned to our respective homes, I began a weight loss protocol that I had been thinking about for some time, something I will write about in more detail in a future book. And after about a week on the plan, just about two weeks following that amazing experience in Brazil, I woke at 5:45 to Jenny's whines telling me she needed to go outside. So, I went out with her and then crawled back into bed because I felt like I needed at least another hour of sleep. But the light was beginning to come into the windows and I couldn't get back into that sleep zone. I decided to put my yoga mask over my eyes and meditate.

I turned my focus inside to see where the controls were that had programmed me to hold onto unnecessary weight and I found myself on the outside of a building that looked really strange. It seemed to be made of a reflective metal, or maybe glass. There were two domes, one was in the forefront of this massive building and the other was to the right, and there were three pillars that looked like smokestacks of some sort to the left. The building was vibrating in a way that made it appear to come into focus and then fade away, only to come back again...all very quickly. It gave the impression of the building shimmering and shaking, sort of existing between two realities, perhaps like a mirage on a desert road.

I thought I wanted to enter the building, and with that thought, I was inside standing in front of a large control panel that appeared to be made of the same material as the building in that it was difficult to actually see, though I know it was there. On the large panel were many buttons, some lighted, some dark. There was a person in front of the panel pressing unlighted buttons to cause them to light up and pressing other buttons that had been lighted to turn them dark.

The person at the controls did not respond to my presence, so I wasn't sure if I was unnoticed or just being ignored. I told the person that it is now time for me to release the weight I'd been carrying for too long because I've become aware of my true power and my connection to the universe, so I wouldn't need to have inflated fat cells protect me anymore.

My awareness shifted to my body organs and I could see fat wrapped around my heart and lungs and all the other organs, as well. I saw an image of an uncooked skinless chicken breast with a thin layer of tissue that made it very difficult for the fat underneath to be removed from the muscle; this image seemed like what was on my own organs so I gave permission for the tissue-like membrane to melt away and flow out of my body. And, I lifted the fat cells and gave them permission to dissolve in my hands and flow away, too.

Then I found myself standing in front of my heart, which was wrapped in what looked like cellophane, and fat cells were attached to that, as well. My heart seemed very constricted and small. In the meditation, I remembered that years ago a chest x-ray revealed that my heart and lungs were small, perhaps, the size of a child's instead of an adult's organs. I was very sad when I first heard that report because I believed it meant that vital areas inside had not developed, as they should have. In the meditation, I gave permission for the cellophane to melt and the fat cells to dissolve. Then I told my heart and lungs to feel themselves stretching, expanding, and growing to their ideal size. But I let my heart know it could maintain the child-like love and openness it possesses while growing into a powerful, strong heart of a healthy woman, able to produce blood flow for a healthy adult body. I let my lungs know they could grow to the size they needed to be able to support a healthy active woman.

I began to feel tingling throughout my whole body, and then I felt pain in my arms that often wakened me in the night. It had been excruciating when I first would wake and begin to move in the morning, as my arms would experience momentary paralysis with excruciating pain shooting from the pain centers in my outer upper arms to my fingers and shoulders. After breathing through all this, I would push against the muscles and in time the pain would dissipate.

My attention went to my shoulders and I felt the pain of being held down so hard that the muscles felt like they were being smashed into the floor, into the ground, or whatever was beneath me. Then I began seeing images of women throughout history who were held down, held back, persecuted, damaged because they were women. I saw little baby girls wrapped up in rags and thrown in the garbage or along side a road in China because parents wanted a boy. Images from all over the world came through my mind of babies, girls, young women, and old women who suffered because of their gender.

***

At this point, I saw the images from one of my client's sessions that had been one of those extremely powerful experiences to witness—it is not unusual for me to enter trance state while doing sessions and actually see what the client sees, and sometimes I notice what the client does not see. She had come to work with her fear of public speaking, and for that matter, even for being seen in a public setting like a networking meeting that required her to take a minute or two, to simply introduce herself. She had registered to attend such a meeting earlier that morning, but canceled because she could not overcome the fear.

When I asked her to re-enter the experience of what it felt like to have to stand up and have all attention focused on her, she felt painful closure in her throat. When I asked if she would be willing to go back to when that feeling first arose in her, she saw an image of herself in the second grade. Though I spoke to the woman, the little girl responded to my question, *"How long have you felt this pain in your throat?"* The child said that it had been there, forever...for many lifetimes. So the woman, her child-self, and I went on a journey to the first time she had felt it lifetimes ago. Though she didn't go to a specific time, she saw another child, about the same age as her second grade child-self. The past life child appeared to be free floating, disconnected from any particular time period. My client noticed the child's throat had been slit.

After I asked if she would be willing to do so, this child took us back to before her death; we found her in what seemed like a tribal or clan-like village, where the people were dressed in animal skins. The child was very happy in her life, and had wandered off into the forest by herself. She happened onto a beautiful clearing with a small pond that drew her attention. She splashed her fingers in the water, and leaned over and was astonished to see her reflection. She looked into her own eyes and was filled with excitement for what she had found and rushed back to her camp to tell the others. She entered the women's tent and with great joy told them about the pond. The women responded so strangely, with both excitement and great fear. They told the child to never speak of the pond again. The client explained that women were not allowed to go to water and conduct water rituals, such as looking into reflections. If they did, they would be killed.

I asked my client if she would be willing to take the child and the women into the present in her lifetime to see that women are now free to do rituals by the water, to see their reflections and look into eyes, as this client has done many times in her life. These ancient women seemed so deeply grateful to be able to see that the future was not like the time in which they were living.

I reminded my client, as well as the souls of the other tribal women who had taken the journey to the present, to notice that true empowerment comes when mind/body/spirit are one and that those who have separated from spirit become weakened; this can happen to both women and men. While women tend to express their loss of empowerment by withdrawing into themselves, men often express their loss by identifying with physical strength and use force to make sure their weakness does not show. Many of these men believe they cannot be the powerful warriors fighting against other powerful warriors if their weakness were known. Out of fear of their own weakness some of the men become brutal. Though this pattern had been more prevalent in men, especially during the tribal times, it is also a pattern women can and do possess, perhaps more in the 21st century than in their time.

We returned to that past life, and the client reported that somehow, the information about the child's discovery of the pond made it's way to the men's tent. The child was called into the men's tent to tell them what she had found. She seemed so excited to tell them about the water and the reflection, and what she saw when she looked into her own eyes. In an instant, a man leaped up and slit the child's throat. After this incident, the clans-women went into great fear that they too would have their throats slit if they ever spoke of any of this to anyone. The child had died in such shock that an aspect of her remained floating between the worlds still struggling with trying to understand what she did wrong and blaming herself for having spoken when she should have kept quiet as the women had warned her.

Understanding what I do about history, I explained to my client that there was a time when worship shifted from feminine gods to masculine gods. This reflected a shift from social groups organized around women's power to men's power. Tribes lost their spiritual connection to Mother Earth and feminine wisdom that knew its inner connection to the Great Spirit and began the process of organizing around male independence and domination when land possession was believed necessary for survival. Women were not allowed to access their source of power and were punished or executed if they did. The unconscious reasoning of the new power structure questioned how they could kill enemies who threatened their tribe if they felt connected to those enemies. As a result, they had to erase all thoughts of connection, and looking into eyes was made unacceptable because it led to feeling connection to self and other, which was unacceptable.

A woman seeing her reflection in a pond would allow her to look into her own eyes and see the spark of God within her. She could see and know her inner God Essence; once she saw it in herself, if she looked into the eyes of others she could see and know God Essence in them, as well. Being able to really know one's own soul allows that one to see into the souls of others, as well. A connected woman would be able to see the disconnection in those around her who were not experiencing the power of their God Essence. Rituals must have arisen around looking into the pond, which empowered women to remember who they were; these rituals were declared to be worthy of death by the rulers, likely because if men were seen, and their weakness known by wise women, they feared they would not be powerful enough to overcome invading tribes or to invade tribes for the benefit of their own people, and everyone in their tribe would perish. These thoughts were, likely, unconscious.

When we asked the one who had slit the child's throat to come forward and explain what made him think he had a right to kill the little girl, the tribal chief stepped out and said he was the one who did it. It was his tribe and he was in control of it. He could do anything he wanted. The client sensed that the chief was attempting to destroy both the child's and the women's connection to their inner power, something that caused those men who were disconnected from their empowerment to feel powerless; and for that reason, they lived in fear, something they believed they had to hide.

I asked my client if she would be willing to take the chief to a higher place where he could see the weakness behind his control and the lack of true power represented in his murdering the child. In the same instant I asked the question, the chief was able to see what he had done as weakness. He was devastated by his action.

***

As a sidebar, this suggestion of going to a higher place is not about a person going to some physical spot above the Earth, but the suggestion seems to allow insight from a perspective that has a higher vibration. If we were to interpret this place as inside the body, it would likely be seeing from the 6th Chakra, a place between the eyes in the middle of the forehead. In Eastern philosophy this is identified as the third eye where truth can be more clearly seen. The higher place allows a perspective not restricted or limited by space or time, but is above time and space where it is possible to see the intricate, infinite connections that are not visible from our normal perspective.

***

A thought came to me while the client was sharing with me her experience on this inner journey, and when she completed her description of the effect this higher sight had on the chief, I shared with her what I was

269

thinking. Not long before the session, there was another one of those polarizing events reported in the news about Caucasian students who had worn American flag t-shirts and bandanas to school on the 5th of May, 2010 when the Mexican-American students were celebrating *Cinco-de-Mayo*. The principal of the school demanded that the Caucasian students turn their t-shirts inside out or go home and change because the shirts represented an act of hostility to the Mexican American students. As expected, this incident split the community and caused uproar on both sides.

Roger Ebert, a well-known movie critic who had suffered cancer that resulted in the removal of his jaw, which greatly distorting the critic's appearance, wrote an article critical of the flag-wearing kids and someone from the opposing side made a vicious comment about Ebert being ugly. The critic's response was that if people wanted to see ugly, they needed not to look at someone's face, but at the mind. After telling the story, I asked my client if the chief heard the story I had just told. She said the chief had dropped to the ground and was sobbing. He heard, and understood.

Though I didn't mention this to my client at the time, I was aware of how that attack energy was present in the *Cinco de Mayo* story and in the response that followed. The kids wearing the flag-shirts, as had been pointed out, were not being culturally sensitive. The likelihood is that their intention was to denigrate the Mexican Americans and throw the proverbial "cold blanket" on the celebration. The principal was aggressive in his demand that the students stop being aggressive by turning the shirts inside out or going home. He could have responded with cultural sensitivity by talking to the kids about cultural sensitivity, but by his demand, he reflected the very behavior he wanted to stop. Then the media picked it up, and people began to take sides hurling all sorts of attacking words at one side or the other. Everyone was trapped in the same fear and anger, the same disconnection as represented by the chief when he killed the little girl. My sense is that the chief could see this really ugly pattern.

With that, I asked the chief if he was willing to ask the soul of the murdered child for forgiveness for what he had done to her. He asked, and the child was ready to forgive him. Love replaced fear and hatred as all the women from the tribe rejoiced.

The souls of the women of the tribe, accompanied the many aspects of my client—those that had inherited the fear of speaking truth to others through many lifetimes, between that child whose throat was slit and my client in this life—together spiraled through time to the present and all of them could see their own reflection and see God Essence within.

Now, they are able to see what they only saw for brief moments before when they snatched glances of themselves in ponds and in each other's eyes. They were able to see, and then feel God Essence within them, and they felt the power, the beauty, and the strength that naturally arises for any of us when we know our true selves. As she connected with her other past life-selves who carried the fear of speaking up and being themselves, they released the fear and opened to the truth. Then other woman in the lives of those past life aspects of my client embraced the wisdom of what she had learned, as well.

My client, then, told me she saw a huge crowd of women doing the "wave" like at sports events, but the wave was a celebration of feminine energy and the rising up in the beauty of the truth. These were women of different ages and sizes, from many periods of time and many lifetimes. They included the client in all her incarnations and all the women that were in the tribe when the child's throat was slit, along with all their incarnations, and women all these others had known in their many lifetimes, too. Their souls had been set free. It was as if a great awakening of feminine consciousness had happened.

My client described what she was seeing in her inner vision. She was in the center of a huge circle of women and she invited me to join her. She said we began to stomp the earth, as if we were sending a message expressing our empowerment by spontaneously breaking into a tribal dance. The stomping took on a powerful expression of celebrating reconnection to Mother Earth and to each other. The others joined in as the dance increased in power and strength as they danced and stomped the Earth, moving in a circle around us. I was amazed to see that the client was visioning a dance so close to what I had experienced at the ceremony in Brazil, something I had not repeated to anyone. It was as if all of us, my client, the many women through all time, and I had been brought together to reclaim not only our voice, but also, our place in the world as equal partners in the flowing of energy of men and women, humans and earth, and all in creation and *Universal God Essence.* I remain in awe of how all of our stories interweave in the creation of healing…if we allow it.

The client explained that what she had just experienced was deep, amazing, quiet, and yet joyful about accessing inner strength. She sensed that these women from the tribe, as well as the child who suffered death back then, were willing to speak, now.

I saw that many of those tribal women had reincarnated into the present and had become or are on a path to become powerful leaders in our world, now and in the future. I explained to the ones who had not yet fully embodied their essence that they might go through some difficult times, but they are on a healing path that is supported by the Universe to restore the feminine energy to its rightful place and to bring balance back into a badly imbalanced world.

Bringing this full circle, I asked my client if she was willing to speak her truth and be her truth now. The woman who had come to me to understand the source of her fears of speaking in public an hour before had been transformed into an empowered woman who was ready to be seen and known for the truths she has learned in her life.

I told her that all of the women, moving into their true power and finding their place in the world as leaders in a vast array of arenas, can say thank you to a woman who was so scared to stand up for 30 seconds and introduce herself at a networking meeting earlier that day and a little girl from a past life who was so excited about speaking the truth that it cost her life. Her courage to face her fear in this transformational session planted the seeds for all those tribeswomen and all their relatives through all their future lifetimes to grow into self-aware women who no longer had to fear their own reflection in the pond.

***

Following my remembering that most profound session with my client, my thoughts returned to my own body and the work I was doing to bring healing, strength, power, and beauty back into my own energy field and into my body. I realized that I would not be able send this energy out into the world for others to see if I didn't experience it inside me. I began feeling a massive tingling going on in my entire body, even more powerful than what I had felt earlier. Then, I sensed that I was one of those women in the tribe who had been terror-stricken by the murder of the child. I believe that is why I was able to see so much of what the client described in her inner journey.

I realized that for me to move to the place I am now in my life, I needed to recognize the fear in me that caused me to withdraw as well as understand the fear in others that causes them to attack. Perhaps the seed of this awareness was planted in a tribal village many, many lifetimes ago. I sent an image of the present to myself in that past life and we both released the fear of allowing my authentic self to be known and allowing my truth to be told, a fear that I carried in so many lifetimes, as well.

I then visited all the children, all the women in my previous past lives and my own child self and my young woman self in this lifetime who had been held down. I visualized the hands of those who held me in the past and my fear of possible hands that could hold me down and do harm in the future…the hands and the fear began melting away and flowing out of my muscles. And I allowed myself to feel the powerful, beautiful, strong *Unique God Essence* in the form of the woman that I am. And, I too, am not afraid to thank a courageous woman for doing her work that allowed me to see my own reflection in a pond.

***

In the work I had done over those months since the Brazilian medicine ceremony, I saw how a past life decision, made by a woman in the 1800s to be disconnected from life by not joining the energy of love displayed all around her, had followed me into this life, likely made easy by the ancient lifetime in the tribe where it was life-threatening to connect to life. To end the power of that decision to disconnect from the experience of life, I had to crack the rigid structures in my thinking. I believe I did that literally by falling on the ice and cracking my skull, a fall that allowed me to discover the side effects of those rigid structures and by confronting my attachment to the rigidity of being a *"medicine virgin."* In that amazing ceremony in Brazil, I had allowed myself to surrender to the love from the magical plant-world, which would then take me on a journey that allowed me to see how I had built a whole set of internal constructs supporting the belief that I don't have a place in this world. *Universal God Essence*, the Earth, and the medicine plants joined together with *Sandy God Essence* to melt away the inner structures that bound me to a lie.

***

Three times I nearly died. The first time I was poisoned by the sister whose birthday I was told I had ruined. The second time I was poisoned by the gas fumes I breathed in because I decided I didn't want to be here any more, and the third time I was poisoned by my body when it didn't want to be in the world of my marriage where I felt unloved and unwanted. After I had awakened from each of these incidents, I had a pounding headache, felt nauseous, and was so weak I couldn't walk for a number of days. It took three current-life experiences to bring healing to those three earlier incidents: the crack on the head, the medicine ceremony in Brazil and the Inipi sweat lodge by paralleling the feelings from the past, which allowed me to finally see the theme that had been ruling my life. Being born into a family that did not know how to love made me believe something was wrong with me; I was a mistake and that I shouldn't have come to this place that had no place for me. When I was given poison by a sibling that I loved I became afraid to receive love. When the abuse I received at the hands of my father escalated and seemed as if it would never stop and no one would protect me from him, I became afraid to be love in this world that I concluded had no love. And when I concluded that God did not want me, either, I believed I must have been the one who was unlovable. And when that conclusion was verified by a husband who seemed to not love me enough to notice

I was dying, death felt like the only answer to stop the pain. I am aware that a part of me did not want to survive that toxic shock of the system wide-infection that was hours away from killing me, just as much as a part of me did not want to wake up after the promise that I could go to sleep and never wake up when I was eight years old.

It took three experiences of going to sleep, believing I would not wake up again into a life and into a world I believed had no place for me, and then waking back up, but fighting it so strongly, for me to finally get what my *Sandy God Essence* needed to teach me. It was only a part of me that had screamed out my whole life that she didn't want to wake up. The rest of me did, and that is what caused me to take the road less traveled when I came upon it in my metaphoric yellow wood that would lead me to become one of the many 1s in the many 50s; I finally did embrace waking up and discovering who I really am and continue to discover more and more that I am not the mask and I am not the stories of what happened to me that I hid behind my mask. I am the unique *Sandy God Essence*, eternally within *Universal God Essence* and eternally in *Unique God Essence* that is within me, learning how to embrace the gift of life and experience all the wonders that life offers, without dread or fear. I am the amazing spark of God, now shining the light of my essence into the world, a light that for so long had been covered over and buried deep within, *Under the Mask*.

***

Not until all this came together in this chapter, did I finally understand how every single experience included here was a part of a series of synchronous events that allowed a major transformation to take place within me. The time spent with David during the third segment of the trip to the Northwest allowed me to feel the deeply embarrassing experience of breaking the bed support that first night that got me in touch with my need to be so still that no one would notice me. The pattern I took on was to move without really moving, as to not disrupt the delicate balance that was unable to support my movement. I needed to reconnect with lifetimes of patterns, repeated in my childhood and adulthood that caused me to feel disconnected from my inner self, something shame does so well, and disconnected from the world around me, and from the universe.

I had to feel the shame of being in my body, as I experienced when I broke the support under David's guest bed, which put me in touch with the pain of being shame-filled for even having a body when I was born a girl. I had to find a way to keep myself from moving too much to not disturb those around me when I was an infant, so much that my mother told me years later how, when I was a baby, she had to peek in the room every now and then to see if I was alive, because I made no noise. My lack of movement kept me alive, but the pattern of non-movement was one of the contributing factors that caused me to gain weight, which if not ended could have cost me my life, so I needed to get moving again, and David was the one who encouraged me to do just that.

I also needed to experience David's decision to stay with me as we walked even though he could have moved on ahead. It was important to feel that I was wanted and belonged in this 3-dimensional world. By finding a home during the Brazilian ceremony, I connected with both my home in my body and my place in the world and was able to release the shame that caused me to hide myself within and keep myself from moving or being seen in my ever-growing body. This led to my beginning to release the excess weight I had carried nearly my entire life.

And, I needed to experience walking in the graveyard very near where my Great Grandmother was buried without knowing that is what I was doing. This allowed me to see the synchronicity related to retrieving her photo, walking near her, and finding out she was buried so close to where I had been walking that very morning. This was a gigantic caricature-like metaphor of the amazing synchronous interconnectivity of everything in the universe. And it allowed me to see how such connection does not just happen on one plane, but happens across time and space, across generations and lifetimes and among us all. Interconnections of the profound web of life can be seen everywhere we look…if we allow ourselves to see.

Synchronicities played out not only in the three-part trip to the Northwest, but they played out as each part of the trip created its own beautiful set of synchronous events over the next year. And the trip became a story filled with stories that reflected on other stories that told the same story over and over again…a story that said I didn't belong because I was not wanted, and, therefore, I shouldn't be here. This story is not unique to me; it is so very common among far too many humans.

What I have expressed in this chapter are my personal stories that reflect that pattern of separation and the pain that results from the belief in separation; the stories reflect the journey to find connection, and the synchronicities orchestrated by the Essence of the Universe to bring me back to connection. And the truths that I am not separate and I belong are the same truths for every one who ever believed that he or she is separate and does not belong. Each of us will find our way to the truth through our own unique path, designed by the union of our *Unique God Essence* with *Universal God Essence.*

If you have not yet found this truth on all the levels of your being, I know you will find your way to it for yourself…because you chose to bring this book and this chapter to you, allowing you to read these words that are speaking the truth to you, right now.

When you make a decision to heal, let yourself take in a deep breath and be prepared for the most amazing ride of your life that is taking you to your true self, who has been waiting for you to come home…for a very long time.

Part Three

After the trip to the Northwest

IT IS FINISHED

MESSAGES FROM THE DAVIDS

LET GO...TURN WITHIN...CONNECT
WITH YOUR GOD ESSENCE

AFTERTHOUGHTS

EPITAPH FOR RACHAEL

Chapter Nine
IT IS FINISHED
A READING OF AN ASTROLOGY READING

What we came to do has been done even if our life experiences make us believe that we have more to do! Instead of living in one of the many possible stories, we can live from this completion when we acknowledge who we believed we were and what we believed we were supposed to do is finished. Finally, we can be aware of the amazing gift of knowing life as the Unique God Essence that we are, expressing ourselves as the conscious love-filled partner in an eternal dance with Universal God Essence, embracing our experience in union with and distinction from the pulse of the universe.

Even though I have had interest in and respect for astrology, I have not focused on it as a source for planning my live or understanding its direction. I see everything as connected, and interrelated, so it is not a stretch to see a relationship between the planets, the stars, the galaxies, the universe and us as individuals. Over the years I have had readings done by astrologers, some good and some not so good. But in retrospect, they all noticed the same configuration, basically interpreting it the same way, because my chart is noticeably left oriented, indicating that much of my life I've been directed toward self-inquiry as opposed to discovery of the external world. However, I have found that it is possible to inquire internally in such a way that an understanding of the external also takes place.

Again, I was not surprised when the astrologer I went to see in the summer of 2009 told me that I had three very strong aspects to my chart. However, this was the first time I really understood the deeper meanings…but not until I heard the reading for the third time, on Christmas Eve, 2009. The astrologer told me I had three equally strong themes in my chart and that one aspect had to do with being a healer whose focus was on purification, cleansing, and perfection. The first time an astrologer had spoken this to me was in the 1980s, when I was considering leaving my husband. My life was in such turmoil a friend suggested I see a reader to help me make sense of my circumstances. I could not even begin to see a truth in what she told me back then, because my life certainly did not feel even close to being pure, clean, or perfect. It felt much the opposite. But as my life progressed into the next decade, it became clear that my interest was drawn to healing modalities, as I began studying with some of the world's great healers. And, while I was learning processes to bring healing to others, I began introspection to bring healing to wounded places in me, as well. In the intervening years, I have learned that focus on purification, cleansing, and perfection are ongoing and are not the same as pure, clean, and perfect. I am, also, aware these three aspects of healing have been important to my understanding of who I am.

The second characteristic of my chart indicated I came to create balance in myself and balance between the world and me. There is no question that I spent my first 45 years very out of balance, because I tried to create harmony in my world by sacrificing my own balance, but not consciously aware of what I had done. If anyone would have asked me if I were happy for most of those years, I would have said yes, while contracting pneumonia at least once but often twice a year from early childhood to the time I ended my marriage. And I would have said yes despite my on-going and ever-growing battle with weight and my eventual solutions that were non-solutions of bulimia and anorexia, which were life threatening.

If I had been asked if I had been a happy child, my answer would have been, yes, despite the fact that I had very few memories of my childhood, and wouldn't have been able to list very many good times. I would have been proud of the fact that our family was very close and that we loved each other so much more than other families, without noticing that we knew very little about what was going on inside the hearts and minds of other family members and without remembering that my mother attempted suicide twice, and my father threatened suicide on a regular basis. And I would have answered that question not recalling the tension that, in retrospect, permeated all our growing up years.

And not until I began therapy in my 40s would I have remembered the horrors of abuse, the evil rituals I was forced to observe, and those in which I was forced to participate. Deeply buried in dungeons behind my mask, I would not have known how to explain the rigidity that ruled my life and all the unexplainable responses to what would be considered normal, everyday experiences. Not noticing how I was living in the world, I would have said, *"Yes, I was a happy child and I am a happy adult"* without knowing this was simply not true.

If someone inquired as to whether or not I had a good marriage, I would have told the one who asked the question that my husband and I had the perfect marriage. But I would not have remembered that I had a dream warning me about marrying Jake before I walked down the aisle, and I had five miscarriages that tore me apart, and I would not have thought about how I felt powerless in making my own decisions. Because I had no idea what it meant to have a voice, I wouldn't have noticed that I didn't have one. I was taught to believe that God required a woman to be subservient to her husband, and I did what I was supposed to do. I would not have remembered the day I met Jake in Hawaii for his R&R from Vietnam and that my young husband told me he didn't think he loved me because he didn't know what love was, or that he left me a few years later while he was trying to figure out if he wanted to be married or be free to pursue a relationship with his girlfriend.

All my positive, loving answers would have come from the part of me attached to my mask, the part of me that wanted all those good things to be true. And in giving the answers, I wouldn't have known I was not telling the truth. I let myself know what the mask needed to believe to feel balanced, while not noticing the profound imbalance that was happening inside.

Before I began to wake up to the truth, when I balanced my needs against other people's needs and valued theirs more highly than mine, I created imbalance that disrupted my internal energy system. Most anyone would not do well with this kind of ongoing imbalance inside and with relationships in the outer world, but a person who is a Libra, as am I, would feel as if such imbalance would be intolerable. When I began to take $5 each time I went to the grocery store for money to allow freedom on my yearly trips to Washington, I was silently and secretly proclaiming the inherent goodness of a more fair balance, though it disrupted my sense of harmony and flew in the face of integrity and honesty, values I held very close to my heart. But I didn't have what it took to be honest and announce that I was taking the money, and I didn't know how to re-establish my internal balance without disrupting harmony. I violated one set of principles to be able to reconnect with another set...until balance finally provided me the lessons for being able to speak my truth with honesty and my own internal strength grew enough to be able to tolerate disharmony in the external world by not taking the external into myself when my actions created internal harmony and balance.

But before I could create a voice and experience personal strength, it was necessary to grapple with those things that created voicelessness and weakness not just in myself, but also, in my interactions with the world. This required me to venture into the darkest places that were connected to the third aspect of my natal chart, which involved a fascination with the dark side. In all the previous times I had gone for readings, I don't recall any of the astrologers mentioning this aspect of my chart. Perhaps they did, but I was unable to hear or remember it, or maybe they said it in a way that would feel less threatening to me in my less conscious state.

By June of 2009, when I had the astrology reading, I had come to realize the value of understanding the dark side, while a younger version of myself would have considered the idea that I was "fascinated with the dark side" to be terrifying. My more mature interpretation of fascination was not that I wanted to be drawn into and overtaken by the dark side, but that I wanted to understand its cause and nature to help me to include it in my wholeness and fit it into a greater awareness of the universe, as a whole, as well. I had come to realize that resistance to something, including denial of it, as well as judgment or fear of it, gives the dark side greater power, so I needed to overcome resistance, denial, judgment, and fear of the dark side.

According to my chart, I came into this world in this lifetime to experience wholeness, created by bringing balance to the dark and the light and to experience balance between the world and myself by creating balance within myself. And, according to the astrologer, I had already done what I came to do. I just didn't know it, yet.

When I began to walk the path of a healer, I recall that I had learned how to heal by taking the other person's disturbance into my body to understand its vibration so I could discover how to heal it in me, not unlike a little child who attempts to put everything in his or her mouth to discover what it is. I used my body, mind, and energy field as a Petri dish in which I could incubate what was causing the other person pain and then administer the energetic antidote when I understood the makeup of the problem. This was not something I was doing consciously, but it did teach me about physical and mental illness and what caused the disturbances. An important component of this process was to be able to approach the illness with intention of discovery, not with judgment, even when the illness included the darkest of the dark behaviors. In time, I learned to only study the disturbance, not to take another's disturbance to heal it for them, something I really couldn't do anyway. Taking it from them to heal it in me could have short term healing effects but was not a healthy path for me and not for the one who came for healing, either, because to be healed the healing energy must come from within the one who is suffering. What I do is reflect to one who suffers both the light and the dark within them; when they

285

are ready, the God Essence within them brings healing to the part that believes it is separate.

It is very possible that, on a soul level, I made the decision to be born into what I have often called the "dark side of the moon" when I referred to my birth in Alaska in October because literal darkness would rule my first months on the planet, followed by the darkness of years of abuse hidden in basements in the cover of the night and never spoken in the day. This allowed me to bring healing to the dark within my own soul, while discovering transpersonal causes for afflictions of humanity. I was not ready to really understand this until I heard it three times, the final time being Christmas Eve, 2009. I suspect it is no accident that as I write these words, it is Christmas Eve, 2010. It has taken an entire year for me to process the meaning of the words spoken by the astrologer 18 months ago when she said:

*Your chart reflects that you came into this world with three major objectives. One had to do with being a healer whose focus is on purification, cleansing, and perfection. The second is that you came to create balance in yourself and balance between the world and you, and the third involves a fascination with the dark side. The first and third impulses might seem to be polar opposites—one of healing through purification coming from the light and the other, fascination with the dark side, but the balance and harmony coming from your Libra aspect has provided a way for you to bring together soul level concerns that on the surface seem opposite. All three of these intentions led you to take on the deepest darkest possible wounds in your early years without closing your heart. Surviving your childhood and in fully embracing the healing process in your adult years **has led you to having accomplished the balance between the light and dark.** You have **completed the task and contributed this vibration to the world, already.***

Before I understood that I really had finished what I had come to do, I had to work with a number of experiences that continued to feel out of balance, unhealed, and dark. These things rose up over the course of the year between the Christmases to allow my experience of being finished to match my understanding of being finished.

AN EARLIER READING

Not long after listening to the astrology reading for the third time on Christmas Eve of 2009, my feelings of inferiority, as well as the more hidden feelings of superiority came to the forefront that allowed me to bring healing to parts of myself still out of balance, which led to a reconnection with *Sandy God Essence* experienced in the form of balance, compassion, and love. But to get to that place, I had to pass through difficult territory.

Quite a number of years ago, I participated in a workshop presented by David Hawkins, author of *Power vs. Force*. His premise was that everything that was ever written and everyone who has ever been alive could be calibrated on a scale of 1-1000 where 1 represents the greatest untruth and 1000, the greatest truth. Hawkins also calibrated human emotions with shame registering 020, the lowest on the vibrational energy scale, guilt was at 030, grief, 075, fear 100, anger 150, pride 175, love registering 500 and Enlightenment or Christ Consciousness coming in between 700-1000. He pointed out that all energetic calibrations below 200 are basically destructive to the human condition and those above 200 are constructive. The lower vibrations use force to get what they want and the higher use power. During that conference, I was calibrated in the upper 700s, which would be considered quite high in the continuum, which interestingly enough caused me to feel a sense of pride, which calibrated quite low.

Sometime later, in 2008, I was invited to participate in a workshop with a man who studied Hawkins' calibrations and developed a code system he proposed could help people increase their consciousness, and he offered to do readings with people who were interested. I had a reading done, and weeks went by before the results were sent, but they had the name Richard, not my name on them. The reader said my potential for this life was 780, which, according to the reader was very rare. He said about 1/100 of 1% of the world population had that number, however, he said I was living at 95 and had been at that number for many years. The reading devastated me and I did not ask for a follow up consultation. In time, I was able to put the reading out of my thoughts until two years later, when I received another communication from the reader, which triggered my memory of the reading and put me back in contact with the feelings I'd forgotten. I sent an email to my dear friend from Oregon,

David, I found out that 1/100 of 1% of the world population that is nearing 7,000,000,000 is about 700,000. Based on the Hawkins calibrations of 1-1000 and the reading I had some time ago, my potential is at 780, which I share with 699,999 other people, or thereabouts. But, according to the reading, I am not living up to that potential, At the time of the reading, I was told I was at 95, not even as high as Hitler, as I recall from Hawkins book. I don't know if you remember just about two years ago, I had a reading from a man who studied with David Hawkins. He sent me the outcome, but instead of having my name on it, he had the name Richard, and when I read the results, I was very sure it was wrong. I called the reader to explain the mistake, but he assured me that the reading was correct, just the name was an error. Out of the 1-1000 calibration, his testing said not only was I a 95, but that I had zero potential of ever being a healing light worker in the world.

I went into a depression, feeling so disempowered by the assessment. I recall wondering if I was completely wrong about my ability to know who I am and what is happening within me. You and I talked some about it back then, and I finally got to the point where I decided it didn't matter what another person thought of my capabilities or whom they think I am or am not as a person. I was supposed to have a phone consult with the reader at the time, but didn't follow through with it, as it felt pointless to me.

A few days ago, this man sent out a group email that announced something about his work, and I decided to write to him, congratulating him on what he is doing and to tell him about my response to the reading from 2 years ago. He emailed me back, telling me that I had misinterpreted the meaning in the reading. He said I had been in my present state of 95/1000 for 38 years, a calibration, which is between grief and fear, but what I had not noticed was that I had a calibration for this lifetime of 780, a reading he said that was very rare, with less than 1/100 of 1 % of the Earth's population being at that number or higher. Apparently, this was supposed to make me feel better.

I decided to take in the information and sit with it for a little while, and discovered that he is probably right that I have been operating out of the 95 in some areas of my life. Grief and fear are common feelings for me, as we have talked about in the past, and a 95 is on the cusp between grief and fear. The reader wrote that, *"at energy levels above 200, abundance in each area is manifested. At energy levels below 200, ideal levels are not possible. Aspects above 200 include ideal manifestation of abundance, vitality, balance and*

harmony in every aspect of your life including mental, emotional, physical, and spiritual experiences, all forms of relationships, career, creativity, recreation, financial etc. All you have to do is take an honest look at every aspect of your life and assess if you are experiencing ideal levels of abundance in each aspect. Those areas of challenge are areas where you calibrate below 200." When I looked at it that way, it was very clear that despite the amazing experiences I've been able to have in my life, I have not felt the abundance, vitality, balance, and harmony that he spoke of, very often.

I went outside on my deck and thought about what I had read. I asked myself how could it be that I could be at 780 in my energy field but exhibit 95 in my life experience. In my mind, I saw an image, a diagram and drew it on a piece of paper.

On the inside of a large circle was another concentric circle, and inside that was a third circle. It could be a geometric symbol of the mask, what is behind the mask, and what is under the mask. In the small inner circle was life force energy, or what I have called *God Essence*. I have no idea why that initial energy would not be 1000 in all of us, since it is God Energy. Outside that inner circle is another circle like the doughnut around a doughnut hole. I sensed that this middle ring taps into life force energy to gain the power to support life processes in the outer circle or to hold down life force energy for all the reasons any of us are afraid to allow our true selves out in the world. This middle ring is like a transformer between the energy in *Unique God Essence* and the expression or repression of that energy in the outer ring.

I clearly could see that it was fear that caused the transformer to turn against life force and try to smother it for all the possible reasons one might not want to be seen in the world. It would make sense that shame and guilt could result in a person wanting to disappear, and that would explain the low registration on a scale from 1-1000 in the outer ring.

It occurred to me that in pushing down life force, we might be mimicking the very separation we believed happened between our unique self and *Universal God Essence*, at the time that non-physical consciousness became many things. This created a conscious experience of separation as one thing observed another thing. This observation of what was interpreted as separation and then judgment of self in comparison to other things may be where shame, guilt, apathy, grief, fear, desire, anger, and pride came from.

And then I saw the outer circle that contains whatever energy is left, which fuels our interaction with the world. This outer circle is like the mask in book one, the mid-circle is like what is behind the mask in book two, and the inner circle is what I'm writing about in book three.

I began writing down thoughts that came to me when I looked at the circles. I could see that Life Force Energy is supported and enhanced through connection with our unique version of *Universal God Essence*, the life force that pulses throughout the universe and through us whether or not we recognize it. I don't believe this is a one-time supply that can dwindle and when it is used up it is gone. But I believe that we can make choices that shut us off from experiencing the flow of that energy in the middle and outer circles of ourselves and as a result can live as if the energy becomes depleted in us.

Without connection to the regenerating energy of *Universal God Essence*, the holding down energy is disconnected from the eternal flow and drains more and more life force from itself, with less and less available to pass on to the outer circle, and the experience of depletion happens. When living in the outer world is disconnected from Life Force Energy, draining also happens, and we experience the depletion as not having enough energy to do what we used to do, which becomes a signal to our bodies to age and die.

I remembered hearing about a magnificent healer, I am not sure who the person was, but the healer stood tall and did great healing for so many people who came to him. He gave all the appearances of being a vibrant man standing in front of audiences, but after the healing session, he nearly withered and was overcome with arthritic pain, along with an inability to move his frail body; he was removed from the stage each night in a wheelchair, only to come back the next night filled with vitality. My interpretation of what I read was that while he was accessing God Essence energy he was strong, but when he returned to his personality-self that held his personal history attached to his mask, he accessed the energy of the depleted self and declined.

In my contemplative state, I also saw images of people doing great feats, far beyond normal human capacity in emergencies and could see how adrenalin fueled by the power of love could force open the usually closed flow of energy between the inner circle and the middle ring to allow a person to do so much more than normal. I wondered what spiritual counterpart in our spiritual body there might be to adrenalin in the physical body. I imagine it might be that surge of love that can flow through us when we are connected within.

I thought about my drawing, in terms of the calibration of 95 I'd been given and about *Unique God Essence* in relationship to *Universal God Essence*. It occurred to me that, in those moments I am called to do the work I came here to do, something happens and the fear that causes a part of me to hold down my Life Force Energy, releases. I know I am flowing in high vibration. And I began to ask myself what is keeping me from releasing grief and fear and embracing who I am.

Even though I know I am not 95 all the time, and that my intellect and heart have a much higher awareness of truth, far beyond a 95, after reading his email, I could see that parts of me remain stuck between fear and grief, and far too often, these are the parts that I feel as I interact with life. After this awareness came to me, I decided to meditate on this whole thing.

From the time I got the response to my email from the man who did the reading, I had a very strange headache. It felt as if a vice had been placed on my head and was pressing in on my brain. The compression was intense and disturbing. I lay down, and asked that my meditation help me understand and release the vice. However, the first thing that came into my inner vision seemed totally unrelated to anything about all this. It was a photo taken of me when I was about 12. My hair was very unkempt, I was wearing the glasses I absolutely hated that were broken in two places and had been repaired with black electricians' tape that, more often than not, made the glasses rest on my nose unevenly or fall off completely leaving a sticky black residue on my nose and making me look like a misfit. The car coat I was wearing was tattered, and the belt was twisted several times. I hated that picture from the first time I saw it. Even as a child, I couldn't understand how I could let myself look so horrible. One thing I could have changed, which was the twisted belt, I didn't. And, I could have been more aware of my hair, and combed it, but I didn't do that either. There was no animation in my face; I had what some might call a frown, but I would call a blank look of dissociation.

About the same time the picture was taken, a painfully shaming event happened as my fellow students and I were lined up at the classroom door getting ready to be dismissed for lunch. The girls were in one line on the left, and boys were in a line on the right. One boy turned around and looked at me and began to point and laugh. He drew everyone's attention to the fact that my nose had green mucus coming out of it. I didn't have a Kleenex or anything at all to blow my nose. For the previous hour or so, when I was at my desk, but not allowed to ask to leave, I tried to keep in the discharge by sniffing, but failed. I was anxiously waiting for the bell to ring so I could run to the bathroom and blow my nose, but the boy saw it before I got the chance and did all he could to humiliate me in front of everyone. I recall feeling so overwhelmed by shame that I wanted to disappear.

In my meditation, I saw this little girl in an alternate reality, standing on the edge of a group of thousands of people. I had the feeling that these people belonged to the group the reader identified as very rare in this world, and though I was a part of the group, I felt as if I were the misfit that did not belong. I was the snotty nosed little kid with glasses that drooped, disheveled closes that didn't fit, and hair that looked like I just woke up from a very restless night of sleep. Normally when I do this kind of work, I go to the child and bring her healing, but this time, I found myself in the presence of the these thousands of people and told them I needed their help to release me from the vice that was keeping me trapped. By this time, the vice that was clamping down on my head seemed to have extended to my entire body. This iron body suit had screws embedded into my flesh at many points, making it impossible to extricate myself. It was clear that if I tried to dislodge one side, the other side would become tighter, embedding the screw-holds deeper into my body.

All of a sudden, I realized that when it came to my being stuck in the vice of shame, grief, and fear, many of these people didn't know how to use their skills to release me any more than I had known. So I began to share with them what I had learned about the elasticity and flexibility of the universe and how matter could be shifted. I have no idea why I didn't use what I knew on myself, but I didn't.

I dropped into a very deep place and spent a long period of time communicating with these people, I believe I was teaching them what I knew and learning from them what they knew, but I have no memory of what I had taught or learned. And I emerged from the meditation with a warm feeling that has remained with me since. The disturbing headache is gone.

Later, I went back to the images of the vice and noticed that it was my adult self that was caught in the vice, and my adult self that participated in teaching and listening, as well as releasing me from the full-body vice in that very powerful meditation. There was still the child that needed my attention.

I entered the photo and held out my arms to embrace the little girl who felt such disdain for her self. At first she felt ashamed of being too dirty with her drippy nose to accept my embrace, but I told her I was her future self who understood how she felt because I felt her same feelings a long time ago in my life when I was she. I helped her blow her nose and gave her a cloth to wash her face. I placed my hand over her eyes and told her she wouldn't need to wear those glasses anymore. She was so, so happy. I helped her unbuckle the badly twisted belt and invited her to sit down in a chair while I washed her hair and used a hair rinse to take out the tangles. Then I combed her hair and curled it to fit the energy flowing from her heart instead of the tangled energy that trapped her in guilt and shame. We went together to buy her new clothes that reflected who she is, rather than how sorrowful she had felt. She was so delighted with the changes. I asked her if she would look at the photo of the little girl with matted hair and a twisted belt to tell me what she saw. She told me she wanted to tell that little girl in the photo that she would be okay...to just wait a very little time and everything would change. I smiled. And as she spoke those words, the child in the photo transformed into the one who was speaking to her.

I know part of what has been happening inside is that I am looking at the 95 that the reader had seen, not as a judgment, but as a thermometer that can guide me to release being in that place still holding on to grief and fear. I am aware of our recent conversation about my fearing to go out into the world, and worse, to be seen by it, a thought that has touched such resistance and attests to the fear part of the 95 reading. My feelings of sadness and accompanying labored breathing is evidence of the grief from the past that still seems to hold on... always looking for something sad in the present to which it can attach itself. As I write this, I sense that a major theme of my grief has been around a belief in loss. The first image that came to my mind when the theme became clear to me was my two dogs I had to leave at the kennel in Alaska when my family moved to Seattle and my father said we could not go get them. As I write this I can feel that under that grief is anger.

For all the years since I was about 12, I believed my father had planned to leave Alaska and intended to leave the dogs behind, but lied to us. Along with the anger and grief was a deep sense of betrayal that stayed with me my whole life. It is amazing that after all these years...decades even...such powerful feelings can still become stirred up so deep inside.

I've never really worked through this, or looked at the circumstances from my adult self's perspective. In reflection at this moment, from my adult's thinking, I don't believe my father intended to abandon our dogs and all our possessions in Alaska. I think he was trapped in circumstances that overwhelmed him, and he didn't know how to get out of them. I imagine he might have felt like he was in a body vice, and no matter how he tried to find escape something would press against him more. I know, now, what that feels like. My father didn't have the advantage of knowing that within him was his *Unique God Essence* or that he could call on others' higher selves to help him, either. He believed he was alone in this world, with no one to turn to. That must have been terrifying. I am sure the choices he made in his younger years set him on a path of more and more separation, so he couldn't even feel connected to his wife and children, much less to his God Essence. Connection was not in his experience. I think I have compassion for him, in a way I haven't felt before. I'm sure he spent much of his life feeling like I did when my nose was running, my glasses were falling off, and my coat belt was all twisted, but from his unique set of circumstances. While I went inside and tore myself down, his path caused him to go outside and tear other people down.

Something I didn't remember until just a few moments ago, was not much after that photo was taken, I took off my glasses and refused to wear them any more. For a while, I took them off after getting to school, put them in my locker, and didn't put them back on until I went home. Later, I just stopped wearing them. My family must not have noticed because no one said anything to me about it. Many years later, an eye doctor told me that had I kept wearing those corrective lenses through puberty, my eyes likely would've developed with a dependence on glasses and I would have had to wear glasses all my life. Interesting.

Yesterday, I went to another Inipi Sweat Lodge. The rocks were not as hot as they have been in the past, but the vibration coming off them was so profound that everyone nearly passed out and, as a result, we did a fair amount of the ceremony with both doors open, letting in the light and a cool breeze. When it was my turn to pray, I asked for all the residues, the stones, the rocks, and boulders of energy patterns that remain holding me back from being in the energy of love and enlightenment to be released.

After the ceremony, the fire keeper—the man who goes to the lodge very early the day of the sweat, builds a fire in the firehouse, and heats the rocks—told us that the fire acted differently than it had ever before in all the years he has been fire keeper. He said the fire burned melon orange the entire time. And though the rocks did not get as hot as in times past, they felt very different to him. He commented that he sensed they were clearing the way for something that was about to happen...though he didn't know what that was. All of us acknowledged that we received the same message from our experience that day in the lodge, that this is our time to trust all that is happening in our lives and in our world is leading us to a transformation in human consciousness. I believe a lot of letting go is happening...

Love, Sandy

Whatever it was that came out of the rocks in the sweat lodge that affected all participants so powerfully, seemed to have a profound impact on my inner experience. I noticed something that I had not noticed before. Everything in me felt open and warm, like love was flowing through me, as I had never experienced before. It was not a love for someone or something; it was love that was emanating from me for everything around me. I began to see pathways for fulfilling my purpose in this world, no matter what the years ahead may bring. I began feeling pure, beautiful joy filling every cell and openings in so many places that had been closed for what seemed like forever. And I became aware that laughter that had been missing for as long as I can remember...that true laughter that most people lose far too early in their lives had returned to me.

One important understanding that came to me, as a result of this work, seemed to shine bright light into my thinking. When I first got the reading that calibrated me in the 700s, I felt a sense of pride and when I got the 95, I felt as if I'd been deeply shamed. I believe that at any given moment, depending on whether or not we are living in our masks, in what is behind the mask, or from our *Unique God Essence* freed from being held down and confined to that deep place under the mask, we can experience all the human feelings and, therefore, any number could be there. Even the focus on the calibration and our longing to make it go higher disconnects us from God Essence and has the opposite effect. I believe if one were to translate what Lao Tzu stated, *"The Tao which can be expressed is not the unchanging Tao; the name which can be named is not the unchanging name."* into this whole calibration concern, Lao Tzu would have said, the 1000 that claims the 1000 is not the 1000.

LIGHT SHOWS UP THE DARKNESS

When something so profound as the experience with my child self and the sweat lodge that followed happens where love is awakened, it is not unusual for those things that do not match the inner truth to come forward, and for the next few months, old beliefs, old fears, grief, guilt, and shame moved into my consciousness for healing. I wrote about a number of those things in chapters six and seven, and there were more to come.

Fear of Being Seen

Writing has always required me to come from my greatest clarity and integrity. If something is missing and I am feeling disconnected from my integrity, I feel a sense of internal discomfort, a distressing emptiness, a lack of alignment that becomes so disturbing to me that I experience a block, not only in my writing, but also, in my life. And I cannot continue until I find what is not clear or not in integrity. I become stuck. As I had mentioned in earlier chapters, I had become stuck in my writing of this third book. Months had passed with no Liberty Quarters coming my way, which didn't seem like a problem, especially because not a whole lot was happening that needed any decision-making. But my writing had slowed down to a crawl, something that was not unusual when ideas were in process of emerging but were not, yet, clear or when

I was avoiding some truth, usually an unconscious avoidance. It was nearly August of 2010, 7 months since I had begun to write *Under the Mask,* and I felt disconnected, not just from my writing, but also from life itself.

I had gone back to Seattle to spend a few days with my Mother for her 94th birthday in July, and returned to my writing place in the mountains of Colorado feeling off balance and completely stuck. I sent a message to Oregon David saying I was feeling ungrounded. This feeling surprised me because of the work I had done before the trip, and I believed I would be able to go into the energy of the "49" and be okay.

Hi David, I arrived home about midnight last night, happy to see Jenny but very tired. I am aware of feeling down. The orange Rufus hummingbirds returned in fair numbers while I was gone, and have joined the many green Fantails. They are all so wonderful, but I am not enjoying them like I did before I left. I feel disconnected from everything. I've been trying to identify the roots of the feelings...but I'm having a hard time. I am sure my lack of insight regarding my future is a big piece of the frustration; I've always needed to have something to look toward, but right now, I don't have anything. I know that will change, but I'm not feeling connected to the future in the moment, and for that matter, not feeling very connected to the present either.

I think there is something that got to me more profoundly than I realized. Last evening, as I sat on the plane, I noticed that people all around me were reading books, paperback novels...one after another after another, up and down the rows. I recall wondering how many would have chosen to pick up one of my books instead of a novel if they had a choice and my intuition told me that most all of them would have preferred the novel. I think I was looking at the 48 or 49 out of 50 and as a result, I felt as if I had collapsed in a heap on the ground in front of the wall of disinterest that I had just flung myself against, and I believe I am feeling the aftershock of that crash today. I kept looking around and wondering what I needed to do to catch the attention of all those people, and as we have discussed before, focusing on those who are not interested, or who are not ready, yet, is self-defeating.

I know I need to pick myself up and turn my attention to those who would find the ideas in my books challenging and rewarding. But then, I get stuck in not knowing how to communicate with the one or two out of the 50 that there is a book that they can choose that will take them into deeper and more meaningful places than the ones they might be reading. I am still very tired from the travel...

and know this is what I need to look at and move through because of how writing this has impacted me.

On reflection of our conversation, yesterday, when I told you I thought the reason I haven't extended myself out in the world is that I am afraid of the danger out there, I realized that I am not afraid of being attacked or hurt by others. You encouraged me to think about getting training in self defense, and maybe even purchasing a small gun to allow my child self to know I plan on protecting her...but after our conversation ended, I knew that some person out there who might be a murderer or rapist was not a fear I possessed.

I am aware that I am far more terrified of a collective of people capable of inflicting wicked damage on others, including me, perhaps imprisoning those who think differently than they do. I realize that I have been afraid, nearly all my life of being noticed by anyone in authority, so I have lived with the intention of staying under the radar. I don't have any sense that I would draw such things as rape, murder, or robbery to me.

I think what has made me feel sad and blocked in my progress is that I have been writing about trusting *Sandy God Essence*, and part of me really believes this, but tonight I have been accessing the part of me that has no trust...I feel like a person in the concentration camp as depicted in *Schindler's List*, where there is some powerful and sinister person randomly taking shots at people on the grounds for his insane target practice. And, those on the ground are trying to figure out what they need to do to protect themselves, but there is nothing that can be done...nothing that anyone does matters if the shooter happens to focus his cross hairs on you for no rational reason.

I am aware that a part of Sandy knows that I am so much more powerful than all this...that it doesn't matter if I am spotted by the radar or not, that I will be fine whether I am seen or not seen or even if I live or die, but I don't know how to get to that knowing from where I am right now. I am filled with tears that don't know how to come out. Holding a gun in a fanny pack, like you suggested in our conversation, does not feel powerful enough to fight the people for whom I have the greatest fear, the ones who feel power in their numbers...maybe another version of the 49, in the form of the ones who take charge of the 49 and rule them with an iron fist through fear.

A while ago, I saw on Google street maps that my car is now visible for all the world to see when someone looks up my address...and I guess the part of me that needs to feel anonymity feels like her little hide out in the mountains is not hidden any more. I let myself feel safe when I come to the mountains, but the frightened part of me doesn't feel that anymore, and she is so close to the surface right now. She feels like she needs to find a way to quietly slip out of sight and not let anyone know where she has gone. I am very sure that I have been blocked in my writing and blocked in my life because this part of me has come forward for healing. I have not yet found the way to bring her healing... and she is so very present.

I realize that I am not afraid of a man attacking me on a trail if I go hiking, as you mentioned. This frightened part of me is afraid of those who control so many with fear that she feels they cannot be stopped. Normally what I do if I am afraid of something is that I take it inside to study it so I can discover how whatever it is, is not so frightening. But the part of me that does this doesn't know how to take the sinister ones inside to figure out how to deal with them, because she is too afraid of them.

A little while ago, I was sitting at my desk, writing, when a huge sound vibrated my whole place like an earthquake. I ran outside to see what was making such an immense sound and saw low flying fighter planes and old looking bombers overhead that were flying over my cabin, just above the trees...so close...too close. I could almost see the pilots' faces. There seemed to be no good reason for these military planes to fly so low. It was terrifying, though I tried not to respond to the fright, as everything shook...and I am sure it triggered a cascade of events connected to a very deep primal fear. I must not be the only one who harbors such fear based on the number of films that have come out in recent years about huge armies of robots or extraterrestrial invaders that look like gigantic unstoppable machines attacking the world.

As I write this, my mind seems to be collecting all the terrifying events of my life and feeding them into my consciousness, screaming out danger, danger. In this moment, I feel like the polar bear running across the ice trying to escape helicopters...and there is no place to escape. I see images of armies of cold-hearted people...like the military people I saw in China, with guns pulled and ready to shoot anyone, while the onlookers have no way of knowing what small thing they might do that would accidentally catch the attention of those who held the guns, causing the soldiers to shoot. This is an irrational fear, but it is so powerful right now.

Earlier, I mentioned that I was in between everything right now, and that I sensed something more needed to happen before I could complete this third book. Maybe this is it. My writing about being *Sandy God Essence* has brought to the surface the part of me that does not know there is any such thing as a God Essence in me or in the universe. I am living in the energy and consciousness of that part of me right now. It is such a troubling place to be.

I don't know how to get a handle on this and find my way to the other side of the fear...it is really huge. Maybe I will find an answer in my dreams tonight. Right now, I feel so very, very alone. Love, Sandy

Two Events

While rereading the letter I sent to David, two events passed through my mind. The first was from my most recent past life as a little child when I died at the hands of the Nazis. I wrote about that shattering experience in *The Mask*. I didn't realize I was still carrying residues of that experience in my energy body. The great fear of that very short lifetime was I needed to be invisible, but when I failed, not only did I die, but the ones I loved died, too. The other experience that came into my thoughts happened one night I stayed at boyfriend Jake's home. I had found his home to be a sanctuary for me, a place that no one in my life knew about but the two of us. But that night, my estranged husband followed me to my sanctuary. He climbed onto the roof and watched from outside as I prepared for bed. While watching, he slipped on something and made a noise that disturbed the peace of the night. Boyfriend Jake said he knew who it was and grabbed a rifle from his closet. He got dressed and went outside in search of the man he knew had come to do us harm. Apparently, my husband Jake had done some investigation and found the house previously. Earlier that day, he put a note he'd written to my boyfriend in the mailbox, which could have been interpreted as threatening. I was filled with terror. I didn't want husband Jake to be shot, and I didn't want boyfriend Jake to be arrested for murder. I no longer felt safe, not there, not anywhere. My sanctuary was gone, forever. It seemed that my daytime soap opera had turned into a possible nighttime criminal investigation plot. Not long afterward, the relationship with boyfriend Jake ended, and I felt truly alone in the world.

After remembering these two incidents, one from this life and the other from the past life, it was clear to me that they were intricately woven together and they connected to what felt like threatening airplanes flying overhead and having my presence in a mountain cabin visible on the Internet for the world to see. My mask, carried through lifetimes had taken on the belief that being seen was dangerous and wanted to be sure I would remain invisible as a way to create safety.

Without realizing it, I had forgotten this truth about safety after having been drawn into what I call the vortex of fear over a number of months, perhaps beginning with my listening to presentations about the end of the Mayan calendar followed by viewing the film *2012* in November and then *The Road* on that marathon day before my December '09 trip to Seattle. The vortex of fear must have taken greater hold as a result of the BP oil spill that seemed to portend what I had learned as a child of the things that would mark the end times…and my child self who discovered she didn't have to place her shoes beside her bed so she could run to the mountain to be saved, was shaken and wondered if she needed to begin to prepare again for the coming of the end that would come like a thief in the night.

I had been hearing so much about the December 21, 2012 date and all the stirrings about the end of the world, the sun aligning with the center of our galaxy, as hadn't happened for 26,000 years, and all the predictions of what that would mean for the Earth. TV specials told of extended periods of blackouts that could result for the hyper activity of sunspots and the disruption in everything electric, causing the failure of communication systems. They pointed to past times when most all life was destroyed in previous epic shifts like the one the Earth is in now, and a possible end of humanity, as there had been an end for the dinosaurs, but I had no idea all this had impacted my unconscious thoughts and feelings as much as it had. I think with the BP oil spill and all the fear that it generated had gotten to me much more than I knew as day after day more information about the death of the gulf coast region filled the airwaves. And, of course, the fears generated from the shift in weather patterns caused people to plug into whatever theories they held about the world, and all this continued to tap on my wondering about my safety in the world.

Fear seemed present everywhere, and conspiracy theorists were using the Internet to send messages of massive government take over of all things human. Some were saying that the BP oil spill was planned as a way to remove all people from the Gulf States and force them into FEMA concentration camps, not unlike Hitler-style rounding up of Jews and others that the Third Reich decided were unacceptable humans.

Even though my mind was not buying into such conspiracies, a part of me, likely the little girl aspect of me still trapped in fear from the life in the concentration camp, must have considered these things were possible. Of course, this played into my childhood training about the end of the world, the coming of the Anti-Christ, and how mass killing would take place. With fear pulsing in so many corners of society, it was almost a given that my frightened child-self would come to the surface.

The next day, I sent another message to Oregon David.

Lots of thoughts are spinning around in my head this morning. Before I left for Seattle to be with my mother on her birthday, I decided to go to the public laundry to wash my rugs because I like to come back to everything being clean. As usual, I bought plenty of quarters to fill the machines, but didn't take the time to do any search through them since I was under pressure to get ready for my trip. But after I returned home, I found three Liberty Quarters in the pile I'd left on the counter before my trip. I separated them out and sat them next to my computer. Last night, when I was in such a low place, feeling so afraid of the powers of darkness in our world, I looked down at the liberty quarters—the three of them—and I was struck by the number in a way that I hadn't when I was so tired from the trip.

It had been so long since I had found any liberty quarters that I had actually thought that they were all gone, taken by collectors or coming from the Sandy part that can so easily be pulled into conspiracy theory, I thought they might have been removed by the government in a way to erase reminders of freedom as we are experiencing less and less of it in our world. Our conversation must have connected all the fears from the past (and I am sure past lives) when powerful dark sided people seemed to be able to do such damage without anyone stopping them. The planes flying over my house did not help and my anonymity feeling compromised by the Google photo stirred fear. But right now, in this moment, I recognize the power of the light in knowing exactly how to communicate to me that I am safe even in a world that can appear unsafe.

It's all connected...all okay and I will discover more. Right now, my eyes are filling with tears...tears of comfort. I am not alone.

I realized that part of what is happening is that I am dealing with the other side of the coin. One side is that I create my life and my experience, and the other side is that I have no power over what others may do to me. It is so hard for me to put my head around both ideas. This is an important part of the struggle. I will work on this. SSS

There is nothing to Fear

Not too many nights after writing this, I was disturbed by something but could not pinpoint what it was. I went to bed feeling frustrated that whatever it was that had a hold of me had not let go, yet. And I woke about 3:00 AM, feeling sick. Instead of writing or turning on the TV, I turned on my electric blanket and decided to do what I had been writing about. I turned inward to find *Sandy God Essence*. I moved toward her but found a barrier between us. It was not like glass or Plexiglas, but was very flexible, more like a thick bubble that was too resilient and resistant to force my way through. And then it occurred to me that I could ask Sandy-God Essence to expand and come to me. The barrier melted and she began to touch me with the most gentle, loving hands. She touched my head where I had been experiencing such difficulty with my sinuses, and she placed her hands on my nose and throat, and moved to touch my chest. I could feel the love flowing from her hands, and felt tears welling up in my eyes. I realized how deeply sad I had been as a child that I had never felt such love coming from my mother, who was incapable of expressing her love for me with such depth, and my body ached for not feeling her love.

As I was experiencing the embrace from *Sandy God Essence*, I felt myself as both the giver and the receiver of love. I completely surrendered to being held and to holding. I felt as if I were the loving mother holding my child and felt as if I were a small child completely surrendering to the arms of the safe, caring love coming from God Essence. Before all this happened, I didn't know there was still so much pain in my chest and throat that needed to be released. *Sandy God Essence* brought me to the healing waterfall of living water, and I, as my child self, felt my whole body surrender to the arms of my inner mother, and I felt myself holding my little child as the water flowed over, around, and through us both. I realized that I had never been held like this, but I had never held anyone like this before, either. There was always a thick energy bubble material that separated me from whomever might have held me or who I might have held. In that moment, I realized that if I had children, likely, I would have held them the same way my mother held me...and I wouldn't have known there was a problem.

After this profound meditation, I fell into a deep sleep and dreamed I was in the high school where I taught for a dozen years for what seems as if it were lifetimes ago. I went to the office and found I had a stack of messages that appeared to have been piling up for years; it occurred to me that I could get fired for not responding to all these messages. The school was a mixture of the one I taught in and the one I attended as a junior high student. I couldn't find my classroom, so I went outside to the steps and began talking with kids. Soon, the courtyard and steps were filled with students. They asked questions and I responded, like we were having this amazing teaching/learning time.

While I was talking, I became aware that there were army tanks and those ugly, menacing army helicopters flying over us. It seemed there was some kind of military action taking place right there in front of us. One of the young girls told me that things were pretty scary and that she suspected the war would soon involve them and threaten their lives. I talked to them about turning inside, just like I had experienced when Michael, in Bellingham, worked with me before Christmas of 2009, and as I experienced just a little while before the dream. I told all the children that no matter what the outside brings, they are eternal, so nothing could ever destroy them. The children began to easily connect with their Inner-God-Essence, and I knew they would be okay.

There was another part of the dream that happened right after I left the children who had been on the steps. I was hurrying home to pack necessities to escape somewhere, because the military was descending on neighborhoods, going from house to house, and arresting people. I knew they were coming after me because of the message I'd been speaking about turning inward. I packed clothing, and realized I might need food to live on if I had to go into hiding. I went to the refrigerator and took out a few items, and then decided to take out a big chocolate cake for my former husband, Jake. Apparently I was escaping to wherever he was and I knew he would want the cake. As I was trying to figure out how to pack the cake to keep it on the trip, there was a loud, demanding knock on the door. At first I didn't want to open it, but I realized if I didn't respond, whoever was at the door might break in and kill me. So I opened the door. Instead of being the military, the one beating on my door was a very large black woman telling me I had better do what the military wanted me to do if I wanted to live. Her voice was threatening, though it was clear she was not the one who would hurt me. It was as if she was giving me a warning.

I woke. But what I felt was not the fear of the military, rather it was the deep comfort that I had shared the message about turning within to all those students at the school. I know this had to do with what I am preparing to do out in the world once this book is finished, but even more, it is about my bringing peace to any of the frightened parts of Sandy who still don't know how to turn within to *Sandy God Essence.* I have some work to do with the military aspects of myself seeking to stop the message, as well as the part of me that was desperately packing to move out to find safety, the part of me that feeds the Jake part of me chocolate cake, and the fat shadow feminine who seems to have sided with the threatening military by cooperating with them to warn me about keeping silent as her way to find safety and encourages me to be obedient out of fear.

Not long after this meditation and dream experience, I took the extended trip to Florida, mid December of 2010 and experienced feeling torn between two friends, the details of which I wrote in chapter seven. It was then that I understood in the cells of my body that it is fear that creates the distraction from turning within as the frightened self focuses on the outside to try to figure out how to keep safe. It is fear that turns away from the amazing feeling of love that is my birthright, a birthright of all humans, yet a gift so seldom allowed to be experienced.

I realized I needed to communicate the truth to the parts of me that still identified themselves with the mask. So I invited three aspects of myself to come to me: the child from the past life who died in the concentration camp, the woman who lost her sanctuary that night at her boyfriend's house, and the part of me from the recent past that was terrified because of seeing her car on the Internet and felt the power of the jet engines that flew too close overhead. As I embraced the three of them, I explained that safety is not found in fear-based invisibility. Safety comes from the inside and is not dependent on life or death for it to be real. Safety, like every other human need comes from the connection we experience when we become aware that the God Essence residing in us in union with the God Essence in the universe all the time. The beings that we truly are can never be destroyed, not by airplanes, by helicopters, by gunmen traveling from house to house, not by organizations of powerful people seeking to disempower any who they might believe are a challenge to their power, and not even by death. I invited these three parts and any others that still are attached to the mask to turn within and discover their eternal connection to universal love expressed in and expressed by *Universal God Essence*. And, within that love is our safety, our security, our place in the world and our significance. It contains everything we need or wish for.

***

As I am coming to the close of this chapter, I can see that I really have learned how to bring balance within me by learning how to trust the light and understanding the dark. In reality, I do know how to live connected to *Sandy God Essence* and live in this world with balance. And, when fear distracts me, I can forget I know that I have finished what I came to do. I am sure I will have more dreams coming to me from still frightened parts of me, and I may never get used to the idea of fighter planes flying close to the ground or military people coming into neighborhoods with guns pointed outward. I also am sure that whatever the future holds, what I came into this world to learn has been learned, and what I came to teach, I am and will be teaching. After all, the worst that could happen to me from the perspective of the mask is that I could die, but from *Sandy God Essence*, who I really am will never die. That I know. And, if the future provides more years for me to live in this three-dimensional reality as Sandy, my *Unique God Essence* flowing with *Universal God Essence* will continue to support me as we dance together to whatever music is playing.

What we came to do has been done! We can choose to live into this truth, allowing ourselves to experience it in an ever-expanding way, noticing when our life reflects something different to us, and bring healing to what is out of integrity with the truth, or we can continue to focus on the struggles that are a part of our stories that cause us to believe we are the stories.

Chapter Ten
MESSAGES FROM THE THREE DAVIDS

When we finally learn to trust, we can discover the support that has always been there for us, encouraging us to be who we are and live the life we came to live.

Christmas Eve 2009, the night before I began writing this third book in the trilogy, *The Meaning of Three*, I received messages on my voicemail, from three Davids, each of whom is very important in my life. I mentioned in chapter one that the calls from these three amazing people acted as a reminder of what I needed to remember just as I was about to move forward in writing *Under the Mask*. And, I wrote about the dedications I had written for *The Mask*, which included appreciation given to China David, Connecticut David, and Oregon David without realizing that each of these men represented one of the three major messages that emerged over the course of the year it took to write *Under the Mask*. These three messages—let go, turn within, and discover infinite connections—were the steps needed to connect with the *God Essence* within us, messages that weaved themselves into me over the year from Christmas Eve 2009 to Christmas Eve 2010, during which time this last book in the trilogy wrote itself in me.

DAVID AS A METAPHOR FOR LETTING GO

Letting go of all that I held onto was the message presented in the first part of the three part trip to the Northwest when I released so much of the past in the form of emptying of the storage crates, which became a metaphor for releasing so much of what I had stored within me over the course of the year between the Christmases of 09 and 10.

Before we can experience full connection to our *Unique God Essence*, it is necessary to release the distracting dark and heavy emotions we've held within us. Letting go is not just about releasing the attachments we made to people and things we believed would provide us safety and security when our experience is that the world is not safe and secure, but also letting go of the emotions we didn't know how to release when we first experienced them. We need to release anything that distracts us from who we are and prevents us from fulfilling the dream our soul envisioned when we entered this three-dimensional world. When I reflected on China David, it became so clear to me, how his life was a metaphor for letting go of what was in his past that could make him believe he was less than who he is and letting go of attachments and distractions that could have gotten in the way of realizing his dream had he not let them go.

David was born in an impoverished village in the very middle of the Middle Kingdom in the year of the great upheaval of Mao's 1966 Cultural Revolution. His parents regretted having given birth to him because he was evidence that they would be burdened by parental duties instead of being fully committed to duties to the state. The only way they believed they had any hope in their lives was to be seen by the authorities as dedicated Communist party members. To free themselves of family obligations and dedicate their lives to Mao, they gave their young son to a pig farming family in the countryside of the poorest district in the poorest province in all of China. He ran away several times and eventually found his way back home but was cruelly beaten by his mother each time and then sent back to the pig farm.

From the time he was small, this frail little boy had a vision of coming to the United States, and from his dismal beginnings, he prepared himself for the coming of his vision by diligently studying English. Because of his linguistic abilities, he was selected to attend a local college, unusual for children coming out of such poverty, and eventually became a teacher of English at that college. In 1989, this young man was asked to write a letter introducing his college to prospective teachers from America, telling them about the wonders of Baoji district and the teacher's college. In *The Mask,* I wrote about the amazing events that brought me to read the letter that this young man had written. Just as he knew he was to come to America someday, I had no doubt that Baoji was the place I was to go after reading his letter. I have come to believe that his *David God Essence* connected with my *Sandy God Essence,* and together, with *Universal God Essence* weaved the life both of us had envisioned without our conscious selves knowing what had taken place.

In a recent conversation with a friend from Ohio, I learned that in natural settings, when a baby chick is ready to emerge from its shell, the hen begins to tap on the egg and the little one hears the tapping and begins its own tapping from within the shell in response to mother. At the perfect moment, both mother and baby mutually tap in exactly the same place; the egg cracks, the chick breaks free of the shell, and it enters the world. In the case of China David and me, I don't know which of us was the chick and which was the mother hen tapping in the form of the letter, on the metaphoric egg; perhaps, we were both to each other.

When my time to leave China was nearing, David found out his name was on a list for re-education. For anyone on that list, this meant they would be sent to the countryside, not unlike the pig farm from his childhood, and forced to do menial tasks, punishment for being in college when the June 4th, 1989 Tiananmen student uprising took place. It didn't matter if any student individually took part in the student demonstrations in Beijing, or any of the other marches and demonstrations that reverberated in colleges throughout China in the days and weeks that followed; just being in school at the same time was indication enough that re-education was necessary. His dreams would have been crushed had he been forced to do farm labor for the rest of his life. This was China's version of imposing required behavior on anyone who might not want to follow the rules, and in this case the required behavior was subservience and loyalty. A loyal communist would accept whatever the leadership determined was the best use of the person in the social order. If this thought is not preeminent, the person would be sent into the countryside to learn from the peasants, who apparently had accepted Mao's thoughts, to release the *cult of the individual*, accept the leadership's orders, and experience re-education. I suspect that this attitude was behind the splitting up of husbands and wives by sending them to distant provinces where they could see each other once a year, and most accepted this without question. Not just his dreams, but also David's soul would have been crushed had this happened.

The God Essences of many other people worked together to create the most amazing miracle that allowed China David to receive an invitation to teach English in Florida, just before his assignment to the countryside was to take place.

Very early on a September morning of 1991, David and I boarded a train in Baoji that would take us across China to Shanghai and from there we were to board a plane to the US. His family and a group of his college friends and students waited in silence for the train to take the young man away from them. And deep inside, they believed they would never see each other again. He knew he was letting go of everything he knew in life even though he didn't know what would be waiting for him on the other side. He simply trusted the dream he had his whole life.

David stood in the pain and excitement of the moment, waiving good-bye to all who had assembled along the track. The conductor closed the door, and when we could see them no more, my dear friend collapsed on the floor in tears for the overwhelming pain of his loss. I knew there was nothing I could do to ease the suffering of his heart, broken open in the realization of all he had let go of in order to fulfill his dream, so I stood beside him in silence, holding him in my heart. I had experienced the same feelings when I left my life behind on my way to China close to two years before, and there was nothing anyone could do for me at time, either. Change, which requires us to let go of something, even when letting go is for the better, can be extremely difficult, but resisting change, when we know it is what we are being called to do, can be devastating. Neither he nor I resisted, though we both felt the pain of letting go.

I know I have lived my life similarly to China David, especially after I separated from Jake. But what David allowed me to see is what it is to live that kind of life with conscious awareness of the dream and the letting go. Too often I have allowed doubt, fear, and distrust of myself to blind me from conscious awareness of the inexplicable knowing that my dream is unfolding and the letting go is happening. Recently, I have identified this knowing as coming from the God Essence each of us has *Under the Mask*, but so few seem to have embraced, or more accurately, so few have allowed themselves to be embraced by it.

From the first day I met David, I knew he was a person of greatness. He would not allow the limitations of his birth to keep him from the world he knew would be his. After the weaving together of those miracles that allowed him to come to this country as an exchange teacher, he enrolled in graduate school with a student visa, and in time received a green card because of his significant contribution to the college in which he taught. Later, he entered graduate school, became a citizen of the US, and then accepted a position with an international corporation developing educational programs that took him all over the world. He returned to China as a citizen of the US to develop a training program and a few years later became the director of the growth market workforce for 147 countries in the world in that gigantic international corporation, and had just received the news that his university has granted permission to complete his dissertation for a PhD. He had been PhD, ABD for 10 years, and normally that would mean he would have had no chance to complete what should have been finished in 7 years. He is now so close to fully realizing his dream because he didn't forsake it and was willing to let go of what would have prevented him from moving forward.

My dear friend from China has been a reminder that it is possible to live consciously in letting go of all that would hold us back from realizing the dreams that have arisen from our *Unique God Essence*. When realized, these are the dreams that fill the places inside that had once felt empty, as if something important was missing and when we do not forsake them, they reward us with living our life in bliss.

DAVID AS A METAPHOR FOR TURNING WITHIN

Turning within was the second message I had received from that Northwest trip in December of 2009 when I went to Bellingham and worked with Saint Michael; it was a subtle message that I lost for many months, not unlike most of us do for many years or decades of our lives, and, perhaps for many lifetimes. And it was Connecticut David who reflected the significance of turning within, through his life. In retrospect, I can see that it was no surprise that I received a message that Christmas Eve of 2009 from David, letting me know that he was thinking about me. In chapter one, I wrote, *"Hearing his voice reminded me of the courage he demonstrated in his life to be himself, willing to release the need to follow the rules society needed him to follow."*

I met Connecticut David in Florida when the two of us worked for the same college and in time, we became very close friends. David spent most of his life from the time he was a little boy into his adulthood trying to feel accepted by family and friends by looking like just another guy, but something in him knew he was not like everyone else. Before he was able to have the courage to be true to himself in the world, he had to know himself. By grappling with the masks he wore, working through what he had hidden behind his mask, and connecting to his authentic self, Connecticut David decided to own his personal truth, that he is a gay man. In speaking his truth, he was willing to risk the loss of his family and so many friendships he had built over the years, as well as risk the friendship and love we felt for each other. Though the risks in being authentic are still present for a gay person in today's world, it was very difficult in the early 1990s. With courage, he not only embraced his true self, he also let go of needing to hide who he is from the world. He had to let go of so much of what he held onto to set himself free. While his path represented the first part of my trip to the Northwest…having to do with letting go of what he spent his life believing would protect him, he released the mask he had worn. His path also represented the second part of that trip, which called for a turning within to find his authentic self. As a result he was able to experience true connection with those who knew the goodness of embracing him for who he is.

In the dedication to him I wrote, *"There can be no greater gifts for any of us to give to each other than our vulnerability and our truth, for in the giving… we…can grow into our most authentic self."* This was Connecticut David's gift to me. With the lesson he taught me about the value of owning as well as professing one's true self, I can now take the lesson more deeply into my self as I release any remaining need to disown *Sandy God Essence* as being who I truly am, and professing this in the world, no matter what the risks might be.

DAVID AS A METAPHOR FOR INFINITE CONNECTIONS

June of my 21st year, my parents and I walked across campus of the University of Washington toward Hec Edmundson Pavilion to join several thousand other students who were graduating that same day. I was dressed in my cap and gown and about to get my BA, when my father spoke directly to me, something he rarely did. He said that he and my mother were very proud of me. I had no idea what to say to him, in response, but I remember as clearly as if it were yesterday, what I thought in response. In my mind, I said, *"Wait until I get my PhD, and then you will have something to be proud of. I'll prove that I can be as good as any boy."* I recall being a bit surprised by my own thoughts because I had never considered going on in school. My plans were to marry about six weeks following my graduation and become a teacher in the fall where I had been hired to take on six classes in history and geography, teaching junior high students, something I knew I would do since I, myself, was a junior high student. Becoming a wife, a teacher, and a decade later, a businesswoman, had taken up all the space where any thought of going back to school might have resided.

The thought never crossed my mind again, until Oregon David wrote a note and addressed it to Dr. Smith, letting me know when his conference was over and where he would meet me for dinner. It was as if his inscription had poured life-giving water on a seed that had lain dormant for over 20 years, and the watering caused it to take root and flower two years later as I entered graduate school to get my doctorate in psychology. Even in the earliest years of our friendship he had a way of connecting me with what I already knew, but had forgotten. His shamanic worldview reawakened my child-self's recollections of her shamanic experiences; his awareness of healing rekindled my innate knowledge of healing energies—both for myself and for other people, and his suggestions of communing with my body allowed me to remember that I could talk to my muscles, my bones, my cells, and my DNA. His love of hiking reconnected me with my love of the great outdoors, walking through the forests of my childhood where I felt most free.

When our physical proximity faded and our connections became far more by way of telephone calls and emails, with visits to each other's states only now and then, he was the first to tell me I ought to consider writing because he believed lots of people would gain from the unusual way I had learned to think and express myself in our communications. Before Alanza, the tattooed psychic from Manitou Springs told me I would write a trilogy, David planted seed thoughts encouraging me to think about writing.

Not only did David open deeper connections between us, he, also encouraged me to make deeper connections within myself, and he became the catalyst for so many connections with the world. He introduced me to people who introduced me to other people, who introduced me to so many more people, many of whom make up the amazing network of people and ideas that have woven themselves into my life, shifting me from being a woman living life in a very narrow arena to one who can now claim the world, and beyond into alternate universes, as a part of her sphere of influence.

I have felt so gifted to have a friend who is capable of knowing me when I am at my best, as well as when I am at my worst…and still loving me. The other side of the gift he has given is that he's allowed me to see his great strengths as well as his flaws, and he has let me see the magnificence of his inner being, something most of us defend against having anyone see, including our selves.

The power of demonstrating true friendship is that it allows the receiver of the gift to reciprocate with true friendship, not just with that one friend but, eventually, with the self and with other beings. Our friendship has provided the template from which I can discern the quality of all other friendships in my life. In the dedication of the first book, I wrote, *"There are only unspoken heart words that can convey the love that I feel for you in being my true friend, for your standing beside me and reflecting to me the strength that I possess, a strength that exists in all of us if we would but look within."* The deep conversations we have had included discussions related to the meaning of life…and death, the existence of God, and the questioning of the value of religion. We discussed ideas related to our creating our own universes, and shared our joy in successes and grief in our losses. We talked about acceptance and judgment, past lives and future lives, and how everything is connected. And, the discussions the two of us had, as well as the experiences we shared, contributed to my discovery of *Sandy God Essence* and my awareness that I really do belong here in this world.

Without knowing it until this writing, I can see that Oregon David represents the truth that though we are all unique, we are all one, connected with each other whether we know it or not, a truth that is knowable only when we are connected to our authentic selves. It is no accident that Oregon David represents the third part of my three-part trip to the Northwest, that was, in fact, a visit to reconnect with him. He represents becoming aware of the need to live from our God Essence, experienced when we surrender to connection within us and with the rest of the universe, not just now, but for all time.

And during the third part of my trip to the Northwest, through his support and encouragement, I reestablished my connection to music and a magical generational and genetic connection with my Great Grandmother and a much deeper one with myself.

When we let go of what holds us back from knowing our authentic self and turn within to experience our *Unique God Essence*, we no longer live in the illusion of separation. This deeply felt experience of connection within, allows us to experience our eternal connection with *Universal God Essence* and also, allows us to see that same connection with everyone in our lives and everything in the universe. This is the experience of infinite connections. It is from this place that we can understand how our *Unique God Essence* draws to us all that we need to fully be who we came here to be and create what we dreamed of creating. This is what Oregon David supported me in understanding.

What we draw to us—especially when we are still metaphorically "asleep" with little or no awareness of who we are—often includes experiences that we could interpret as terrible and certainly nothing that we ever chose to create. But from this broader and deeper perspective, it is possible to see that what we might call *"the worst of the worst"* comes into our lives to work together for our good because things such as this, hold the potential for us to awaken and finally discover who we are. And, we can know that all the people who we might have believed wronged us have also played a role that can lead to our awakening. Knowing this allows us to embrace even those we would normally see as extremely separate and, finally, we are capable of experiencing our connection with them.

I don't think I would have taken the trip to Brazil without David. Our connection allowed me to experience the life-altering ceremony that helped me make the connection to the parts of me that didn't believe they were connected, to me, to any one else, or to the Essence of the Universe. And they believed they had no place in this world. Before I could complete *Under the Mask,* it was necessary that I reconnect with the truth that I have a place, I am loved, and I belong. I am able to say with honor and gratitude that Oregon David opened the pathway for so many completions and connections.

When we have learned how to release all that we believed was the truth and our hope dies…the answer to the question, "Then what?" is that we can finally discover the truth about ourselves and the world, a truth we hid *Under the Mask,* without realizing that is what we did. We can be grateful for everything that crosses our path and everyone who walks along our path with us, whether for a short time, for a lifetime, or for many lifetimes. Because everyone and everything is a part of the creation of our awakening to the *Unique God Essence* that has been calling us to become conscious of that which we are, we can experience our connection to everything. And, as we awaken into consciousness, the Universe becomes conscious of itself, as well. This has been the ongoing gift of Oregon David.

***

The calls from these three amazing Davids in my life acted as a reminder of what I needed to experience, as I was about to move forward in writing this last book in the trilogy. And, now, as book three is coming to a close, the deeper message within the messages of these calls is the same that continues to proclaim I can trust being me in the world. The message is that I contain the God Essence that creates my safety, my security, my ability to experience giving and receiving love, and like each of us, I am a significant being, a radiant spark of God; I am a holder of *Unique God Essence* in an amazing Universe. And, I can trust that I have always been supported in discovering and creating the path I came to walk.

These understanding, gained from the contributions of the Davids in my life provided the completion of *Under the Mask* before I began to write it…and before it wrote itself in my life. I am now ready to pass on these contributions to anyone who is prepared to receive them.

It feels almost poetic, that as I was beginning this chapter about the meaning of the Davids in my life, it was Christmas Eve 2010, and again, as last year, I received Christmas calls from each of these Davids. Oregon David, the man who represents connectivity to me, called while he was celebrating the holiday with his mother and sister to wish me a Merry Christmas. Then, I got a call from Connecticut David, the man who represents turning within; he was celebrating the holidays with his partner and his partner's little niece and nephew for whom they have guardianship, along with two cats and four dogs, many of whom they rescued. From the time he was a small boy, David wanted to feel a part of a family that loved him for who he is, and he has created that through the integrity he discovered when he turned within. Finally, I received a call from China David, filling me in on all the newest adventures in his life as he continues to move in the direction of the dream he first dreamed when he, too, was a small boy.

Each David in his *Unique God Essence* reflected to me an amazing aspect of *Universal God Essence* that I can experience when I connect to my unique *Sandy God Essence*. And, I can do that when I let go of whatever distracts me from experiencing my essence, when I turn within and open myself to experience the gift of connection. All the stories that fill the pages of the preceding chapters, as well as the stories in the previous two books were included to demonstrate, by way of vicarious experience, how we can become stuck or move through the three stages of life lived in the story that begins with the feeling of separation, continues with the hero's journey in search of connection, and is completed when authentic connection is found.

On Christmas Day 2009, when I began to write the first chapter of *Under the Mask,* that unique essence within me let *Writing Sandy* know that the three-part story of my trip to the Northwest would contain all that would be told in the rest of the book, although I had no idea how it would play out. And, I had the feeling that what I wrote would contain, not just the essence of this book, but also all three books, as well as the essence of the collective human story wrapped in whatever stories I would live through in the months to follow. As I look back over the past year, I am amazed at all the synchronicities that occurred, at the microscopic and macrocosmic levels, as well as so many other levels in between, synchronicities that weaved together to support my being able to not just discover what I came to teach in the world, but what I, myself, needed to experience so I could know the truth and power of the message inside me in my body, not just know it as a thought. The message—*let go, turn within, and connect with Unique and Universal God Essence*—is very simple, but profoundly transformational as expressed through the David's in my life whose calls became the cornerstone and the capstone of all that unfolded in the year between the Christmases.

Sandy Sela-Smith
December 25, 2010

Chapter Eleven
LET GO...TURN WITHIN...CONNECT WITH YOUR GOD ESSENCE
REFLECTIONS ON UNDER THE MASK

We shall not cease from exploration, and the end of all our exploring will be to arrive where we started and know the place for the first time.

T.S. ELIOT

From the time I was a small child, I searched the eyes of others to find someone who possessed, kindness, gentle but powerful justice, radiant light, and heart warming love to protect me from the emptiness and terrifying darkness that lived in me because of the wickedness, injustice, and bone chilling indifference that permeated my world. Without conscious awareness of what I was doing, I was longing for my childhood hope to become a reality, that the Lone Ranger would ride in and rescue me. When the masked man didn't come, I looked for someone else who held the promise of taking his place; I believed I found my Lone Ranger in the eyes of Jake. It took me decades to realize that the one I was looking for couldn't be found in the outer world, despite cultural programming to the contrary. But I wouldn't be able to find the one who could rescue me from my childhood until I let go of the one I hoped would do so.

So many of our generation's childhood fairy tales promised each little girl that someday her prince charming would come to save her from whatever was the poison or curse of choice that put her to sleep and stole her free spirit, her laughter, her light, her birthright, her soul, and her life. Her rescuer would be a younger version of the loving protective father—whether or not she had such a father in her childhood—who would save her from whatever frightened her; he would be the one to sweep her off her feet and carry her into safety, security, and love. She would surrender to the loving support of his arms and his heart, and they would live happily ever after.

The more boy-friendly tales encouraged each little boy to don a mask or a cape that would transform him into a powerful man, who would jump on the back of a dragon, mount a wild stallion, straddle a fire burning motor cycle, or climb into a super powered car, truck, tank, fighter-plane, or rocket ship to claim his manhood by defeating evil in whatever form it might take…and his reward was possession of the beautiful princess who would provide all his hearts desires and fulfill all his wishes and needs. She would be a younger version of the perfect mother—whether or not he had such a nurturing caring, perfect mother in his childhood—who could create a warm and comfortable place to which he could return whenever he was ready to take a break from his conquering duties, and she would anticipate his every need with a ready and open heart to take care of all of them with ease and grace.

In stark contrast to the *"Disneyfied"* version of the 20th century fairy tales were the original versions that were not so gentle. There were many versions of Sleeping Beauty, some as far back as the 1300s coming out of England, France, Italy, and Germany that included the lovely daughter being put to sleep by her jealous queen mother, raped by her king father and when she awakens she discovers she has given birth to his children. In other stories, sleeping beauty was raped by the prince as she slept, a young man who was already married with children. Some of the tales had the errant prince's jealous wife, or his wicked mother, making arrangements to have the illegitimate children and their mother murdered, cooked, and eaten intentionally by the angry wife or unknowingly by the cheating prince or king.

Whether the fairy tales are the fanciful, cleaned up versions of life as we wish it to be or the sinister stories representing what life is like for people, in reality, they represent a metaphor for the struggles faced in life. No matter which version be told, the story contains innocence, joy, and celebration, followed by jealousy, evil, betrayal, pain, suffering, anger, rage, revenge, loss, longing, desire and so much more, not unlike the contents so many lives lived in the 21st century. This one story reflects the many stories lived throughout the world now and in the past, that are, in fact, one story of connection, separation, the journey to find connection, and either the success or failure to connect, which leads to a repeat of another story with the same pattern, told over and over again, with different details, but still, the same story.

What many have a hard time accepting is that there is no prince charming and there is no princess, there is no perfect soul mate that will make all the bad old days go away. What makes any relationship work is the same thing that makes our individual lives work, and that happens when we let go of the protective patterns of the past that keep us focused externally causing us to lose connection with and balance within us. Lives work when we let go of all that we have attached to with the hope that something outside ourselves will provide safety, security, significance, and love. Instead of looking for a person or thing in the outer world, we become free to turn within to find who we truly are and discover that what we have wanted our whole lives is within us. Often this requires a journey into the dark side, a hero's journey, behind the mask to release what blocks us from finding the essence we have buried deep within us. And, when we have released the resistances and fears that have prevented us from accessing who we are, we finally allow ourselves to see and then experience being our true selves, our *Unique God Essence* that has been waiting for our return, likely since we were very tiny children, or perhaps, for many lifetimes.

This is the central message written in *Under the Mask,* told through the stories of my life and the lives of others, which are really the same story, just like yours, only told with details unique to you, to me, and to the others.

Once we let go of the stories and the patterns that create the stories, reflected in the meta pattern of connection, separation, searching, attachment, separation, searching, attachment…on and on, we can finally discover the connection we have been seeking all our lives, the connection that nearly every human has been seeking for generations, for eons, since creation first experienced what it interpreted as frightful separation instead of joyful uniqueness.

Once we discover that each of us is the drop of water that contains the ocean, and experiences life from our *Unique God Essence*, as T. S. Eliot proclaimed, we will arrive where we started and know the place for the first time. From years of exploration, by way of introspection, studying the great philosophers, researching the great religions and spiritual traditions, and learning from many master healers, I've come to an awareness that I am a spark of God, a drop in the ocean that contains the ocean, eternally connected to that which spoke, and from the speaking created the universe out of itself.

As I was writing this summation of *Under the Mask*, I remembered words from the Gospel of John I had memorized as a child, but at the time I had no idea what these words meant:

In the beginning was the Word, and the Word was with God, and the Word was God. The same was in the beginning with God. All things were made by him, and without him was not anything made that was made. In him was life, and the life was the light of men. And the light shineth in the darkness; and the darkness comprehended it not.

After all the years of study, of meditation, of introspection, and contemplation, I believe I have come back to where I started and know for the first time what I had only memorized when I was a child. When I was first studying scriptures, I was taught to believe that this passage was telling me that God created everything, including me, and that he provided a light for me to see, but because I was evil, I couldn't recognize the light. But now, after all these years of exploration, what I see in this passage is what I have seen reflected in nearly every major religion of the world, in everything in the world, itself, in all the stories I have ever heard, and in myself.

I finally have gotten it that in what some call God, some call the universe, and I call *Universal God Essence* is the pulse of life and light and this is what is *in* us all. We were in God, with God and were God from the beginning and out of God came everything that exists...but for oh so long, we didn't know it...though we contained the life and the light of God, our awareness was in the dark, and we didn't know who we were. This passage doesn't say that the life is the light *for* us; it suggests that the same life and light in *Universal God Essence* is in everything, in humans...in us; that light and life is who we are.

When we identify with what is behind the mask, we are in darkness and from that place cannot understand the light in us. If we identify with the mask, we are focused outward and cannot see the light in us, but when we turn within, we can see that which we are. We are the light of our world, the candle that glows in the darkness within us. However, the darkness caused by what we have hidden within, behind our collective masks, has covered over the light within us, causing the aspects of our consciousness identified by what we have hidden to not know the light and to believe the light is separate from us. In fear, consciousness became lost in the darkness and created the mask into which it could escape and began to identify itself with the mask. Consciousness, which attached to the mask, tried to make the mask alive and light filled so we could feel safe and secure again. Until the mask crumbles and the darkness is entered and released, we will not know the light that is within us; we will not understand what Joseph Campbell said when he explained *"You are it. The whole sense of these religions...is to evoke in the individual the experience of identity with the universal mystery, the mystery of being. You are it. Not the "you," however, that you cherish. Not the "you" that you distinguish from the other."*

An old song suggested if everyone lit just one little candle what a bright world this would be. What the writer may not have understood is that the candle that is the Spark of God, our *Unique God Essence*, has already been lit; it is not something outside of us. It is in us...it is who we are, waiting for us to wake up from our proverbial sleep and recognize ourselves. This waking and connecting is told in the metaphor of the prince kissing the princess and waking her, but so often, we have taken the metaphor and made it factual...with little girls growing into women who are waiting for their prince charming and little boys growing into men, waiting to kiss and awaken their sleeping princess.

The prince or the princess that you believe you want is not the one that you cherish, not the one that you see as the other. You are it. When you finally understand this truth and merge with the Unique Pulse of Life that is in you, your true being in the world, you will be ready to see and experience your connection to all else in the world. You will see that you, me, and, all others are not separate. You, me, and us are three aspects of the one…and this is the deepest and most profound meaning of three.

We are both unique and united; we are a part and apart. We are distinct aspects of the One, even if we do not know this truth. Let go of what holds you back from knowing yourself, turn within to find who you are and discover your eternal connection. Only then can you gaze into the eyes of another and see who you really are.

AFTERTHOUGHTS
ABOUT THE MEANING OF THREE

You are so much more than you have thought. Embrace your whole self in all the mysterious, magical, mystical, meanings of three that are within you.

Many years ago, before I knew anything about awakening from the dream that has kept humanity from knowing the truth of who we are, long before *library angels* brought me books that helped me to recognize what I already knew, and before I had heard about being on a path toward higher consciousness, I was involved in a philosophical discussion with a business acquaintance about who we really are. Our discussion was going down an esoteric road that felt disembodied from experience, so I made an attempt to explain my understanding of this subject by asking him a series of questions. I asked him if he severed his finger while cutting something, would he still be himself without that finger. *"Of course,"* he said, *"I'd still be myself."* Then, I asked if he were in a car accident and lost his legs, would he still be himself. After a little thought, he more reluctantly said, yes, and following that question, I asked him if he were in a fire and his face and body became burned beyond recognition, but he was alive, would he still be himself. This question was harder for him to consider, but after a time, he agreed that though an accident or a fire might change his attitudes or feelings about himself and about life, he suspected he would continue to be himself.

Then, I asked him if he lost consciousness, would he still be himself. After an even longer time, he hesitantly said, maybe, but he wasn't sure. He thought it would depend on whether or not he regained consciousness. I sensed he was avoiding feeling what was going on inside him and finally, when I asked him if instead of waking, he died, would he still be himself, he ended the conversation by saying, *"I don't like thinking about that kind of thing. Let's talk about something else."*

What I had hoped for my friend as he considered the questions was that he might move beyond thinking about who he is with the normal identifiers he placed on himself to be able to *experience* himself, for whom he really is at the very core of him. I thought that through the questioning he would experience himself, not as a man, a job, a role, or not as a collection of attitudes, thoughts, or feelings, or even as consciousness, but something far more than he could ever fit into descriptive boxes; however, it turned out that going there disturbed him.

Although I had no words for it at the time, I hoped he would be able to experience the amazing flowing being that exists inside him, under the images, the thoughts and feelings, under the roles he had taken on, the rules that guided him, the beliefs that had defined him, or the things he had accomplished in his life. I hoped he might discover the *Unique God Essence* that exists in him—the essence that exists in all of us, unlimited by the life we are living, the layers of explanations and images we hold, or anything else that we use to define us. Of course, I wouldn't have known to use the words *Unique God Essence* back then, but that was the experience I hoped would come of our conversation. As much as I wanted him to become aware of this essence within, I wanted the same for myself. This essence in cooperation with the essence of the universe is what produced the original organizing principles that created the physical universe and the physicality that embodies and expresses that essence through these wondrous bodies that allow *Universal God Essence* to experience being in the physical, three dimensional world through our *Unique God Essence.*

The God Essence in everyone is the ineffable something that *is* who we are, as well as is that which is in our bodies and our minds, but also, is beyond our bodies and minds. The *Unique God Essence* is inextricably flowing in, with, and through our being; it is eternally connected to the Being of *Universal God Essence.* In my youth and early adult years, I had fleeting experiences of this essence within me, without having words to explain it. And, now in my later years, the awareness of my unique essence has extended more and more into my lived life, with less time absorbed in the false identities I used to believe were me.

Many years before the conversation with my friend, when I was in junior high school, my class was given the assignment of memorizing the *Bill of Rights*. I remember feeling so very sad that it had been necessary to write out the rights soon after our constitution was formed, because it felt like writing them would eventually limit them and, in time, would destroy them. I tried to explain this to my teacher, who of course, took great exception to what I had attempted to express but failed to communicate.

My child self had an inexpressible understanding that once the experience of an ideal is formed into words, the words create meanings that too often become limited by the definitions needed to fit the categories those words had formed. Over time, the definitions become more precise to clarify the meanings and the ideal becomes something that is thought rather than experienced and, in time, even more limited until the experience of the ideal is eventually lost.

Back then, all I knew to say was it was sad. And, I now can see how I still carry some of the sadness of my childhood, because like the eventual destructive limitations formed in words that were attempting to express an ideal in the Bill of Rights, I find myself feeling sad that along with my fellow brothers and sisters, mothers and fathers, children and grandchildren, I myself have experienced the destructive limitations of identifying myself with definitions that are not my essence, rather than knowing myself through experiencing myself experiencing the world. Self-definitions, too often, are disconnected from the true self.

In my youth, I had understandings that I didn't have any way to express. What I knew within me was not something that could easily be explained with words, but came from experience, from visceral feelings that flowed inside me; it took years—if not decades—to find the most effective words to place on the knowing, and sometimes, I still have trouble finding the most effective words.

Decades after my child self attempted to explain her feelings to her teacher, I began to write a trilogy to support the junior high child and the businesswoman in expressing what was so difficult for them to articulate back then. Even in writing of the trilogy, *The Meaning of Three,* what I wrote was subject to similar limitations as my 13-year-old self sensed about the *Bill of Rights*, because what I have written in this trilogy can become just words to those who read it, and to me who has written it. As a way to lessen the chance of this happening, I wrote most of what was included in the three books from experience, and much less from a place of reasoning thought, In writing this last volume, as in the other two in the trilogy, I have counted on the decades that have come and gone since I was a child to have provided me the means to express the deeper truths that my child-self knew and experienced but could not explain, and that my 40 something self tried to communicate to my business associate, but instead, took him to a place that made him feel uncomfortable.

In retrospect, I can see that what I wanted to communicate when I was a child and when I was a businesswoman is the same message I've been writing about for the last four years in *The Meaning of Three.* The deepest message in what 8th grade Sandy was saying, without conscious awareness, is when humans attempt to take an experience and turn it into words and then focus on the words, life shifts away from the experience and the experience can be lost, just as the experience of life can become lost in the mask, believing the mask is the self as we can believe the words are the rights. The deepest message of what my 40 something self tried to communicate is that inside us there is something that is ineffable, something that is so much more than any definition can explain about who we are. It is that same "something" that the 8th grader knew was under the words, that the 40 year old knew was deep inside…something that could only be known through experience. And together the message was that when we lose the experience of that something, it is sad.

***

Just as Joseph Campbell acknowledged that the you that you think you are is not the you that you really are, I found that I was communicating the same message, but instead of saying this with philosophical theory, I presented the message through my personal experience, with the intention that through the stories that are really the same story, you would be able to find yourself somewhere in the experiences.

Even though most of us identify with the mask and believe the mask represents who we are, we are not the masks we wear. We can know when we have attached to the mask because its focus is on the external world…what people think of us, how they judge us, whether or not we are good enough, smart enough, worthy enough…and in the process, we become our own judge, doing the same thing to us that we believe the outer world is doing to us. In taking on the role of self-critic, judging ourselves for all we do wrong or for all of our inadequacies or ineptitudes, and all of that is not good enough about us, we live our lives as observers of ourselves rather than participants experiencing life. In the observation, we can become more critical of ourselves than others are of us, or we can become defensive against what we sense as underserved external criticism, and become critical or attacking of others.

When we are living from the mask, we can never rest in feeling fully satisfied with ourselves; any joy that might be felt is fleeting, and we feel inauthentic, often sensing that we are playing a role instead of living our lives. We live from patterns, repeating stories over and over again. And even if we make tremendous progress in our lives, as far as the world is concerned, we feel as if our accomplishments are insufficient or empty.

While living from the mask, it is not uncommon for us to seek another person to make us feel safe, secure and loved, looking for reassurance about ourselves in their eyes, but never really feeling like what we get is genuine. We can become trapped in the codependent triangle, sometimes feeling like the victim who needs rescuing, the rescuer who needs someone to take care of to feel a sense of meaning in life, or a persecutor who feels used and abused by a victim who is taking advantage or a rescuer who is taking away our independence.

The mask cannot offer freedom or flow; it is trapped in control…of the self and of others…because it can never fully feel safe or secure; it cannot experience the surrender to love in the fullest because, in the end, it cannot trust love. Because it is always criticizing, the mask cannot feel the joy of our significance and because it measures its significance as in comparison to others, the mask cannot feel joy for another's success. Somehow, another person's success means failure of the self that has identified with the mask.

When coming from the mask, the drives we experience to contribute to the world come from needs other than our doing based on our being's loving wish to share what radiates from our essence with a world that we love, even if we receive no recognition for what we have shared. The mask creates attachments rather than connections that are not satisfying in the long run.

Living from the mask is ultimately a lonely experience. It feels disconnected from life...because it is. Life, disconnected from God Essence, is made up so many stories like the ones I told in this book as well as the two books that came before. And yet, when we identify with the mask, we are terrified to release our attachment to it for fear we will lose what we have.

Despite all the discomfort the mask can bring us, it also has found a way to construct the world around us to help us feel as if we are in control, which can cause us to falsely believe that it makes us safe and secure and it promises that we will be able to feel loved. Because the world gives accolades to what the mask might do, we can become attached to the feelings of significance we gain when we wear the mask. If we begin to sense that the mask is crumbling, we do all we can to patch it up, or we distract ourselves with our addiction of choice to avoid looking in the mirror and seeing that the mask is falling apart. Drug counters are filled with every kind of painkiller imaginable that we hope will take away the pain we don't want to face because of the lifeless emptiness created when we wear a mask, and pharmacies are filled with prescription medications to cover over our depression or anxiety so we won't have to feel what is going on deep inside us. And of course, both legal and illegal substances offer the same promise of killing or covering the pain, which can be successful for a time, but requires more and more to provide some relief. But eventually all that we try fails to stop what the inner system is pushing to the forefront for healing.

Perhaps the biggest fear for the part of us that identifies with the mask is that it will see what it has hidden behind the mask. And the terror most all of us have been avoiding our whole lives, if not lifetimes, is that we are what is behind the mask.

Most of us do anything to avoid identifying ourselves with what is behind the mask. But some have become attached to or trapped in this dark place. These who identify themselves with what is behind the mask could be sociopaths who have disconnected from the wish to connect with other humans. They experience the thrill or sensation that comes from doing harm to others, without knowing they are actually wishing for the feelings that come from connection to life and light. The sought after rush that comes from committing evil is really a camouflaged longing for feeling the flow of life inside, but the person is so lost in the darkness, they know of no way out to connect with authentic life. The likelihood is that such people were so badly wounded early in their lives, or perhaps, in past lifetimes that they have turned the hatred for their abuser on all people, blaming everyone else without looking inward to see that what they hate most about other people is what they have become.

Persons, who get caught in the guilt, shame, depression, or anxiety, that lives behind the mask feel unable to extricate themselves from the feelings and may feel too broken or too unacceptable to connect with anyone, especially the God Essence within. Instead of turning on the world, these people usually turn on themselves, attacking, criticizing, blaming, shaming, guilting, or frightening themselves, while remaining stuck in the belief that there is no way out of the darkness. Living in pain or anger about what the world is, who they are, or what they believe the world will do to them, they are unable to feel the flow of life within or look beyond the darkness to see the light.

The painful story that took nearly the whole of *Behind the Mask* to tell, on one level, was about the people in my life who inflicted damage on me, as I was, in the words of the astrologer, *learning to dance with the devil so I could discover how to create a boundary with darkness*. But more so, it was about my own sense of guilt, shame and self-blame for the dancing. While most of me had learned to live beyond the horror of those early years in my life by dissociating from them, a part of me still identified herself with what was behind my mask. Subtly, and sometimes not so subtly, that part of me robbed from the rest of me my spontaneity, my laughter, my joy, and my sense of wholeness, always leaving me with the feeling that something was missing, or was not quite right.

Just as much as the part of us that identifies with the mask needs to know we are not the mask, any part of us that believes we are what is behind the mask needs to know we are not what is there, either. **We are not the story.** The answer I found for myself as to how I could release the attachments I had to my mask and what was behind my mask, was to open to the courage to turn within and face the pain and the anger that created a belief in separation from my true essence that was covered over and relegated to existence *Under the Mask*. Turning within does require death…death to what I wanted to believe was me but really was my false self, death to the structures I built to provide safety and security for that false self to feel somewhat alive, and death to the beliefs that were a part of that false world. When we are ready to accept the death of what is false, for the first time we can open to and connect with authentic life, that amazing, mysterious, mystical, magical, *Unique God Essence* that is who we really are.

***

Once we discover, experience, and choose to live from the light that is *Under the Mask,* our lives are transformed. We experience the flow of life within us that is ignited and for the first time felt in our bodies and consciously known in our minds. We viscerally feel the coming together of *Unique God Essence* and *Universal God Essence* in a cosmic dance. We are free to fully live because we are no longer afraid to die—death only happens to what is not who we are. Our *Unique God Essence* does not die. We live in bliss doing what we came to do…primarily, to become conscious of who we are, and secondarily, to express our unique being in the world, sharing the gift of our unique magnificence with all the other magnificently unique aspects of *God Essence* in human form.

We have no need to fear the ending of Tuesday when we know there is a Wednesday and we do not mourn the loss of middle school when we leave it to enter high school. When we move from one location to another, we may experience sadness for a change in relationships that have meant a lot to us, but we can find ways to communicate when we want to maintain connection. The same can be said regarding the times when one *Unique God Essence* moves from the experiences in a lifetime into the next point on the soul's journey.

The mask fears death and as a result is afraid to live; what is behind the mask often longs for death and as a result seeks ways to end life, and the light that calls us to let it expand beyond its confinement under the mask knows there is no such thing as death. There is only change in form. I have come to believe that if we do not learn this in this life, we will be given opportunity to learn it in some future life, but until we learn it, we will be living the stories, which is really the same story, over and over again. I am eternally grateful for all I have learned in the journey that has taken many lifetimes to understand, and I am grateful that I've finally gotten it that this lesson I came to learn is finished. I'm, also aware there are many more lessons...

The ultimate intention of all life expressed in the Being of Universal God Essence is to experience life consciously. The love filled gift you have been given in your Unique God Essence is that you are able to consciously experience living that life in your unique way that can only be expressed in the world by you. And, the gift you can offer to Universal God Essence, in return, is the irreplaceable conscious experience of being you as you share your uniqueness with other aspects of Universal God Essence... experienced as other Unique God Essences in all the ways of being, all One with the giver of life.

Until next time,
Sandy Sela-Smith
1-11-1

POSTSCRIPT

For my entire life, I had lived with an unconscious belief that I needed to be invisible, to not make waves or draw any attention to myself, especially from people in authority. Lifetimes of suffering at the hands of powerful people, replicated by extreme abuse by equally powerful people in my childhood, taught me that being in the world was excruciatingly painful if not fully life threatening, and the only way to survive was to not be seen.

As I began to write this trilogy in the late summer of 2007, I knew I had so much to learn about letting go of the mask with its futile attempts to create the protection of invisibility, while assuring some semblance of acceptance and love. I, also, had to find ways to release the fear of anything that still remained behind my mask that I believed could destroy me if it ever was revealed. But, when glimpses of what was to be in the trilogy began coming into my inner vision, I knew I would be teaching the lessons the books were to contain, a direct challenge to the belief that invisibility was essential to my survival. As book three was forming, I knew that my life and my work would soon become far more visible, yet, I knew I still held fear about stepping out in the world to offer perspectives that likely would not be well received, at least, by some people.

In a July, 2010 entry in chapter nine of this third book, I shared with you my distressing discovery that I was no longer invisible in this world when I saw my car on Google, followed by experiencing the bombers that flew over my mountain cabin causing me to feel vulnerable and unprotected, both experiences catapulting me back to events in my past and into past lives that I had to work through. Eight months later, in March of 2011, after having completed writing Under the Mask, and while waiting for the galley to come back so I could review and make whatever changes were needed in the manuscript, an experience opened my eyes to all that changed inside me.

Late one evening during that waiting time, on a nearly starless night when it was very dark outside, I was working with a client on the phone who was struggling with a major loss in his life when a helicopter flew over my carriage house and dropped so low it made my entire home shake, as violently as the hurricane winds I had endured in Florida. The beating of the rotor blades sounded like they were less than 20 feet above me. My walls and windows were pulsing with the pressure from the downdraft. The pilot hovered over my house for at least a couple of minutes, though it felt longer. Birds went crazy in the trees that surrounded my place and one crashed into my window; they must have been as terrified by this highly unusual occurrence as the polar bear who attempted to outrun the helicopter that I wrote about in chapter six.

After what seemed like a very long time, the helicopter ascended just a little . . . and slowly flew off in the same direction the bombers had flown months before. I would have gone outside to see what was happening, but my client was at a critical point in the session, and I couldn't abandon him to appease my curiosity. What felt so good was to notice that I was not frightened by this strange event. I was more disturbed by the insensitivity exhibited by the pilot who had flown so close to a private residence in the dark of the night for no apparent reason. This was such a different response than when the bombers flew over my house, and I went into panic. The bombers flight was in the daytime, not in the night, and they did not seem to be targeting my place, as did the pilot of the helicopter.

In retrospect, I consider the two experiences I had, one with the bombers and the other with the helicopter incident, an amazing gift that allowed me to see how far I had come since book three began writing itself in me. It seemed as if the universe had given me a pre and post-test in a scientifically based experiment to discover the effect of book three on my internal responses to apparent threat. And, I can report results that indicate I have learned what I had wanted to learn, not just as an idea in my head, but knowing in my body, that I am safe no matter what is happening in the world out-side my window. I believe the helicopter experience allowed me to really get it that I have accomplished what I wanted to accomplish and have made the connections I needed to make with my true self as Sandy God Essence in physical form, an eternal part of Universal God Essence. My response to the "mechanical predator" let me know I no longer need to respond from old patterns and programs that linked safety to invisibility, patterns that were based on a belief that I had been abandoned in a world that was out to get me . . . believing I was lost and alone, not wanted, and that I didn't belong.

For the first time since that July day in 2007, when the Tattooed Lady told me I would write three books, I realize I have come to trust the world and my place in it . . . and I know I have been set free to teach what the trilogy wrote in my life and in my consciousness. For almost 1230 days, my life was focused on living the lessons the trilogy was writing in me, all contained in close to 1150 pages, pointing to one idea that is in no way new, an idea that is as old as time, but one that still has not been embraced by the vast majority of humankind. And that is each of us is a unique expression of Universal God Essence, the embodiment of the magical, mystical, mysterious union of the spiritual and physical worlds. A corollary to that understanding is, in my being this Unique God Essence in union with Universal God Essence, I am creating my own life experiences to support self-discovery to allow me to become consciously aware of the being that I am.

I have been humbled by the power behind the synchronicities that conspired to wake me up and teach me what I needed to learn in order for me to offer to others what I came here to teach. I am no longer afraid to acknowledge what I have come to know about my true identity, and I no longer need to act as if invisibility is an option. And, as I have said on numerous occasions, I know that as long as I live, there were be more lessons to learn.

As one final humorous reminder of the interconnection of all that exists in the universe—with a subtle message of the wisdom and safety of that connection set into play by the great mystery that is the Universal God Essence—on the very day that this galley was returned for my review and submission for final production, I received a call from the Tattooed Lady telling me that she had returned to Colorado after having been gone for a couple of years and wanted to let me know that she would be available for readings should I want to reconnect with her work. The psychic, Alanza, is the one whose message acted as the catalyst that began my writing the first book in the trilogy almost 4 years ago, and she reinserted her presence the very day this last book in the trilogy she had predicted was completed. This reminder of connectivity has to be up there, somewhere close to receiving Liberty Quarters just when I needed them, and all of this has come to me in a way that brings a smile to my face, a sense of fascination and wonderment to my mind, and joy to my heart. Life is good!

AN EPITAPH FOR RACHAEL

Rachael came into my life in the early 1990s. At the time, I had no idea that she was to be a most important teacher in my life. She was with me all during the time I wrote *The Meaning of Three,* more as a silent third partner with Jenny and me. But a third of the way through my writing of the third book, *Under the Mask,* Rachael became sick and her partnership was no longer silent or invisible. Her illness, her healing, and her passing brought expanded understanding to so many principles I learned as I walked the path of greater awakening into my spiritual consciousness. As she became the focus of my life, she supported me in knowing experientially, many concepts I had previously embraced in my thoughts and experienced in my life, but never as deeply as I know them now. Being with her during her time of releasing experiences in this life allowed my knowing to be transformed into the integrity of body/mind/spirit oneness.

It took her passing for me to know in my DNA what I have learned, about so many things, and I no longer need to question that everyone who comes into my life, everything that crosses my paths, or any event that happens to me has the potential to be my teacher, letting me know something of myself, whether it is positive or negative, something I have hidden in myself or know in myself, but maybe can appreciate more, if I decide to allow myself to be a receptive student. And I know I do the same for any whose life I touch in all the ways one can connect with and touch another. I know in my oneness that there is an essence of the universe that is eternally connected to the essence of every one of us, whether we recognize it or not. This essence—*Universal God Essence* that resides in all that is—allows us to experience the interconnection of everything that exists in the universe if we are open to accepting this truth. And, it brings to us whatever we may need to expand this awareness through amazing synchronous events that cause us to be at the right place at the right time…even when it might not feel like what has been brought together is "right."

I learned about the meaning of family in the highest form of that word, and I learned about the meaning of death when it was time for Rachael to leave our partnership, which meant I also learned about the meaning of life more deeply than before. What Rachael had to teach me was not just about who she was but who I am, as well. She deserves to have her story told.

***

The afternoon was warm even though it was December, not unusual for that time of year in Florida. I was out for a walk with my tiny 6-year-old Lhasa, Sara, meandering through the apartment complex wondering if she might be lonely during the day because my work had increased substantially, causing me to be away far more than I had been at the beginning. I thought Sara might be less lonely if I got her a little sister, perhaps another Lhasa to keep her company during the long days I was at my office.

As I was pondering the possibility of a sister for Sara, I noticed the apartment manager walking toward me. She stopped in front of us and asked if I had ever thought of getting a kitten. I was surprised as well as intrigued by her question because at the very moment she approached me, I was having second thoughts about another dog because I suspected Sara might be jealous of puppy, and the manager seemed to have provided a perfect answer, a cat. When I told her just that very minute I had been thinking about bringing another member into my family of two, the manager smiled and then explained that a recently departed resident had left a pregnant cat in his unit, and she delivered her litter of seven kittens in an empty apartment. The maintenance man had found the helpless little family all huddled together in a corner of a totally empty apartment only a few minutes before.

The manager decided she would take mother and babies home for 8-weeks, and in the meantime, find families for them. She mentioned I was the first person she had approached, so I could pick the one I wanted, and she would deliver my new pet in about 2 months when it was old enough to be weaned from its mother. I left Sara at the entry so she wouldn't disturb mother and kittens and went in to see the cat family.

There they were, seven little babies with their eyes still unopened. In the middle of the group of wiggling little creatures, mostly all black and white, was the only calico, a female that seemed to be sending a message through her squeaks that she was the one that belonged to me. Without any further thought, I pointed to the lovely black, rust, white, brown, and orange, kitten and told the manager. *"I want that one."* The deal was sealed; this little newborn had joined Sara and me as an expanded family of three.

Later that day, I was aroused by Sara's loud barking, foretelling that someone was approaching my front door, followed moments later by a knock. The manager had come to tell me that between the time she'd shown me the kittens and when she had come with a box to take the mother cat and her babies from the empty apartment to her home, mother had found an open window and managed to carry all seven babies from the second story window, hiding them somewhere in the forest behind the complex, and no one was able to find them.

In Florida, helpless animals do not survive long because of so many predatory birds, wild animals, and alligators in constant search for their next meal. Even though humans have managed to create places to live that look civilized, people have really only carved out places in nature, while in reality, Florida still belongs to the wild things. I was saddened by the news of having lost a member of my little family even before she had come home to be with Sara and me. And, at least for a time, the idea of adding to our family of two faded into the background.

***

Two months later the apartment manager stopped by my place to tell me the grounds keeper was doing some work along the edge of the forest when he saw the mother cat with her babies, grown to about 8 weeks. He was able to capture all of them and brought them back to the management office. She told me the calico was alive and well... though in desperate need of a bath, and wanted to know if I was still interested in the kitten. When I said yes, she went back to her car and carried the now not so tiny creature to me in a towel. I reached for the kitten, but instead of a loving or shy response, my arm received her razor sharp teeth and claws that penetrated into muscles. The two months in the forest had turned the precious little kitten into a feral creature, making her very unsure about any human contact. I quickly set her down to let her discover her new home, but even with her freedom, she hissed and arched her tiny back like a mean Halloween cat, ready to attack anything or anyone in her sight. Noticing that she was covered from ear-tips to toenails with fleas, I filled the bathroom sink to give her a bath, but not before her claws sunk into my arm again, a painful experience she provided on so many occasions for a very long time, not just for me, but for visitors and friends, as well.

While I washed off the dirt and sent hundreds of flees down the drain, a name came into my mind, almost as if she was telling me who she was, and I decided to call her Rachael; the name seemed to fit. Rachael, Sara, and me...we three...were now a family.

***

Not long before Rachael's arrival, I felt a distinct need to move from where I had lived for a year to another place and had begun a search but had not found something suitable. And finally, just a few days after the little calico kitten had come into my life, I found a most perfect place. It had cathedral ceilings, with skylights, a fireplace—unusual for Florida, but something I really liked—and its entrance was above a most beautifully manicured courtyard with blossoming cherry trees and flower-lined paths leading to picnic benches and outdoor grills for the residents. The moment I stepped into the living room, I could feel this as my new home. The manager seemed pleased that I might choose to live there. She began going over the rules, but I stopped her when she got to the statement about one small pet being allowed. I asked if I paid an extra deposit would she allow two, because I had a kitten and a dog. She insisted that the rule could not be broken, so I sighed and told her I would have to keep looking. She asked about my pets, and I told her I had a small 6-year old Lhasa and a 2-month old kitten that I had just brought into my life only a couple of days before. She seemed relieved, and without any hesitation said, *"Oh, just give the kitten back. You haven't had it that long."* I was surprised she would suggest something like that, and thanked her for her time.

When I got home, Rachael and Sara greeted me at the door, and I told them that I thought I'd found a place for us, but they wouldn't accept all three of us, so I'd need to keep looking. I stooped down to look into Rachael's eyes and said, *"Honey, whether you want to be or not, you are family and I am not giving you back to anyone. Your place is here with us…you are stuck with me."*

Not long afterward, I found a place that allowed two pets. It was a lot bigger than the other place, though not as beautiful…but it allowed us to stay together, which made it extraordinarily beautiful to me. It was up on the second floor and had a 6 X 24-foot screened in deck that ran the width of the living room and master bedroom. The deck overlooked a grassy area and a row of flowering oleander trees that stretched the full length of the apartments. They were at least 25 feet tall, very full, and oh so lovely. Every morning, birds of all kinds, including parrots and songbirds filled the branches that made waking up feel so calming.

Rachael was a free spirit and loved the deck. She spent most of her time either sleeping in the sun or stalking the birds that glided into the trees on the other side of the screen. It didn't take her long to discover that she could get a better perspective of the wildlife by climbing up the screen and hanging there outstretched looking like a decorative animal skin until she turned and jumped from her spot 6 or 7 feet to the floor, and then she delighted in running as fast as she could from the deck, into the living room, and down the long hall to the front screen door, a distance of about 45 feet. She clawed her way up the screen door and hung there for as long as it took for some unsuspecting neighbor to walk by. At the perfect moment, she would let out a Halloween-yowl as only a cat can do, shocking them so badly that words I thought only kids knew came out of the mouths of some of the most dignified of the elderly people who lived there.

After that little game, Rachael would release her claws, and drop to the floor to make the run back to the deck where she would look for birds, attempt to catch little geckos that had found a way under the screen and into her domain, or she would lay down in the sun again. She seemed to really love our new home.

Perhaps, the best word that fit Rachael was independent. She liked to do everything her way. When a friend and her cat came to stay for a while, Rachael decided to mark the whole apartment, claiming it as her territory, which resulted in my having to carry a spray bottle of cleaner around with me much more than I wished. She had a disturbing habit of jumping onto guests' laps, purring with delight, and with unexpected fierceness, teeth and claws went into arms. Finally, I had to have her front claws removed, which broke my heart, but probably not as much as it broke hers. Never again was she able to climb screens and play Rachael games.

I don't think I ever heard a cat purr as loudly as my calico cat could purr. Her favorite spot to crawl into was a paper bag I kept beside my computer desk. Her purring made the sides of the bag vibrate. She was happy in that special place, fully in touch with her unique cat essence.

I began to travel more in my work, which required leaving Sara and Rachael more than I would have liked. One of the first times I was gone for several days, Sara became despondent, sighing a lot, and refusing to eat. Her sitter told me when Sara was in a particularly despondent mood, Rachael picked up Sara's stuffed Tigger animal, the one from Winnie the Po that Sara had completely gutted, and dropped it next to Sara, an act of kindness we usually don't believe animals are capable of doing. Sara responded with apparent appreciation and her mood shifted from that time on. Sara and Rachael became buddies after that though they would still get into turf wars when their food bowls were at stake.

One day, I took Rachael to the vet clinic for the required yearly shots, but when she was back home she had a reaction that nearly killed her. She spent several days in the hospital and from that time on, she was on medication that compromised her immune system, but allowed her to maintain a near normal platelet count that had been destroyed by the vaccinations. The vet told me that in time the medication would cause her to die, but if she didn't have the medication, she would die, anyway. Not long after that catastrophic event with Rachael, Sara developed heart trouble and died. Along with me, Rachael went into mourning.

Sometimes, in the middle of the night, my little calico cat would let out the most mournful howling cry. I would turn on the light to find Rachael walking around the apartment with Tigger in her mouth, as if it were her kitten, seeking a hiding place to keep it safe, or perhaps looking for Sara. I cried, too.

It took a long time for me to recover from the loss of Sara, and when I felt it would be fair to all of us to add another member to our partnership, I brought Jenny into our lives. Rachael was 5-years-old by that time and had an apparent need to be put Jenny in her place. The two got into batting matches at times, especially when it came to food and toys. As Jenny grew, it was hard to tell which was the pack leader...the role flipped back and forth depending on which one felt wronged by the other. But when any threat from the outside came across their paths, the two joined together into an unbreakable team.

For years, she seemed to be doing fine, taking her pills twice every day, until Rachael decided she didn't want them anymore. I began finding tiny pills hidden away under pillows and beside her water bowl or food dish after I had given them to her, which concerned me because she needed the pills to stay alive.

While working with a client from another state, I found out that there was a world-renowned naturopathic veterinarian not 15 minutes from my mountain cabin, a person I had never heard of before, but people all over the country had. She told me she travels to the Colorado Mountains for her pet care. I scheduled an appointment and Rachael began a process to rebuild her badly compromised immune system.

We were going to the clinic once and sometimes twice a week. She was making such good progress and then, suddenly, she developed a tumor under her tongue. It was a very fast growing cancer that was inoperable because of its location.

The vet began a regimen that called for 12 shots a day, that I was taught how to administer, and Rachael seemed to be improving. But, I never felt good about putting needles in her body. For several months she seemed to hover between slight improvement and slight decline. The Doc let me know that as long as she wasn't suffering and I felt good about seeing if a little more effort could help her beat this disease, we could continue.

Each day, I asked Rachael if she wanted to be here, and using a pendulum, I kept getting the same answer that she was not ready to go. I promised Rachael that I would support her decision, and then I prayed asking the God of the Universe and the helping angels to support me in my support of Rachael. Each time I received a new vet bill, within hours, clients would call and schedule appointments that covered the bills completely, sometimes within a dollar or two of the amount that was due.

Rachael began experiencing more difficulty eating and drinking because her tongue couldn't work effectively with the tumor getting in the way, so I began to feed her and give her water with a syringe. She also needed to be hydrated with a saline drip twice a day. Despite the challenges, Rachael seemed to be purring more than ever before. She was a very happy cat and didn't indicate she was suffering. I was aware that others thought I should put Rachael down because of all the complications, but I promised her I would support her to be here as long as she wanted to stay.

One night, Rachael seemed to be having difficulty breathing and I was afraid I had waited too long to make the decision to euthanize her. I took Rachael to an emergency clinic and the vet told me that I ought to consider putting her down, right then. But when I asked Rachael, she indicated that this was not the time. Whatever was happening for her that night passed, and she seemed to be doing better: I decided to continue to support her to live.

My naturopathic vet examined her the next day, and decided to make a change in the regimen she was under, cutting down on the number of shots she needed each day, something that improved her test results for awhile. And I continued to pray for what was best for Rachael. Not long afterward, Rachael began to fight the shots and instead of resting in my arms accepting the saline drip, she began to fight that as well, causing the needle to pull out from under her skin spewing the solution and antibiotic medication everywhere but in her. I told her I wouldn't poke her any more with needles and began feeding her and giving her water with a syringe.

Later one night, Rachael began to howl cry, the way she did after Sara died. I turned on the light and found her in her bed with Tigger curled up next to her. Her breathing was labored even more than it had been the night I took her to the emergency clinic. I couldn't stop crying as I held my little calico cat in my arms.

The next morning, my naturopathic vet told me it was time to stop our efforts and put her down. But I couldn't do it that day. I said we needed more time. I brought Rachael home and asked her if she was ready to go, and despite everything, her response was no. She was not ready. It broke my heart. I bought baby food and began feeding her every hour or so. She loved sweet potatoes and purred when I gave her turkey and broth. She would jump off the bed and walk over to the kitchen, lift her head up and make purring sounds letting me know she wanted to be fed. For a time, it felt like feeding her was the central purpose of my life. All the work the naturopathic vet had done with Rachael over the months had rebuilt her immune system and strengthened her body organs making her wonderfully strong and healthy, all except for the cancer in her mouth.

So many times, I would look up from my work and find Rachael just looking at me. Her eyes seemed extremely large as if she were taking in all there was to see, maybe seeing far more than she had ever seen before. I would look deeply into her open eyes as she looked directly into mine; we connected soul to soul, sometimes for long periods of time.

Rachael became more loving than she had ever been in all her 18 years. She somehow still had the strength to climb up on the bed and snuggle with me...and all the while, she purred. The feral habits that had been a part of her behavior all her life were gone, but it was clear she was becoming much weaker. And then, one day, when I asked again, she said she was ready to go, but she didn't want me to take her to the clinic. I was puzzled by her response, because the people at the clinic were lovely folks, but when I re-asked the questions, I discovered that she wanted to let go of this life at home, not at the clinic.

With pain in my heart, I called a local vet that comes to people's houses to put pets down, and though she normally would not do this procedure on an animal she had not had as a patient, she agreed to be with Rachael and me for this process. We scheduled the time for 3:00 in the afternoon of October 13, 2010. I wished that my calico baby would have chosen to leave on her own instead of having to do it this way, but apparently that wasn't what Rachael wanted.

Waking on the morning of the 13th was so painfully raw. It would be my last day with my sweet Rachael. I couldn't hold back the tears as I fed her and gave her water, and she curled up next to me all morning as I sang to her and told her she would never have to go through all those shots or eat nasty pills again. I explained to her what was going to happen and told her that when she left her body, she would be without pain. I let her know she would always be welcome to visit if she wanted…and that if she chooses to come back, she could come as anything she wanted. She didn't have to limit her choices to being a house cat if she wanted a different experience. As the time neared, my baby girl buried her face in the space between my left arm and breast. I could feel her warm breath as she lay there beside me…waiting for 3 o'clock to come, while dreading it at the same time. A few minutes before 3:00, I heard a car drive up. We both became still.

When the time came, Rachael accepted the injection to knock her out before the lethal injection that would stop her heart. But instead of responding like other animals, Rachael stood up, walked across the bed, hopped on the chair and jumped down to the floor. She walked over to the kitchen and stood with her head up, asking for food. The vet was astounded. No animal had ever done that before. Rachael had decided to do this in her own way, too. I took out the feeding syringe and filled it with turkey and broth baby food. Rachael stood for a little while and dropped to the floor in slow motion. In that most painful moment, I remembered when I was a child; I had been given injections to stop me from fighting some of the most vicious abuses. When I was such a little kid, I struggled against the anesthetic coming into my system, and when I could no longer stop the drug from taking effect, I blamed myself for not trying hard enough as I lost control of my body in that slow motion way, just as Rachael had done.

Heartbreaking shock waves exploded through me as I realized what Rachael had done for me. Had she not communicated her choices to me exactly as she did, and had she not demonstrated the drug-induced collapse as she did, I would not have found little Sandy still buried in her guilt for collapsing in a drug-induced state. As she was letting go of her life, *Rachael God Essence* had participated in a healing so deep for the part of me who believed she had not deserved to live because she didn't try hard enough to prevent being overtaken by drugs. For the first time in my life, I saw, there in front of me, in the form of my sweet calico cat, the proof that no matter how hard little Sandy tried, she could not have stopped the power of the drugs, nor could she have stopped what those who drugged her did to her afterward. Standing over collapsed Rachael, too drugged to stand and so very close to death, I felt as one who had just survived a near death experience to find out that someone I so dearly loved had died so I could live. Everything in me cried as deeply as Rachael cried when she carried Tigger in her mouth so many times in the past after she lost Sara, and again the night before her passing.

I picked up my Rachael and carried her back to the bed. She was still not under enough to administer the lethal shot, so the vet gave her a second shot. That didn't do it either. The vet asked me if Rachael and Jenny struggled with who was top dog, and when I answered in the affirmative, the vet said that explained why Rachael was responding to this whole procedure like a dog instead of a cat. Finally, she gave the amount she usually gives to dogs, and in a short period of time, it worked. When she checked for the vein to put in the final shot, the vet told me how sorry she was that because Rachael was so very dehydrated, she might not be able to easily find a vein that would work and was afraid all the prodding would hurt my little girl. I didn't want her to suffer with such pain as the last remembrance of her life with me; I asked Rachael if she would allow a vein to come forward so getting the medicine wouldn't hurt her. In that very moment a vein raised up on Rachael's arm. The vet was in awe of what Rachael had just done and slid the needle in. Within a moment, Rachael's heart stopped beating; my sweet little calico was gone.

For days, I struggled with whether or not I had taken Rachael's life prematurely. If I had waited longer, could she have survived the cancer? Was this really what Rachael wanted or was she doing what she thought I wanted her to do? I wondered if she let her vein rise up because I asked her, not because she wanted to do it.

Not long after all of this, I had another session with Shar, the Tibetan Cranial therapist. While she worked with the grief energy in me stirred up by all the doubts that had been swirling around in my head, Shar stopped for a moment and reminded me that Rachael was a very independent cat. If she had not wanted to go, she would have made it very clear to me and impossible for the vet to put in the needle. Rachael did it her way. She had chosen to leave her body in our home, not in a clinic. She had chosen to resist the first shot enough to walk over to the kitchen to get food and she had chosen to fall onto the floor in such a way that would reconnect me with something from my past that so needed to be healed. And in that moment, I realized that Rachael in collapsing on the floor after she had fought the anesthetic so very hard allowed me to reconnect with my child self who believed it was her fault for not having tried hard enough to stop what was being done to her. This child-part's belief connected with so many other incidents from my childhood where I blamed myself for not trying hard enough. By demonstrating the energy of collapse, I was able to connect with the feelings from parts of me who had been separated for decades still holding on to a belief that all that happened was their fault. Rachael let me know that it was time to let go of blaming myself…for what happened in my childhood, and for what had happened to her. She had decided it was time to start moving towards her end when she rejected the pills and then later when she rejected the shots and the saline drip. It was her decision. In letting go of her life as she did, Rachael helped separated parts of me open to receiving life, for the first time in decades.

If I had followed what other people thought I should do, and put her down earlier at the clinic, Rachael would not have been able to help me in my own significant healing, and we would not have had those special days of closeness we shared together, we would not have had those most beautiful moments of soul to soul connection as we gazed into each other's eyes and saw the beautiful God Essence in each other. We both learned how to surrender to love without needing to protect ourselves from being hurt. She played an important role in my life and I am very sure I played an important role in her life, as well, perhaps letting her know that it is possible to overcome a difficult and terrifying beginning of life, as she did as a kitten, and I did as a child, and find love, even if it takes a long time. Maybe that was a lesson we have learned from each other, a lesson that brought healing to us both. Her timing was impeccable. She came into my life exactly when she needed, she demonstrated exactly what she needed and she left exactly when she needed…and all of it was in a way that supported both of us, as we both needed.

I miss you very much my sweet independent Rachael. Even though you are gone, we are still family. We are eternally connected, and I look forward to what we will share and learn from each other when we meet again.

With honor and respect for who you are,
Love, Sandy

About the Author

Dr. Sandy Sela-Smith has an MA, and Ph.D. in psychology from Saybrook University. She is a mind/body/spirit psychotherapist, is licensed as a mental health counselor in Florida and Washington State, and is a licensed professional counselor in Colorado. She is nationally certified by NBCC as a mental health counselor, and has been certified by ACHE as a clinical hypnotherapist. Sela-Smith is a part time faculty member at two graduate schools, is a published, author, and has recently enjoyed her work as a professional photographer and producer of greeting cards. Her home is in Florida, and she lives part time in the mountains of Colorado with he Lhasa, Jenny, where she finds the environment is conducive to writing.

Licenses: FL MH6984, CO LPC5184, WA LH00010277

Sela-Smith speaks and presents workshops on the healing processes presented in the trilogy, *The Meaning of Three,* related to the letting go, turning within, and finding connection with *Universal God Essence,* eternally connected to the *Unique God Essence* that resides in each of us. To arrange for workshop presentations or individual sessions email her:

sselasmith@aol.com

To purchase any of the books in the trilogy or to find other information about Sandy Sela-Smith and her work, go to her website:

http://www.infiniteconnections.us

The Trilogy can also be purchased from the publisher:
1-888-728-8467
And it can be purchased online from:
www.barnesandnoble.com or www.Amazon.com

CPSIA information can be obtained at www.ICGtesting.com
Printed in the USA
267831BV00001B/5/P